Some Wore Bobby Sox

GIRLS' HISTORY & CULTURE BOOK SERIES

Miriam Forman-Brunell, Series Editor

This series, which focuses on the diversity of girls' lives as well as shifting constructions of girlhood, examines girls and female adolescents as subjects, objects, and agents of American history, culture, and society. Placing girls at the center of historical inquiry, the books in this series investigate the varieties of ideologies and institutions that have shaped gender ideals, framed identities, and generated girls' subjectivities and subcultures.

About the Series Editor

Miriam Forman-Brunell, Professor of History at the University of Missouri-Kansas City, is the author of *Made to Play House: Dolls and the Commercialization of American Girlhood* and the editor of *Girlhood in America*, a two-volume encyclopedia. Her forthcoming book is entitled *Desire & Dread: The Rise and Fall of Babysitting*.

Advisory Board

Joan Jacobs Brumberg
Stephen H. Weiss Presidential Fellow and Professor of History,
    Human Development, and Gender Studies
Cornell University

Susan J. Douglas
Catherine Neafie Kellogg Professor
Department of Communication Studies
University of Michigan

Jane Hunter
Professor of History
Lewis and Clark College

Sherrie Inness
Professor of English
Miami University of Ohio

Steven Mintz
Professor of History
University of Houston

Viviana Zelizer
Professor of Sociology
Princeton University

Some Wore Bobby Sox

The Emergence of
Teenage Girls' Culture,
1920–1945

KELLY SCHRUM

palgrave
macmillan

SOME WORE BOBBY SOX

Copyright © Kelly Schrum, 2004.

First published 2004 by
PALGRAVE MACMILLAN™
175 Fifth Avenue, New York, N.Y. 10010 and
Houndmills, Basingstoke, Hampshire, England RG21 6XS.
Companies and representatives throughout the world.

PALGRAVE MACMILLAN is the global academic imprint of the Palgrave Macmillan division of St. Martin's Press, LLC and of Palgrave Macmillan Ltd. Macmillan® is a registered trademark in the United States, United Kingdom and other countries. Palgrave is a registered trademark in the European Union and other countries.

ISBN 1–4039–6176-X hardback

Library of Congress Cataloging-in-Publication Data
Schrum, Kelly.
Some wore bobby sox : the emergence of teenage girls' culture, 1920–1945 / by Kelly Schrum.
    p.   cm.
Includes bibliographical references and index.
ISBN 1–4039–6176-X
    1. Teenage girls—United States—History—20th century.   2. Teenage consumers—United States—History—20th century.   3. Popular culture—United States—History—20th century.   I. Title.

HQ798.S328   2004
305.235'2'09730904—dc22

                                                                        2003063271

A catalogue record for this book is available from the British Library.

Design by Letra Libre, Inc.

First edition: June 2004
10 9 8 7 6 5 4 3 2

Printed in the United States of America.

To Cory and Cassie
with love and gratitude

Contents

Figures

Acknowledgments

I am grateful to the many people, archives, and institutions that have enriched my research and made this book possible. First I would like to thank the women who offered their memories of high school life in the 1920s, 1930s, and 1940s: Louise Armstrong, Alma Bond, Jo Nelson Booze, Nancy Boyce, Mary Streeter Farber, Betsy McDonald, Alleyn Moore, Nancy Winslow, and Dorothy Barry Wolff. Special thanks to Betsy Hughes, who shared her stories and friendship as well as her keen wit. June Calender, June Goyne Corotto, Betty Goldstein Friedan, Beth Twiggar Goff, Adele Siegel Rosenfeld, Katherine Rosner, Arvilla Scholfield, Yvonne Blue Skinner, Ruth Teischman, and Frances Turner opened their lives through diaries and letters. Their honesty, enthusiasm, and humor kept my research lively. I would also like to thank Estelle Ellis, *Seventeen* magazine's first promotional director, for granting me an interview in 1994. That interview, along with her papers at the Smithsonian Institution National Museum of American History Archives Center, opened the door to this research.

Many libraries and archives provided access to the materials included in this research. I thank the Maryland Department of the Enoch Pratt Free Library; Smithsonian Institution, National Museum of American History Archives Center; Library of Congress, especially the Motion Picture and Television and Recorded Sound Reading Rooms; Scholastic Incorporated; Maryland Historical Society; Bryn Mawr School; Frederick Douglass High School; the Charles Sumner School Museum and Archives; the Archive Research and Study Center, UCLA Film and Television Archive; the Center for Motion Picture Study, Margaret Herrick Library, AMPAS; the Schlesinger Library and the Henry A. Murray Research Center, Radcliffe Institute for Advanced Study at Harvard University; Gutman Library, Harvard University; Goucher College; and the Institute of Human Development, University of California, Berkeley. I owe a special debt to many archivists and librarians for their patience and persistence, including Peggy Woodward, Margaret Stevaralgia, Jeff Korman, Judy Capurso, James Friedman, Mimi Minnick, Faith Ruffins, Shirley Hunter, Joseph Smith, Scott Curtis, Margie Simon, and Zachary Jaffe. Dr. Philip Cowan allowed me access to the Oakland Growth Study and Berkeley Guidance Study data, for which I will always be grateful. Natsuki Aruga encouraged me to explore this rich resource and generously shared her ideas and research. Additional thanks to Stephen Provasnik for sharing his research on the history of public education. In addition, I am grateful to the institutions that have supported this work. Johns Hopkins University, George Mason University, the Schlesinger Library, and the Henry A. Murray Research Center provided valuable re search grants and support.

I also owe many intellectual and emotional debts. Ronald Walters shared his enthusiasm for social and cultural history and supported my project from its inception, generously offering insightful analysis, encouragement, and guidance. I am grateful for his willingness to share his family's personal papers, including diaries, drawings, and photographs. Many thanks to Paula Fass who has encouraged and mentored me for many years. I would like to thank Toby Ditz, Sherrie Inness, Kathy Peiss, Kathryn Fuller, and Roy Rosenzweig for their careful readings and perceptive comments. I am grateful for the support and guidance from my editors at Palgrave, Brendan O'Malley and Deborah Gershenowitz, production editor Donna Cherry, and to Jim O'Brien for his careful reading, indexing, and thoughtful advice. I would like to thank my parents—their support, compassion, and confidence in my work have been truly sustaining. And finally, I thank my husband, Cory, whose patience and intellectual curiosity have made this work better, and our daughter, Cassie, whose enthusiasm for life, generous hugs, and ready laughter have inspired me to finish and provided wonderful distractions along the way. She will one day teach me about teenage girls in the twenty-first century.

Introduction

Now don't get me wrong. . . . I get around. I read. I listen to the radio. And I have two older sisters. So you see, I know what the score is. I know it's smart to wear tweedish skirts and shaggy sweaters with the sleeves pushed up and pearls and ankle-socks and saddle shoes that look as if they've seen the world. . . . I'm not exactly small-town either. I read Winchell's column—you get to know what New York boy is that way about some pineapple princess on the West Coast, and why someone will eventually play Scarlett O'Hara. It gives you that cosmopolitan feeling. And I know that anyone who orders a strawberry sundae in a drugstore instead of a lemon Coke would probably be dumb enough to wear colored ankle socks with high-heeled pumps or use Evening in Paris with a tweed suit.

—Maureen Daly, "Sixteen" (1938)[1]

Maureen Daly won first prize with her short story, "Sixteen," in a *Scholastic* magazine high school writing contest. In this opening paragraph, Daly identifies her protagonist, a small-town high school student, as a "typical" teenage girl through her knowledge of the latest teen trends in fashion, beauty, music, and movies. The narrator understands her peers as well as the latest news from the New York society pages and Hollywood gossip columns. By 1938, growing awareness of teenage girls as a distinct group allowed Daly's story of unrequited love and self-awareness to resonate with teenage and adult readers nationally.

Daly could not have written her story in 1900. At the turn of the twentieth century, teenage girls received little, if any, attention from creators of consumer culture or commercial popular culture and wielded little power as a group—in fact they were rarely defined as a distinct group. The period from 1920 to 1945 proved crucial in the formation of teenage girls' culture in the United States. Daly's assumptions and tone reflect important changes that shaped public and industry understanding of teenage girls during these years.

In the twenty-first century, it is hard to imagine a world without teenage girls. Terms such as "teen" and "Girl Power" circulate widely. From dELiA's clothing to Buffy the Vampire Slayer, from Jennifer Lopez (J.Lo) products to *Teen People, Teen Vogue,* and *CosmoGirl,* stores, catalogs, clothing lines, television series, movies, magazines, music, and websites designed for teenage girls abound. By the beginning of the twenty-first century, these teenage fashions and trends supported a multi-billion dollar industry. According to Teenage Research Unlimited (TRU), teenagers spent $170 billion in 2002, about half of that on clothing and the rest on personal care products, entertainment, electronics, and snacks. These numbers include boys and girls, but among teenage consumers, girls are the primary spenders and the central advertising market for the majority of teenage products.[2]

In the public imagination, teenagers first appeared in the 1950s, complete with distinct dress, habits, music, and culture. And they were primarily white and male. The preceding decades, however, tell a remarkable story of the formative years of "teenagers"—especially teenage girls as we know them today—as high school students, consumers, and trendsetters.

One of the unique characteristics of high school girls' consumer culture has been its enthusiastic "discovery" year after year. The *Washington Post* declared in February 1999, "Gone is the time when only parents, shrinks and educators worried about what teens wanted. Now they're the darlings of the marketers, who see abundant dollar signs attached to this latest bulge in the population." In 1998, a *Boston Globe* article heralded the success of dELiA's mail-order catalog and website designed for high school and junior high school girls, and quoted Michael Wood, director of TRU, "Everybody's waking up and taking notice that this group is growing for the first time." Steve Kahn, president of dELiA's, proclaimed, "the history of retail will declare dELiA's as the company that turned teenage girls into a viable market segment."[3]

In 1959, forty years earlier, *Life* proclaimed "A New, $10–Billion Power: The U.S. Teen-Age Consumer." The title championed all "teen-age" consumers, but the article featured girls, such as seventeen-year-old Suzy of Van Nuys, California, who "delight[ed]" in a new luggage set from her father and shopped for china to store in her hope chest. The article stated that "until recently businessmen have largely ignored the teen-age market." *Life,* however, was not alone in its latest "discovery." *Consumer Reports* noticed in 1957 that teenagers had been "coming in for special attention from advertisers in the past few years." The *Wall Street Journal* announced in 1956 that not only were 16 million teenagers "getting increasing attention from merchants and advertisers," they readily identified television sponsors and items they wished to purchase, often describing their needs in the language of advertisements. Once again, the reporter interviewed only female teens.[4]

Fifteen years earlier, a young entrepreneur named Eugene Gilbert called himself the "George Gallup of the teenagers." He hired a vast network of high school students to conduct market research on teenagers around the country and profited from his promise to "translate" high school consumer desires. By 1946, his clients included Quaker Oats, Maybelline, Studebaker, and United Airlines. By the early 1950s Gilbert wrote several monthly columns, including "Girls and Teen Merchandise," and in 1956 he introduced a syndicated newspaper column, "What Young People Think." Gilbert argued that teenagers spent billions of dollars annually on clothes, food, and entertainment for themselves and, equally important, they influenced family purchases. Gilbert simultaneously argued that teenagers, especially girls, were quick to follow the latest trends and highly responsive to material "developed for their special interests." But Gilbert did not originate many of these ideas.[5]

When *Seventeen* magazine debuted in September 1944, its first issue sold out quickly—400,000 copies in six days. Circulation exceeded 1 million copies by February 1947 and 2.5 million by July 1949. *Seventeen* declared that through copies shared with friends and family, it reached more than half of the 6 million teenage girls in the United States. *Seventeen*'s first promotional director, Estelle Ellis, played an important role in ex-

panding the mode and messages of advertising to teenage girls. Ellis saw her job as one
of translation: to translate the buying power of teenage girls for advertisers, retailers, and
manufacturers. She emphasized girls' demographic strength, their autonomy in buying
certain products, such as clothing and cosmetics, their ability to influence parental purchases, and their future as adult consumers.[6]

The postwar era, remarkable for its proliferation of teen consumer goods, still did not
mark the beginning of teen consumer culture. The years before 1944 witnessed the
emergence of a teenage market and the development of teenage girls' culture. Even before 1920, movie fan magazines identified young women as avid moviegoers and consumers of fan culture. Media and advertising attention to youth markets in the early
1920s focused on college students, aged eighteen to twenty-four, introducing many of
the marketing tools later used with teenage consumers. Attention to those under eighteen, however, was growing.[7]

High school played an important role in the development of teenage consumer culture, bringing young people together in large numbers in an age-segregated setting for
the first time. An article in *Printers' Ink* in 1915, "Campaigning on Future Big Buyers While They Are Students," mentioned high school students. *Scholastic* magazine
started in 1920 by reporting on high school sports in Western Pennsylvania. In 1922,
it expanded to a national magazine designed to present current events and literature
to high school students, and by 1930, circulation exceeded 100,000. Advertising revenue, inspired by belief in the ability and desire of high school students to purchase
goods and influence family spending, played an important role. By the late 1920s,
Scholastic boasted an eclectic mix of advertisers, from baking powder to Arthur Murray dance lessons to Coca Cola, although the advertisements did not yet address
young people directly.[8]

By the early 1930s, *Scholastic* envisioned high school readers as reliable consumers,
promoting movies and books through columns, contests, and surveys. A survey in 1932,
"Are You A Buyer for Your Family?" declared that *Scholastic* "would like to know more
about you in relation to the purchase of foods, tooth paste, etc., for your family. By
'buyer' we mean—a person who goes to the store to spend money, whether it be your
own or that of your mother or father, etc." The authors presented the survey as "a favor
we are asking of you" and offered five pencils to each respondent. During this same period, companies as diverse as Metropolitan Life Insurance, RCA, and Deere & Company also began to notice the rising number of high school students. They attempted to
capitalize on their immediate potential as customers while fostering brand loyalty for future purchases through school contests, educational materials, and product samples for
classroom distribution.[9]

Who were these young people? Why did some industries begin to notice them long
before others? How effective were they in shaping the consumer choices of high school
students? Why did these forces take shape in the 1920s, 1930s, and 1940s? Why did
girls receive more attention than boys did as teenage consumers? As high school girls developed a separate peer identity and began to recognize their collective strength, they established themselves as important arbiters of clothing, beauty products, music, and
movies—consumers with decided opinions and preferences. Before World War II, manufacturers, marketers, and retailers in some industries, such as fashion, were among the
first to recognize high school girls as a discrete social group with purchasing power.
Other industries, such as music and movies, interacted with teenage girls but remained
unaware of them as consumers with special interests and needs.

By 1938, when Maureen Daly's short story was published, her references to radio, shaggy sweaters, and ankle socks worn with saddle shoes but not with pumps were the norm rather than the exception. Many of these trends emerged out of the 1920s and early 1930s; others were still being formalized in the late 1930s and early 1940s. But by 1938, teenage culture, most notably teenage girls' culture, was identifiable.

Not all girls participated in a single, unified teenage girls' culture. The very concept of "culture" is problematic, used by some to imply a static, coherent system of symbols and meanings. Culture here may be understood instead as fluid, impermanent, and loosely defined. There were multiple teenage girls' cultures across time and space and within individual high schools. Yet these cultures increasingly overlapped. High school girls across the country began to share a set of styles, practices, and behaviors, of symbols and meanings in relation to each other, to their parents, and to the larger world of consumer culture and popular culture that helped to define the emerging teenage girls' culture at the heart of this analysis.[10]

Historians have traditionally described teenage culture as a postwar phenomenon and, until recently, have emphasized boys. These are related, as the focus on boys has played an important role in understanding the timing of teenagers, placing the emergence of "teen" as a category after 1945. Teenage boys were the main focus in the discourse on juvenile delinquency. Although teenage girls have been criticized periodically regarding sexuality and sexual behavior, they primarily received attention as consumers. In the consumer world, girls were the first teenagers. And they became the first teenagers in the decades before 1945.[11]

The lives of teenage girls are undoubtedly influenced and shaped by teenage boys, but boys were not the primary "other" during the formation of teenage girls' culture. Teenage culture, as defined by girls and by marketers, focused more on distinguishing high school girls from younger girls and from female college students than from boys. In part, this reflected societal norms. In the highly gendered arena of adolescence, high school boys and girls operated under different restrictions and demands and received different kinds of attention from adults and media.

Studying the transitional decades before World War II allows an investigation of the emergence of teenage girls' culture and the teenage market as well as the relationship between group identity formation, popular culture, and consumer culture. High school girls mediated desires for age-specific goods and vacillated between interest in comfort, fads, and sophisticated styles. How did girls integrate mass culture and mass-produced commodities into their lives? How did they respond to products intended for adults, children, and increasingly for high school students? Were high school girls initiated into the norms and practices of heterosexuality and femininity through products and popular culture? Did they challenge or accept these messages?

As boundaries of age, maturity, and consumer responsibility shifted, some advertisers, manufacturers, and retailers recognized high school girls as a potential market and tried, with varying degrees of success, to earn their consumer dollars. Girls responded to these efforts, but they also demonstrated their interest in products created for adult women. Exploring these trends helps to explain how an age group was defined and a market formed, as well as how industries responded to unintended consumers.

High school girls and producers of goods and culture were not the only ones involved in these complicated negotiations. Professionals, social scientists, educators, and parents created and resisted change and engaged in an extensive dialogue over the nature of "adolescence," high school, and the emerging concept of the "teenager." Parents interacted directly with girls, fighting daily battles over clothing, beauty, sexuality, and music and movie preferences. Others studied, analyzed, or advised girls, interacting in less immediate ways. These adults often found themselves at odds with manufacturers and marketers, as well as girls' growing consumer independence and attention to teenage trends, exacerbating generational differences. Parents lost some degree of control over their daughters as peer, consumer, and popular culture gained new importance in the lives of high school girls.

The best word to describe the development of teenage girls' culture from 1920 to 1945 is uneven. Changes did not begin exactly in 1920 and did not end in 1945. In between, change was not constant, nor did it follow a predictable trajectory. Change within various industries—fashion, commercial beauty products, music, and movies—happened at different times and often with no attention to similar efforts by others. Some industries attempted to shape the teenage market; others remained unaware as teenage girls became major purchasers of their goods. Chapter one outlines the social and cultural factors that made the emergence of teenage girls' culture possible, from academic theories to the rise of high school. It explores the roles teenage girls played and the significance of these changes.

Awareness of high school girls as a distinct market originated with the fashion industry. Local department stores were the first to experiment with teenage sections and with strategies for attracting and selling to high school girls. Chapter two examines this formation from the perspective of manufacturers, retailers, and advertisers, locally and nationally, beginning with nascent efforts in the 1920s. It compares these efforts with high school girls' relationships to fashion and clothing, examining the impact of high school culture on size and style changes and the importance of girls' creative efforts to shape their wardrobes in order to express their developing peer group identity and personal interests.

Chapter three explores the relationship between high school girls and the commercial beauty, health, and cosmetics industries. These industries were less aware of high school girls than clothing manufacturers and marketers were. A growing market of advice literature helped shape girls' experimentation, but girls read a range of magazines and advice books creatively. They adopted some beauty ideals and regimens and rejected others, sometimes mimicking adult styles while at other times creating teen-specific looks. Eventually, primarily after 1945, industry insiders began to see potential profits and teen cosmetics became a booming business.[12]

The music and movie industries were even slower to devote special attention to high school students. Before 1945, high school girls developed an important relationship with commercial music. Chapter four examines how high school girls and boys listened to music. In relation to popular culture in the form of music and movies, boys and girls both participated actively and often together. Yet they also participated in different ways and this chapter explores how girls integrated songs, dance, and radio into their daily lives, shaping trends and surprising some industry analysts.

Similarly, male and female high school students watched movies regularly. As avid moviegoers and fans, high school movie attendance attracted attention from scholars and cultural critics decades before studios recognized the devotion of young people and understood their movie preferences. Chapter five outlines adult responses to this phenomenon, as well as efforts by the movie industry to create teenage characters. It compares this attention with girls' responses to movies, rarely anticipated by studios, including the teenage movie culture they constructed. Moviemakers preferred to envision high school girls as innocent and asexual, not noticing their strong preference for handsome or glamorous adult characters played by Rudolph Valentino, Clark Gable, Greta Garbo, or Hedy Lamarr over wholesome, juvenile characters played by Mickey Rooney and Judy Garland.

In all of these situations, girls created a unique teenage culture. They utilized the materials of popular culture to do so, reshaping adult or multi-generational products into teen-centered trends. They re-created popular stories and fantasies of heterosexual romance and love, reading advice literature and expressing anxiety about popularity. Yet they also pushed boundaries of sexuality, exploring various looks and consequences. Failure to recognize this impeded the efforts of some marketers and manufacturers to connect with teenage consumers, especially in the case of movies. In other instances, such as formal dresses, a range of choices demonstrated important differences between ages thirteen and seventeen as well as continued confusion and conflict between parents, daughters, and peers over how sexy girls should or could be in their teens. Some dress lines gained popularity with mothers but failed with teens because they were too frilly; others failed because they were too sophisticated or revealing for fourteen- or fifteen-year-old bodies. Some of the most successful combined the two. This was not a unified, static culture, yet it emerged in similar ways at high schools around the country.

The history of youth culture in America changes with the examination of teenage girls from 1920 to 1945, before the postwar explosion of teen culture and rock 'n' roll. Teenage girls' culture began with high school girls' definitions of themselves as individuals and the growing tendency to locate themselves within—and thus helping to create—a group identity. Beyond the girls themselves, various forces worked to create a distinct identity based on age and gender. The complicated relationship between producers of culture and goods and their intended (or sometimes unintended) consumers, through a period of trial and error, helped shape a new market for consumer goods and popular culture and pave the way for a mass consumer market focused on teenagers in the twenty-first century.

999

A Note on Sources

The findings in this book are largely based on the voices of high school girls gathered from unpublished sources, including diaries and letters, and published sources, such as yearbooks and short stories. The research also draws upon a range of local and national industry and scholarly materials, such as corporate newsletters, advertisements, academic studies of high school habits and anxieties, and longitudinal studies that included high school girls in the 1920s, 1930s, and 1940s. Additional information comes from contemporary published material such as the Sears catalog, *Women's Wear Daily, The Parents' Magazine, Scholastic* magazines and books, *Ladies' Home Journal, Calling All Girls,* and *Seventeen* magazine.

Although the trends discussed occurred across the United States, these data have allowed for the comparison of national trends with individual experiences and comparison of national business interests with the interests of girls. National advertising efforts, as well as those of local merchants, illustrate enormous uncertainty about the high school market. Yet they demonstrate continued efforts from some industries to understand and control it, while other industries overlooked it completely. Although the voices of high school girls do not represent a random sample, they illustrate patterns across the country that coincide with the messages of individual diarists, letter writers, and yearbooks in various locales, as well as stories and poems from high school students throughout the country.

There is a significant literature by and about the scholars, educators, and experts who played an important role in structuring and defining the lives of girls in their teens. These professionals helped create the vocabulary of angst and engaged in extended dialogue with parents and other professionals about the roles of young people. Although they are not the main focus of this book, they provide important context throughout as observers and advice givers. In addition, since the high school experience is central to this discussion, the declining number of young people, aged thirteen to eighteen, who did not attend high school, are not included.

High school yearbooks provide an important source of information on the lives of young people, recording scattered information on a wide range of girls—the studious and the popular, the athletic and the musical. Filled with snapshot images, yearbook descriptions such as "Eager to . . . ," "Happy while . . . ," or "Purple passions" present a wealth of detail on student habits, preferences, and peer culture. The yearbooks in this study come primarily from schools in and around Baltimore, Maryland, including four African American high schools in the Baltimore and Washington, D.C., area, with yearbooks from the West Coast for comparison. They represent students from all socioeconomic backgrounds, drawing on exclusive private schools, small parochial schools, large public schools, college preparatory schools, technical schools, and evening high schools. Students attending these schools came from a range of ethnic and religious backgrounds, including Protestant, Catholic, Jewish, immigrant, native-born, African American, Polish, Italian, and Irish.

Washington, D.C. opened the first high school for African Americans, the Preparatory High School for Negro Youth, in 1870. By the 1920s, the city offered three options for African American youth—an academic school, a technical school, and a commercial (initially a business) school. These divisions were similar to those in white schools: the academic high school emphasized college and work; technical schools emphasized practical skills for the girl "who goes directly out into life." African American high school yearbooks were more likely to discuss race and prejudice, increasingly so in the 1940s, but the main themes in relation to teen culture mirrored those in the broad range of high schools. Similar references to bobbed hair and flappers, to popular women's magazines such as *Vogue* and *Harper's Bazaar,* and to famous movie stars appear throughout. The wish lists are similar as well, recording desires for cosmetics, chocolate, bridge, boyfriends, music, movies, and dancing.[13]

The diaries and letters used in this research tell more individual stories, yet they also recount important national stories. They record personal responses to national trends, as well as the individual experiences of moving through an increasingly significant stage of life. These were primarily written by white, middle- or upper-middle-class girls who attended high school and often college.

The earliest writings are from Frances Turner. Turner lived in Baltimore, Maryland, and graduated from high school in 1922. She corresponded frequently with girlfriends, and their letters address the changing roles and fashions of women, from bloomers to driving to bobbed hair. Beth Twiggar, an aspiring writer, wrote frequently and passionately in a long series of diaries. Born in 1913, she grew up in Ossining, New York, entered high school in the mid-1920s, and filled her diaries with rich, colorful descriptions of her life, friends, activities, and relationship to popular and consumer culture. Beth's writing often reflects the "jazzy" style of the 1920s culture that she longed to emulate, and her wit, prescient analysis of the changing world around her, and knack for self-reflection make her diaries entertaining and insightful. She offers a valuable perspective on high school culture because she articulates trends found throughout all of the data presented here, coherently discussing developments expressed more abstractly by other girls.[14]

Representing other parts of the country, Yvonne Blue grew up in and around Chicago, Illinois. She began writing her diaries at age eleven, and at age twelve, in the fall of 1923, she enrolled in high school. Precocious, creative, and intelligent, she recorded her rich fantasies, friendships, and social life, as well as her rapid transition from a carefree child to a self-conscious high school student. Arvilla Scholfield grew up in a small town in Northern California. She kept a diary in 1926, at age sixteen, and recorded the events of her life at school and at home. She particularly enjoyed dancing and movies, and many of her brief yet telling entries describe these leisure time activities. Katherine Rosner lived in upstate New York and kept a diary during her sophomore year of high school in 1929. She recorded conflict with her parents, primarily her father, as well as her school and social activities, interests, and dreams. Adele Siegel grew up in one of two Jewish families in a Staten Island suburb. She wrote her diaries from age fifteen to seventeen while attending high school in the early 1930s.[15]

In the late 1930s, Betty Goldstein, later Friedan, wrote an autobiography and a diary for a high school English class in Peoria, Illinois. These documents offer a more formal perspective on being a high school student in this era. June Goyne Corotto attended high school in the early 1940s in Ashland, Pennsylvania. In 1984, she wrote about her life and reminisced at length about her teenage years.[16]

Two later diaries provided material for comparison. June Calender was born on a farm near Versailles, Indiana. Her extensive and lively diaries, primarily written during her high school years in the mid-1950s, record the strong influence of national popular and consumer culture on high school girls outside of urban centers. Calender read *Seventeen* magazine and regularly attended movies, adopting various styles and attitudes. She romantically envisioned herself a fashionable intellectual misplaced in a rural community. Finally, the relatively brief diary of Ruth Teischman, a twelve-year-old from Long Island, New York, provides comparison with later years as she records her self-conscious development into a teenage girl—physically, emotionally, and socially—in 1959.[17]

Published sources, such as volumes from *Scholastic*'s yearly writing competition and books of high school poetry, provide access to an even wider range of voices—geographically, racially, ethnically, and socioeconomically. Published and unpublished letters also offer insight into high school girls' friendships and interaction with consumer and popular culture in the form of clothes, beauty, music, and movies. In addition, a series of interviews conducted in the 1990s with women who attended high school during the 1920s, 1930s, and 1940s provided valuable insights into teenage girls' culture.[18]

Another central source for this research was a series of longitudinal surveys conducted in Berkeley and Oakland in Northern California. Psychologist Harold Jones began the Oakland Growth Study (OGS) in 1931 at the Institute of Child Welfare (later renamed the Institute of Human Development [IHD]), affiliated with the University of California at Berkeley, to research the physiological, intellectual, and social growth of adolescents. Jones selected the original sample of 212 subjects from fifth and sixth graders at

Oakland elementary schools likely to attend the junior high school affiliated with the university. In the early 1930s, when more than 90 percent of the population of Oakland was white, the researchers determined that there were not enough non-white children to constitute adequate subgroups for analysis, so the children selected for the study were all white. The children represented all socioeconomic groups, with roughly one-third from lower-class families, one-third from middle-class families, and the remaining third from upper-class families.[19]

OGS data were collected primarily through the schools and at a clubhouse adjacent to the junior high school. Participants spent much of their free time at the clubhouse throughout their junior high school and high school years and visited the institute every six months for formal exams and tests. At the clubhouse, social scientists recorded and commented on the behavior, activities, and conversations of participants. Most of the material was collected openly, although subjects could not read their files. Participants were aware of the constant attention, but they enjoyed the benefits of the clubhouse, from music and magazines to social activities, and became somewhat inured to the observations over the years. Only one set of data was consistently collected without permission. As subject participants dressed and undressed for physical examinations, observers secretly listened to dressing room conversations. Although a few participants suspected that observers were eavesdropping, most did not. Some subjects criticized the study and observers during these "private" conversations and others spoke about personal topics, such as menstruation and budding breasts, but in general this dialogue did not differ significantly from that recorded openly at the clubhouse.[20]

Additional IHD data comes from the Berkeley Guidance Study (GS), a personality development study that followed every third child born in Berkeley, California between 1928 and 1929. These families were also predominantly white, Protestant, and native-born due to the demographics of Berkeley in the late 1920s; they represented all socioeconomic groups. Interviewers recorded information on "Habits and Regimes" as well as similarities and differences between parents and children on a variety of topics. Data collected were similar to those for the OGS. Subject participants in both studies were assigned numbers, and data was recorded according to these numbers. Contemporary names have been assigned for the purpose of readability.[21]

The IHD data offer many rich layers for analysis. The varied tests and observations traced the lives of high school students during the Depression, during World War II for the GS, cataloging their attitudes toward consumer culture and burgeoning high school culture through interviews, questionnaires, tests, and writings. In addition, researchers freely recorded their opinions throughout the observations, allowing insight into adult perspectives on high school culture and on definitions of "growing up." The raw data include extensive observations from the clubhouse, dances, parties, and field trips of participants' physical, social, and cultural interests and development, as well as dress, hairstyles, and habits.

These notes often contained reports of participants' formal and informal discussions. Dialogue was written out by observers, sometimes verbatim, and other times reconstructed or summarized. Although the notes are not always clear on this point, they allow unique insight into girls' lives and a rare opportunity to "hear" the voices of high school girls in the 1930s and 1940s. Responses to self-reported questionnaires on personality, attitudes, interests, and activities, as well as letters, essays, and other material written by participants for school, provided further insight.

999

Integrating these myriad sources allows for an exploration of how teenage girls related to popular culture as producers and marketers sought to understand, create, shape, and eventually capture the teenage market. Although the data are limited in some respects and may not be scientifically representative, they merge individual stories with national sources and inspire confidence because they are consistent. A teenage girl in a remote part of Northern California shared enough with a Jewish girl on Staten Island and a farm girl in Indiana to demonstrate a distinct teenage culture in the making.

Emergence of
Teenage Girls

In the second half of the nineteenth century, the lives of young people changed significantly. Those in their teenage years received increased attention within the family as the birth rate declined, urban life outpaced rural, industrialization changed the shape and nature of work, public education expanded, and middle-class strategies for success focused on education and nurturing of the young. By the late nineteenth century, reformers, educators, social scientists, and legislators began to conceive of those in their teens as separate from adults and children, young people who deserved limited freedoms yet required special protection. The legal system created separate courts for accused juveniles. State and federal governments began to legislate age requirements for marriage, school attendance, and work, and later for voting, driving, and consuming alcohol. There was little consistency in these legal definitions of maturity and immaturity, and some legislation further divided age boundaries by gender. Girls, for example, could marry at a younger age than boys, but boys could legally consent to sexual intercourse at a younger age than girls could.[1]

Psychologist G. Stanley Hall is often credited with establishing the modern concept of adolescence with his seminal work, *Adolescence: Its Psychology and Its Relations to Physiology, Anthropology, Sociology, Sex, Crime, Religion, and Education,* published in 1904. Hall interpreted adolescence, from thirteen to eighteen, as a distinct period of crisis and preparation for life. Some psychologists and educators disagreed with Hall's definition of adolescence as tumultuous, but his work firmly defined adolescence as a separate stage of life.[2]

Hall's theories influenced the scholarly study of child development, but his ideas spread far beyond academia. They shaped school reform, leading to the rise of physical education, the development of adult-sponsored recreational and extracurricular activities, and vocational education. They also shaped home life, defining standards for middle-class parenting disseminated through manuals for raising youth. Parents, educators, and other professionals changed the way they taught and understood adolescents as Hall's ideas spread.[3]

This dialogue occurred primarily among adults, but attention to age changed the lives of young people. Age became an increasingly important factor in America in the late nineteenth century, defining the individual's role in society in relation to family, school, work, and community. In the early part of the twentieth century, "youth" often referred to those in their late teens and early twenties who worked, started families, or attended college. But the categories were fluid, and a fifteen-year-old factory worker could be categorized more easily as a "youth" than as an adolescent. This changed during the first decades of the twentieth century as psychological theories, the changing shape of the family, and shifting economic structures led to the rapid growth of high school attendance. High school, based on biological age, transformed the life experiences of young people aged thirteen to eighteen as a period of schooling came to define a stage of life. The dramatic increase in high school attendance proved to be the single most important factor in the development of teenage culture.[4]

Between 1910 and 1930, enrollment in secondary schools increased almost 400 percent. Compulsory education laws, primarily passed between 1870 and 1910, required young people to attend school, usually through age fourteen. States did not enforce these laws rigorously and exemptions were easily attained, but the legislation reflected a growing societal desire for young people to remain in school longer. Furthering this trend, the average number of days per school year increased, as did the average number of days attended. In 1900, students spent an average of 99 days in school; by 1940, that number rose to 152. This growing student body spent more time together each year, expanding the role of high school and peers in their lives.[5]

As seen in graph 1.1, the proportion of fourteen- to seventeen-year-olds in high school grew from 10.6 percent in 1900 to 51.1 percent in 1930 and to 71.3 percent in 1940. The percentage of seventeen-year-olds who graduated, as seen in graph 1.2, remained

Graph 1.1   Percent of 14- to 17-Year-Olds in U.S. Enrolled in High School

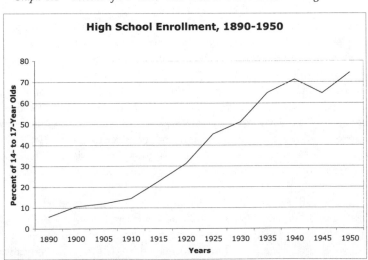

Graph 1.2   Percent of 17-Year-Olds in U.S. Graduating from High School

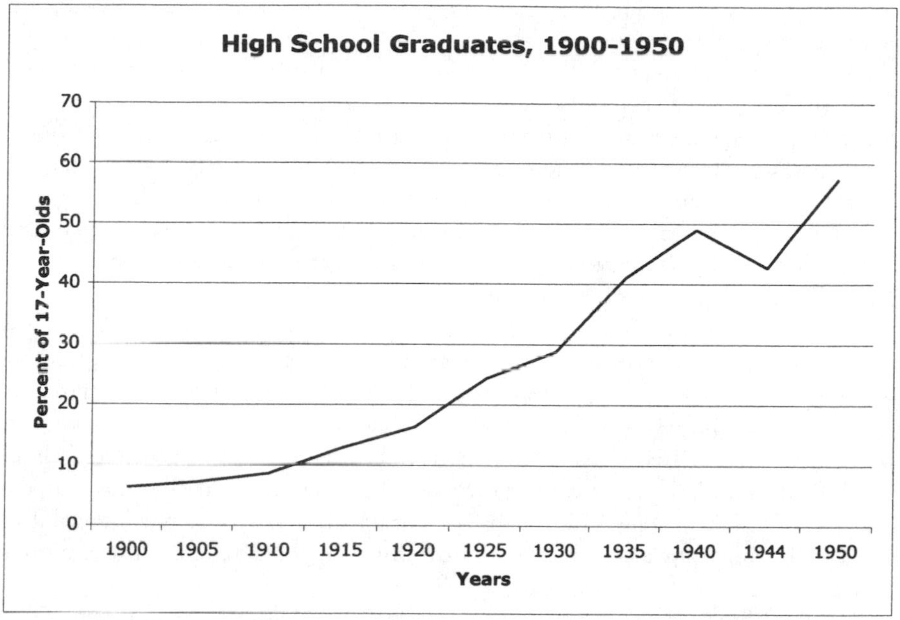

High School Graduates, 1900-1950

lower but still rose steadily from 6.3 percent in 1900 to 28.8 percent in 1930 to 49.0 per-cent in 1940. These numbers did not represent all fourteen- to seventeen-year-olds equally. In urban areas, 60 percent of youth attended high school in 1930, compared with 30 percent in rural areas. Girls made up slightly more than half of the student popula-tion and graduates.[6]

As enrollment grew, the student body changed and the number of rural, immigrant, African American, and poor young people who attended high school increased. High school shifted from an elite institution to a universal one, attracting students from all socioeconomic groups. Middle-class and upper-middle-class youth were more likely to stay in school longer and graduate, but many working-class and immigrant families also made high school education a priority for their children. The number of African Amer-ican youth in high school rose as well, although more slowly, especially in the South and in rural areas. Nationally, African Americans comprised roughly 10 percent of the total population in 1920 and 1930, but only 1.5 percent of the high school population in 1920 and 3 percent in 1930.[7]

By 1930, high school was an accepted step on the path to adulthood in America. Ed-ucators, business leaders, and parents waged heated debates about the changing nature of high school education and fought over curriculum, the role of education in "Ameri-canizing" immigrants, and the separation of academic and vocational classes. Educators designed rapidly expanding high schools to create responsible citizens, promote social order, and, during the Depression, keep young people out of the labor market. Yet unan-ticipated results occurred. High school had a dramatic effect on students because it pro-vided a place for constant peer interaction without parental supervision. In classrooms and through extracurricular activities, high school students discovered an unprecedented opportunity to develop friendships and peer culture free from adult control.[8]

Peer culture played a new, central role in shaping the experience of adolescence, especially for girls, by promoting conformity and age-specific norms and allowing for the development and dissemination of teenage culture. In the 1920s, fashion changed dramatically and high school became a site for struggle between students and school officials, students and parents, and among students themselves. At high schools around the country, girls experimented with new styles, wearing makeup, high heels, and shorter skirts to school. In response, school officials—and sometimes peers—created rules to control these behaviors. Student support for these rules could represent a desire to please school officials as much as disapproval of particular styles. Student involvement—official and unofficial—also demonstrated early consciousness of peer influence and its role in the growth and regulation of teenage culture.[9]

During a radio broadcast of high school student discussions in 1937, one girl summed up the advantages and disadvantages of the intense peer culture high school provided, "One of the greatest benefits is the association with classmates in a group of one's own age. One gets poise and confidence." She added, however, "I know students who have gotten inferiority complexes because they haven't been taken into a clique which they particularly admired." High school culture was often divisive, and competition and exclusivity among social groups was not uncommon. Yet despite internal divisions, high school provided the institutional setting for the development of a distinct teenage culture across social divisions.[10]

Although high school played a central role in establishing the concept of the "teenager," it was not the only factor. Many social and cultural changes influenced high school girls and their relationships with consumer and popular culture. Production of consumer goods rapidly outpaced population growth between 1900 and 1930, and mass-produced goods largely replaced homemade items. Advertising in national magazines increased 600 percent from 1916 to 1926 while newspaper advertising doubled. In addition to rising volume, the nature of advertising changed. New attention to consumer anxiety and satisfaction reshaped advertising as a guide to products, but more importantly a guide to being socially acceptable and stylish. This proved important for teenage girls who welcomed clothing and products designed for their bodies and lifestyle and craved recognition of their emerging status as individuals in a distinct stage of life.[11]

By the early twentieth century, middle-class women had become the primary consumers as well as a central target for advertisers, and they received significant attention from newly established advertising agencies. This partially explains the focus of teenage consumer culture on girls—females were already considered a receptive and appropriate audience for advertising. A *Printers' Ink* article rejoiced in 1922, "Girls seem to be doing their buying at a younger age than ever before." Although young women shopped predominantly with their mothers before 1920, they began to shop alone more frequently in the 1920s and 1930s as they gained access to public and commercial space. Much to the delight of advertisers and storeowners, this article reported that girls often entered stores with advertisements in hand.[12]

Teenage girls did not read all advertisements equally, but ads became part of their everyday world. In 1937, at age sixteen, participants in the Oakland Growth Study in Berkeley, California, demonstrated their ability to connect advertising slogans with brand names on a questionnaire. A remarkable 95 percent answered Coca-Cola to the prompt, "The Pause that Refreshes." High school students even played word games based on this growing phenomenon, casually noting, "played the advertising game" or "We played 'Advertisements'" in yearbooks and diaries.[13]

During the first decades of the 1900s, women, and especially young women, also gained access to public space through the rise of commercial leisure, including amusement parks, dance halls, and movies. This was true for young wage earners in the early part of the twentieth century and especially true for high school students as their numbers increased. Social commentators throughout the 1920s and 1930s noted, often disapprovingly, a marked decline in the amount of time young people spent at home within the realm of parental authority. Tension with parents emerged frequently over this decline as school, peers, and the expanding world of consumption and leisure increasingly influenced children and young people in their teens. This expanding world had a hold on the lives of teens that would only increase over the coming decades.[14]

Girls' interest in consumer products and popular culture merged with attention from businesses and advertisers to hasten the development of teenage girls' culture. Mass media, such as magazines and newspapers, played an important role by raising awareness, disseminating information, and in some cases spreading fads. By the 1920s, publishers and writers began to notice the market value of stories on "wild youth" as well as a new reading audience of high school girls.[15]

As in advertising, "youth" in mass media generally referred to young people between the ages of eighteen and twenty-four, although some writers included high school students in tirades against the younger generation. This attention to college-age youth set in motion the "discovery" of a separate high school culture and, eventually, its promotion as an object of interest to middle-class and upper-middle-class readers. Although many articles on youth denounced the dress, attitudes, and behavior of flappers, others sought to ameliorate intergenerational conflict, emphasizing the value of a "questioning spirit" and the overall continuity in moral values.[16]

Society columns had heralded debutantes before the 1920s, but this interest demonstrated a fascination with the lives of the wealthy more than an interest in youth. In July 1928, *Ladies' Home Journal* unceremoniously introduced a "Sub-Deb" column to speak to and about upper-middle-class girls. The column initially addressed girls with plans for college, debutante balls, or marriage and offered advice on growing bobbed hair "gracefully." By 1931, the tone shifted and a new editor, Elizabeth Woodward, wrote breezier columns, addressed high school students directly, and discussed ways to attract boys, gain teacher approval, and decorate bedrooms.[17]

The 1920s supported the development of teenage culture through the celebration of youth, the evolution of commercial leisure and consumer culture, and the steady rise in high school enrollment. The Depression in the 1930s also shaped teenage culture in several important ways. Despite economic hardships and more limited access to cars, consumer goods, and leisure, teenage girls' culture grew to a national phenomenon during the 1930s. Some young people could not afford to stay in school and looked for work at home or on the road. At same time, government and societal pressure on young people to remain in school and out of the labor force increased, and enrollments continued to rise. Less money was available, yet young people still pursued teen trends, finding creative ways to alter existing clothes and establish new fads. Manufacturers and marketers, faced with declining revenue, showed new interest in niche markets such as high school girls as they sought smaller, more focused groups of consumers and furthered market segmentation. The onset of World War II led to shortages and an economy focused on war production. Yet teenage girls merged patriotism with consumption, making necklaces to promote scrap collection and painting Red Cross symbols on their hats and nails. High school enrollment dropped slightly as older teens enlisted in the armed services or filled wartime work shortages, but it marked a momentary decline within the overall trajectory of rising high school attendance throughout the twentieth century.

Impact on Teenage Girls

A new consciousness of age accompanied the rise of high school attendance. Girls in this era expressed acute awareness of the transition from childhood into the teenage years and from the teens into adulthood. In 1929, a girl named Eleanor confided her ambivalence about turning thirteen in a letter to her friend Adele: "I'll have to wear dresses, stop slamming everyone, get settled down and learn how to be civilized." Eleanor accepted social norms of femininity regarding dress, manners, and domestic duties and of the teen years as the appropriate time to begin to adopt these norms, but she only reluctantly sacrificed her childish exuberance and freedom. Turning thirteen often meant loss of freedom in dress and action for girls. By sixteen and seventeen, the end of the teen years loomed large, and many girls expressed similar apprehension about the transition to adulthood. Leaving high school and one's adolescence could mean new opportunities, but it could also mean a more prescribed life.[18]

In addition to high school life and peers, advice literature and advertisements shaped the lives of teenage girls. Twentieth-century literature for boys emphasized education, work, independence, and rebellion, but literature for female adolescents addressed behavior, appearance, and relationships, promoting domestic skills and consumer goods. While offering solutions for improving appearance, dress, posture, figure, weight, and relationships, media messages created new problems for girls, fostering anxieties and providing a language for insecurities. These messages, and their popularization in women's magazines and other media, introduced high school girls to the world of commercial "looks" culture, prescribing femininity, heterosexual romance, and strategies for changing from young girls into women. The growing commercial attention to teenage girls both empowered and exploited them. For example, teenage sections in department stores allowed girls to congregate with less parental supervision and select clothes more likely to fit their bodies. But the increased attention also fostered dissatisfaction and exacerbated girls' concerns about their bodies, wardrobes, and "popularity."

In private writings from the 1920s through the 1940s, girls articulated awareness of their role as consumers, some advertising and media savvy, and enormous anxiety about popularity and appearance, frequently couched in the language of advice literature and advertisements. Beth Twiggar, a high school student in Ossining, New York, in the 1920s, frequently expressed desire for popularity and envy of her peers, "Gee I bet that girl's popular! Peppy, jazzy, cute, personalitied, and fascinating! Wonder what it's like." She also wrote dramatically, "I'm worthless and tearful. My inferior complex is killing me. I've got to cry." Advice literature, mixing the language of popular psychology and the marketplace, offered commercial solutions—usually booklets, clothes, or beauty products to help attain "popularity."[19]

As a high school sophomore in 1929, diarist Katherine Rosner also wrote extensively about her anxieties and perceived shortcomings, similarly parroting the language of advice literature for adolescents, "I'm so unhappy! I'm not popular with the girls or with the boys, and I don't know why. I wish I could see myself as others see me. Then I'd know my faults and be able to correct them." She continued, resigned, "I suppose the fault is partly my detestable self-consciousness, and partly my disgusting Inferiority Complex, and partly—the important, unknown part—a million other things."[20]

Several months later, Katherine explicitly linked her anxiety to a "clever" magazine essay called "Dates": "Among other truths, it said that if it gets around that a girl is unpopular, she might just as well move to another state or enter an old ladies' home! Whoopee! You'd better hurry up and make yourself popular, Katherine my girl." She joked about the magazine's gloomy predictions, yet she pushed herself to seek the ever-elusive "popularity." A few weeks later she wrote in desperation, "Oh, Diary, I think I'll go mad. I want a date so badly. Oh, I don't know what's wrong with me—why am I not popular? . . . I want to be popular—I want to be loved." Her tendency to blend popularity, dates, and romantic love with self-worth was common in the magazines and girls' writings.[21]

During the years between World War I and World War II, dating rose as an accepted social activity and way for organizing relationships between boys and girls, especially in towns and cities and among middle-class youth. As high school enrollment increased, dating became a more formalized part of the emerging high school culture. Dating in these years differed from nineteenth-century courtship in several important ways—young people on a date were usually alone or with other young people, without adult chaperones. In addition, dates increasingly occurred in public venues, such as movie theaters, in automobiles, or as a group at one young person's house. Dating provided more opportunity for premarital sexual contact, from kissing to petting to sexual intercourse. During this period, according to Kinsey data, the number of girls who "petted" before age sixteen increased from 29 to 43 percent and for boys, from 41 to 51 percent.[22]

Advice literature created a complex set of guidelines and mixed messages, telling girls to focus on attracting and pleasing boys but to avoid becoming "boy crazy" or too serious about one boyfriend. Learn to be sexually appealing to boys, magazines counseled, but not too sexy or too sexually active; flirt, but do not flirt too much; be coy, but be yourself. High school girls spent a good deal of time writing, talking, and fantasizing about boys and about interactions with other girls, from camaraderie to competition. This was often related to feelings about clothing and beauty, such as whether or not an outfit would attract a certain boy or receive approval from girlfriends. They also expressed excitement and anxiety about dating and the complications of exploring one's sexuality while controlling a date's sexual desire. Teenage girls' private writings, such as letters and diaries, are filled with euphemisms for sexual activity and sexual intercourse, from petting and necking to "going the limit" or "trespassing." Some girls were adventurous sexually; others relied on a slap on the face to deter a boy who was "terribly thrilly" or too sexually excited.

Advice on attracting and interacting with boys was routinely contradictory, telling girls not to act helpless, yet always to be a lady and let boys open doors. Girls were advised to be good at games but not *too* good; smart in school but not *too* smart. Katherine Rosner wrote in 1929 in response to such advice, "I really think it's true that boys don't like clever girls. That's why, lately, in school, I've tried not to appear too smart." She did not want to sacrifice her grades, though, and fretted about how to reconcile this contradiction. Beth Twiggar wrote in 1928, "I wish now I hadn't let him neck me though. Been reading stories about modern girls who didn't and the boys preferred them muchly." Such stories, common in contemporary movies and magazines, usually opened with a popular "bad" girl mocking a newcomer who refused to smoke or kiss. By the end of the tale, the new girl converted the "whole crowd," gaining popularity, respect, and a date with the most popular boy.[23]

Many teenage girls avidly read these messages, especially as media and markets began to target them directly. They followed some advice but not all, debating various points in writing, with friends, and through yearbook parodies. Yet they also lived in a broader social context. The twentieth century saw a rise in the number of single and married women who worked outside the home, often part of the new white-collar workforce holding clerical and retail jobs. In the 1930s, the marriage rate fell and the average age of first marriage rose. Girls who attended high school, especially those who graduated, found new work opportunities between school and marriage. Conceptually, though, the Depression strengthened societal desire for an idealized "traditional" household with a male breadwinner and a female homemaker. Most mothers did not work, and marriage remained a goal for many young women.[24]

This image of an idealized family permeated advice literature and the growing consumer market aimed at teenage girls. Despite the reality that it did not represent all households, advertising and advice literature emphasized products and strategies to help a successful girl secure a husband and financial stability. Some girls included marriage or an "Mrs." degree on their high school wish lists; others dreamed of careers in medicine, teaching, or fashion design. Some married and worked in the home while others led non-traditional careers and lives. But overall, the young women who attended high school from 1920 to 1945 followed a path toward marriage and a future as a homemaker. Some of these women married and raised children in the postwar era, becoming mothers who experienced what Betty Friedan termed "the problem with no name." The 1950s witnessed a rise in the number of married women who worked, but the work was often part time or temporary. While in their high school years, though, many of these young women were part of an important demographic group becoming a recognizable peer culture. They experimented with various styles and products, with their strength as a group, and with new freedoms.

This culture was defined in part by a new language centered on the word "teenager." The first half of the twentieth century witnessed the development of a group identity among high school girls, bounded by age and to a large degree by gender. It was shaped in part by important changes in the definition of the teen years by adults. The institution of high school played a critical role, as did rising commercial and media attention to high school girls as consumers of fashion, beauty products, music, and movies. Language also became important as the words "teen," "teenage," and "teenager" were defined.

Popular Science Monthly is often credited with being the first to use the word "teenager" in 1941. The *Readers' Guide to Periodical Literature* first listed it as a separate index entry in the 1943–1945 volume. Both the word "teenager" and the concept, however, existed before the 1940s. By the late nineteenth century, adaptations such as "teener" defined one in his or her teen years. By the 1920s, the words "teen," "teen-age," and even "teen-ager" referred to young people aged thirteen to eighteen or nineteen, especially in advice literature such as *The Trend of the Teens* (1920) and *Teen-Age Tangles: A Teacher's Experiences with Live Young People* (1923).[25]

Separated from the professional term "adolescent," "teen" and "teenager" were closely tied with high school and most frequently used for girls. These terms were also linked with consumer culture as manufacturers experimented by the early 1930s with "teen," "teen-age girls," and "teener" when marketing products for high school girls. Although spelling varied for decades, the language of a distinct age cohort linked with an educational institution, peer culture, and gender was underway by the 1920s and 1930s.[26]

Girls: The First Teenagers

America's Youth, a film in *The March of Time* series from 1940, claimed that "youth" created a "vast and glamorous society," setting styles and leisure trends. Integrating dominant stereotypes, the film used girls to represent "upper income" and college-bound young people, emphasizing weekly clothing allowances and preparation for marriage. Boys represented workers, from white-collar to factory and city to farm, as well as the unemployed. In 1943, *Life* magazine, buoyed by the success of photographic essays on high school jitterbugs in the 1930s, photographed a high school slumber party, "an old and honored institution" that "answers the need for gregarious interchange of ideas and gossip." Stories on high school girls' styles, fads, and language followed. The 1944 *Life* story, "Teen-Age Girls: They Live in a Wonderful World of their Own," depicted a gendered sphere defined by consumer goods. *The March of Time* film, *Teenage Girls,* furthered this link in 1945, and proclaimed that the high school girl had emerged "as an American institution in her own right. Where once teenagers were without group identity, lingering indifferently in the uncertain period between childhood and womanhood, today they constitute one of the most highly individualized and acutely noticeable groups in the nation." The film unequivocally equated "teenager," in the context of social gatherings and consumer behavior, with female—teenagers lingered between childhood and "womanhood," not childhood and adulthood.[27]

An important part of the history of teenagers lies in consumer culture and popular culture where girls were unequivocally the first teenagers. Although teenage boys received significant attention through media reports and academic studies on male juvenile delinquency, manufacturers, retailers, and advertisers focused their attention on high school girls. Girls were active consumers, searching for fashions that met their needs, pursuing commercial beauty products and popular culture before being targeted as a market distinct from adults or adult women. In the twenty-first century, teenage market research firms focus on boys and girls for some products, such as electronics, but teen and junior departments are still created almost exclusively for girls. *Seventeen* is a top seller in a market crowded with magazines aimed at teenage girls, while no magazine has tapped such a specific demographic for boys.

Some writers in the 1950s equated the rise of teenage culture with the rise of business interest in teenage girls. The Parent Teacher Association (PTA) magazine declared in 1956, "The trouble with teenagers began when some smart salesman made a group of them in order to sell bobby sox." Cultural critic Dwight MacDonald similarly wrote in 1958, referring to girls, "the teenage market—and in fact, the very notion of the teenager—has been created by the businessmen who exploit it." Girls, however, actively participated in such developments far more than these writers recognized. Some industries overlooked teenage girls entirely until forced to acknowledge that girls were important consumers of their products and messages. Girls were influenced by industry attention to their consuming habits, but they also shaped that attention and demanded that other industries notice them.[28]

These trends began not in the 1950s, but in the 1920s. They increased in the 1930s and fully emerged in the early 1940s. Rock 'n' roll, movies aimed specifically at teenage audiences, and segmented products such as teen deodorant did not exist. Growing awareness of high school girls as consumers with disposable income, influence over family purchases, and future status as adult shoppers, however, did. And the resulting impact on teenage girls, who had already begun to shape their culture based in part on their appropriation of consumer and commercial popular culture, was significant.

999

Throughout the twentieth century, a teenage consumer market evolved as high school culture strengthened and as interest in high school students' purchasing power intensified. Did businesses create high school girls as a distinct culture? Or did high school girls drive the development of teenage consumer culture? Some mid-century critics placed the agency squarely with the producers. Others, such as those within the world of production and selling, envisioned high school girls as leaders whose fickle interests and tastes they tried desperately to understand.

There are no simple explanations for these complex interactions that occurred at individual, local, and national levels. Consumer and popular culture are created for profit. Teenage girls were active consumers who used fashion, beauty products, music, and movies to construct their group identity, yet they also sought messages and goods that further inducted them into commercialized femininity and adult beauty culture. When producers and marketers first identified high school girls as a potential market, albeit tenuously, they shaped girls' sense of themselves as individuals, consumers, and actors in a complex social and economic system. And as girls began to develop strong peer affiliations, to experiment more freely with fashion, makeup, music, movies, and the notion of constructing their identities in imitation of—and in opposition to—adults, they were perceived as a ripe market opportunity.[29]

The growth of teenage girls' culture and a teenage consumer market is in part a story of celebration, of girls finding friendship, pleasure, and meaning by defining themselves through their high school lifestyle. It is also a larger story of capitalism, marketers and manufacturers whose bottom line involved profit. Some helped shape a niche market for earning that profit while others profited and only later began to understand the significance of teenage consumers. Teenage girls drove some of this development, based on their interest in establishing a peer identity. They used consumer products in innovative ways, forging a space for themselves in markets where none existed. They found freedom to make certain choices, challenge parents, and experiment with different personas. At the same time, they were constrained by the prescribed gender roles embedded in the cultural forms they encountered, guided by advice literature for women—and increasingly for teenage girls—to focus their energy on pleasing others, especially boys, and on not appearing too smart or competent. They adopted the language of literature and advertisements and agonized over the almost inevitable failure to achieve the mysterious "popularity."

From the early twentieth century until mid-century, professionals defined adolescence while advertisers, media, educators, parents, and girls experimented with the related but distinct concept of the "teenager." In the midst of these debates, girls in their teens helped define a unique culture based on age, gender, and participation in the institution of high school. This culture was also shaped by commercial forces—by the interest, and at times lack of interest, in teenage girls from the fashion, beauty, music, and movies industries, as well as by girls' active engagement with their products and messages. Girls controlled some of these interactions and were controlled by others. Fashion proved central to this transformation. High school girls expressed strong interest in clothing and in developing teenage styles. Manufacturers, marketers, and retailers were the first to notice this interest and the potential for establishing a new market.

"Oh the Bliss"
Fashion and Teenage Girls

FATHER: Your mother never dressed to catch a husband the way you girls do to-day.

HIS DAUGHTERS (IN UNISON): No, but look what she got!

—Joke, 1926 high school yearbook[1]

This joke's presence in a high school yearbook signifies the growing importance of dress in the social world of teenage girls as well as important fashion developments that shaped teen consumer culture in the twentieth century. It demonstrates increased access to fashion as a tool for constructing one's image as well as consciousness of the power to manipulate social status through appearance. Teenage girls' emerging group identity and interest in fashion, developments in the fashion world, and the growing interest of manufacturers, advertisers, and retailers in high school girls as consumers nurtured these trends.

Poodle skirts and bobby sox are powerful symbols often equated with the beginning of teenage culture in post–World War II America. Even historians of fashion or youth generally place the beginning of teenage fashions in the late 1940s or early 1950s. While fashions for high school girls entered a new phase in the 1940s, with clearer style divisions, size ranges, and marketing strategies, they actually first appeared during the preceding decades and tell an important story of market identification and group development.[2]

The 1920s, 1930s, and 1940s proved to be an important time of formation and negotiation for the teenage girls' market. Clothing manufacturers, marketers, and retailers were the first to recognize the financial significance of teenage consumers. They noticed potential for profit but were only beginning to understand how to attract high school girls. And these girls were only beginning to perceive themselves as a discrete group of consumers. Efforts to capitalize on this recognition were at best uneven and often unsuccessful throughout this period, beginning with local department store attempts to attract high school girls, primarily white and middle-class, through teen clothing sections, yearbook advertisements, and contests. Manufacturers created teenage clothing lines and then dropped them. Marketers focused on teenage girls, then ignored them. Often these efforts were isolated, operating separately rather than building on one another. With little infrastructure and no market research, confusion often prevailed. These decades did not witness one dramatic turning point nor a gradual, steady rise in awareness of teens. Instead, the years were marked by uncertainty and bursts of interest followed by quiet, a time for reinventing concepts and definitions of age groups and styles. Throughout this period, though, manufacturers and marketers increasingly assessed teenage girls' sizes, styles, and interests. Studying the years from 1920 to 1945 allows insight into the learning process for sellers as well as for teenage girls.

By the end of World War I, the styles and customs of everyday fashion were changing. Ready-to-wear clothing spread quickly, fueled by simpler styles, affordable prices, increased demand, and the growing fashion marketing and retail industries. Paris and New York still dominated design, but mass-produced imitations made fashionable clothes widely available for the first time. The wealthy began to lose their status as fashion leaders, replaced by movie stars, athletes, and "youth." "Youth," symbolized by college life, was idealized in the 1920s in fashion as well as popular culture. Youthful styles emphasized short dresses and boyish figures, leaving behind the exaggerated female curves of the early twentieth century and separating young women in their twenties from older women.

The rise of ready-to-wear clothing was significant for teenage girls. It fostered autonomy by emphasizing shopping over home production of clothes, shifting style and purchasing decisions partially outside the purview of mothers. Although parents still had primary control over clothing expenditures, girls increasingly shopped with friends, allowing peer approval a new, central role in clothing decisions. Yet despite the advantages of ready-to-wear clothing for girls, there were no styles or sizes designed for their growing bodies or increasingly distinct lifestyles and fashion interests. High school girls admired college styles, but they still had to choose between larger sizes in children's clothing or smaller sizes in women's. By the 1920s, high school girls sought out clothing tailored to their changing bodies, as well as appropriate styles for school, casual wear, and dates. As their numbers grew, so did their buying power. The teenage girls' consumer market developed simultaneously, trying to understand high school girls and at the same time to shape them into responsive consumers.

Parents, educators, and advice columnists encouraged girls' interest in fashion, pushing the linked acceptance of consumerism and femininity. Yet they also promoted strict limits on sexuality, barely keeping pace with changing definitions of "acceptable" dress and the fashion industry's growing efforts to capture the high school market. Conflict with parents, schools, and occasionally the legal system over what clothing was appropriate for certain ages and situations, from school to dances, became an important factor in shaping high school girls' fashion culture. Parents and concerned adults feared losing control of their daughters to the expanding world of peer culture and consumer goods, and to a large degree their fears were well founded. During these years, young people gained a greater degree of autonomy from parents, especially in the consumer world. Manufacturers, unsure at times who was selecting and paying for girls' clothes, alternated between addressing mothers and talking directly to girls, between presenting "girlish" fashions and highlighting more sophisticated styles.

Equally important, how did the teenage girls' fashion market emerge from the perspective of high school girls? What meanings did these girls bestow upon clothing? How did they negotiate shopping and clothing selection? How did they work within existing size ranges and shape the creation of new sizes and styles? And finally, how did they actually wear the clothes they purchased? Teenage girls wrote frequently about clothing and fashion, at times adopting the language of fashion advertisements, comparing themselves and each other to idealized images of teenage and adult life. They bought clothes in the hopes of gaining popularity or a boyfriend, accepted newly established dictates of fashion, and desired the "latest" styles or colors. Yet girls also questioned or even ignored fashion advice. They preferred to dress according to local fads that identified their friendships, group loyalty, and individual interests. Sometimes they hid their emerging sexuality and pushed gender boundaries, even when strongly discouraged by parents, schools, and media. Some fashions allowed girls to imitate adult women and adopt standards of femininity; others served to define them as teenage girls. Throughout, they used the materials of mass culture to voice their opinions and preferences while furthering sales.

Adult Interests: Professionals, Parents, and Popular Magazines

The fashion industry responded positively to high school girls' clothing interests in the 1920s and 1930s, but it was not the first group to notice. By 1900, psychological, sociological, and educational studies reported that girls ranked clothing and appearance as very important and that they willingly traded comfort for attractiveness. Researchers defined this link as normal, even necessary, for a girl's development. Educational psychologist Leta Hollingworth argued in 1928 that having the "'wrong' clothes is one of the keenest tortures to which an adolescent girl can be subjected." The trend continued in the 1930s. High school educator Lucretia Hunter equated appearance and contained sexuality with popularity in her 1936 advice book for girls. It was a girl's responsibility, Hunter wrote, to "present a pleasing and satisfactory appearance" and to "refrain from wearing that which makes her seem unduly sophisticated, rather than girlish and naive." These studies were always highly gendered—literature on boys never questioned their feelings about appearance or clothing and rarely focused on popularity.[3]

Parents also played an important role in shaping the emerging teenage market. One aspect of growing up is learning to make clothing decisions independently—from dressing oneself to purchasing clothing. By the 1920s, teenage girls modified existing clothing options and created unique styles for school according to peer standards. *The Parents' Magazine* (hereafter *Parents*) reported in 1931 that parents and adolescents disagreed over clothing more than any other topic, leaving parents shocked that "a formerly meek, docile girl" would fight to wear a desired outfit.[4]

Conflicts between parents and teenage girls about clothing reflected larger tensions related to sexuality, femininity, age-appropriateness, and peer culture, but they specifically centered on three issues: clothing purchases, upkeep, and daily appearance. The conflict was most intense in early adolescence, as teens learned responsibility and parents adjusted to their children's newfound independence. While some parents controlled every purchase, others allowed great freedom. In either situation, girls could be resourceful in gaining permission or circumventing rules. Although mothers often encouraged their daughters' interest in clothing, they lagged behind teenage girls and even manufacturers in awareness of teenage styles, insisting on clothes deemed too childish or too formal by teens. In the 1920s, 1930s, and 1940s, the teenage girls' fashion market increasingly created teen-centered spaces for shopping, promoted teenage independence, and offered new sizes and styles designed for teenage girls. These innovations created more common ground but also allowed more room for conflict.

Social scientists involved in the Oakland Growth Study (OGS) compiled extensive observations of study participants, providing a unique record of teenage life in the mid- to late-1930s. In addition to recording parent-child conflict, OGS observers often expressed strong opinions about girls' dress, asserting middle-class values and equating character with attire. Although some observers demonstrated greater fashion awareness than others, all commented on consumer and fashion choices. These descriptive and often value-laden observations recorded some of the most interesting aspects of teenage girls' consumer culture, detailing color, size, and style as well as perceived age-appropriateness of clothing items and peer responses. Girls in the study represented a range of class backgrounds and exhibited variation in dress. They knew that observers watched them constantly, but they did not always recognize or care about observer disapproval. The observations make clear the level of experimentation among teenage girls—imitating women's styles one day and wearing "teen" clothes the next day—and the growing differentiation among teenage girls' styles. School clothing grew more casual in this period while demand increased for new styles appropriate for secular social events such as school dances, informal parties, and dates.

OGS observers praised girls who wore the "regulation high school uniform" of a skirt, blouse, and sweater, especially matching ones, and criticized those deemed inappropriate, such as the girl who "wore straight waistless dresses long after she needed more mature attire" or one whose sweater "showed up her stuffy bosom." These observers presumed that both were unintentional. These critical comments reflected expectations that high school girls should be aware not only of the style, size, and condition of their clothing but of their body shape and of the opinions of others. One observer bluntly stated her opinion of a thirteen-year-old participant: "When the 'grown-up' idea in clothes first burst upon [Sharon], she came out in an outfit which reminded me forcefully of that worn by Jeanne Eagles as the prostitute in 'Rain.'" Descriptions of boys rarely included attention to clothing or appearance unless a boy wore exceptionally tasteful or noticeably ragged clothes.[5]

Disagreements with parents and sometimes peers, similar to disapproval by observers, attest to the importance of fashion—imposed from within and from without—in the world of high school girls. Parents forbade high heels at age thirteen or tight skirts at sixteen, but they still strongly encouraged girls' interest in clothing. Debates over how much sexuality or peer affinity a girl could express through clothing did not lessen this encouragement. In fact, mothers and other involved adults, such as educators or OGS observers, explicitly and implicitly worked to induct girls into the "looks" culture and to shape it, not to hinder it. They pushed girls into adult grooming habits and controlling undergarments, yet wanted girls to avoid overt displays of sexuality. Tensions arose regarding the appropriate age for beginning to experiment with "adult" styles, as well as over acceptable standards of femininity.

Although parents and other adult observers had well-defined ideas about what teenage girls should wear, high school girls were more receptive to fashion trends, women's magazines, and advice literature. Peers had great impact as well, often deriving fashion ideas from the same sources. Girls frequently read fashion magazines together, sharing ideas and incorporating the language into their discussions of clothing and shopping. By the late 1920s, fashion advice permeated girls' yearbooks, diaries, and stories. Girls discussed fashionable colors and styles and assessed their wardrobes. Beth

Twiggar exemplified this trend when she sadly proclaimed at age seventeen, "My adored fur coat is now passé. . . . They are all fitted this year, mine is straight & baggy." Sixteen-year-old Adele Siegel wrote excitedly in 1931, "'Burnt orange' is now 'Spanish tile' the most fashionable color, so my dress is very much up to date. It matches my coat." These girls paid close attention to fashion literature and to the "latest" trends. When Parisian couturier Paul Poiret visited America in the mid-1930s, he advised high school girls in Oklahoma to wear clothing suitable to their own coloring and bodies, not the latest fashions. To his dismay, they immediately inquired about the fashionable colors for the upcoming season.[6]

By the time OGS participants reached their early teens, they referred frequently to *Vogue, Mademoiselle,* and *Harper's Bazaar.* Girls requested current issues, sketched clothing seen in magazines, and discussed fashions. Yearbooks from a range of high schools— white, African American, parochial, public, private, academic, and technical—similarly reflected the impact of fashion magazines, labeling one student a "mirror for *Mademoiselle*" and praising another who "wears clothes like an ad from *Vogue.*" Before magazines in the 1940s, such as *Seventeen,* emphasized teen sizes and styles exclusively, teenage girls avidly read women's magazines, translating the messages for high school interests.[7]

Not all teenage girls shared this intense interest in fashion, but clothing played an important role in high school life. And of the many factors influencing wardrobe decisions, fashion magazines and advice literature held a special place. Although few read the magazines reverently, girls turned to them for information, advice, and reassurance. The advice cultivated further dependence on magazines and consumer goods—those who wore the right clothes and followed the magazines' advice would achieve beauty, popularity, and dates as defined by perfected images of models and fictional characters. The inevitable lack of sufficient beauty, popularity, and dates necessitated more magazine advice on how to attain them. Girls did not always accept this blindly and expressed strong ideas regarding clothing, but the messages of fashion and consumption were decidedly influential.

Teenage Girls Meet Fashion

Not all commentators agreed that fashion improved girls' lives, but the criticism further demonstrates the entrenched nature of this ideology. In 1923, Leora M. Blanchard's advice book, *Teen-Age Tangles,* warned parents of the dangers of fashion and advised that clothes "do not make the woman." The message that clothes did make the woman remained a popular theme in advice literature and fashion magazines, however, and was frequently reflected in studies of girls' self-perception. Sociologists Robert and Helen Lynd wrote in their 1920s study of social life in Muncie, Indiana, entitled *Middletown,* that upon entering high school girls became increasingly fashion conscious, leading to conflict with parents. When the Lynds returned to Middletown in the mid-1930s, they found a more highly self-conscious teen subculture, "the whole high school is said to be dressed down . . . but the social pace has continued." This dressing down was also due to a rise in teenage girls' fashions, marked by increasingly casual styles.[8]

Although styles grew less formal, anxiety intensified. In a study undertaken in 1937 of 3,000 girls from public, parochial, rural, and urban high schools, Mary Knoebber asked girls why they cared about personal appearance. Their responses demonstrate the impact of beauty and fashion messages aimed at women and increasingly at girls. Some echoed the advice literature mantra that beauty was a female duty: "'Because I am a girl.'" Others mimicked fashion magazines and advertising slogans: "'Appearance shouts out a personality,'" "'I like to be thought modern,'" and "'The sheer joy of looking "smart."'" Still others saw power to control their world through dress: "'It helps my chances of doing things I want'" and "'Rates with friends and teachers.'"[9]

The influence of advice and fashion literature on teenage girls is equally evident in Alice Barr Grayson's 1944 book *Do You Know Your Daughter?* Child psychologist Jean Schick Grossman, under the penname Grayson, edited a column in the first magazine for girls in their early teens, *Calling All Girls,* first published in July 1941. Grossman advised parents and teachers, after reading hundreds of letters from readers, that girls wanted to look and act like their peers. Yet the letters reflect stronger concerns, including intense anxiety about looks and popularity. One sixteen-year-old girl wrote, "I don't neglect anything in personal cleanliness and wear just the right shade of make-up. But I still don't have dates." This girl, and many who wrote Grayson, accepted the notion that the "right" clothes and makeup as well as access to consumer goods should equal popularity and dates. Letter writers also demonstrated an acute awareness of age-appropriate fashions in relation to peers. Several complained of mothers forcing them to wear "'babyish cotton dresses'" while peers wore longer, more "grown-up" clothes.[10]

The short story "Janie," published in the *Ladies' Home Journal* in 1941, attempted to illustrate humorously teenage girls' relationship to clothing. Casual skirts, jeans, and sweaters prevailed throughout the story, but dressing to meet a boy causes anxiety for sixteen-year-old Janie:

> She had decided, the night before, on her new rose-colored sweater and rose-striped skirt and her high-heeled pumps. The pumps were too obvious. She changed to saddle shoes and the whole thing was too ordinary. She took off the sweater and skirt and put on her white sharkskin dress. She removed the white sharkskin immediately and went to the closet for the blue dress with the little bolero jacket. The old blue dress was becoming but casual. . . . She was putting on the high-heeled pumps [when they arrived]. . . .

In this passage, Janie experiments with several "looks," equally frustrated when she looks as if she is trying too hard to appear grown up as when she looks too much like "just" a teenage girl. Finally, at the last moment, she finds the desired combination for appearing effortlessly attractive yet age-appropriate.[11]

High school girls increasingly wanted to dress like teenagers, a middle ground between children's styles and women's styles. Adolescent girls' interest in appearance was cultivated by adult fashion and advice literature and intensified with attention to teenage styles and consumer solutions related to "teen" problems. Sylvia Silverman reported in 1945 that feelings of inadequacy increased dramatically with age. At twelve, 24 percent of the girls questioned felt that their wardrobes were insufficient; by age eighteen, that number reached 100 percent. And further demonstrating the influence of advertising and advice literature, 95 percent believed that dressing well facilitated personal, social, marital, and vocational success in life; three-fourths of respondents believed the "right" clothes were required for happiness.[12]

Girls' writings illuminate some of the positive and negative emotions they connected with clothing. In 1928, at age fourteen, Beth Twiggar wrote, "Oh the bliss, the positive bliss of being well clothed. Mother and I to the city did went. . . . My coat is delectable, my dress delicious, my skirt most succulent." Her diary entry exudes happiness with the adventure of shopping as well as the clothes purchased. In addition to her rich, vivid language, Beth writes whimsically, playing with the order of the words to make the experience, and its retelling, even grander. Beth articulates the relationship many teenage girls had with clothing, illustrating a tendency to credit a dress or a sweater with the ability to bestow happiness or sorrow, confidence or insecurity.[13]

A short story written by a high school student in 1931 further demonstrates this power as a coveted scarf transforms its owner: "Standing before her little mirror she reverently lifted the scarf and tied it around her neck. . . . The reluctant red seemed to creep into her cheeks, and her dull eyes seemed to steal some of its blue. Suddenly she felt warm, splendid, powerful—beautiful." In the story, an awkward girl in a "shoddy" coat sacrifices her lunch money for a month to buy the scarf. Wearing it to school, she becomes funny, smart, and confident. When the wind pulls it away, she reverts to a hunched girl who "trudged off into the thick, gray streets." Her inner strength and beauty, summoned by the scarf, cannot withstand its loss.[14]

OGS data similarly demonstrated a strong interest in clothing across socioeconomic class that increased with age among female participants in the 1930s. A questionnaire about leisure time recorded a yearly increase in shopping and caring for clothing. By age fifteen, more than 75 percent of female participants read about styles or clothing regularly. While only 30 percent read *Cosmopolitan* in sixth grade, 75 percent did so by grade twelve. The number of girls reading *Harper's Bazaar* similarly increased from 17 to 83 percent and *Ladies' Home Journal* from 54 to 86 percent. As high school seniors, 80 percent talked about clothing "often" or "very often."[15]

High school yearbooks frequently mentioned clothing as well. Mabel the "fashion plate" was "always in style though a few minutes late." Another senior always looked "as if she has just stepped out of a bandbox." These sound remarkably similar to captions for fashion layouts, indicating not only that girls read magazines, but that they applied the stated ideals to themselves and their peers. Not all high school girls cared about clothing, and those who did could not always afford to buy the latest fashions. But the strong interest in clothing and adult fashion magazines among high school girls does demonstrate that many were ready and eager for teenage fashions.[16]

Creators of the teenage fashion market exploited peer pressure whenever possible. It was the essence of *Seventeen* magazine's extensive campaign in 1944 to convince marketers that teenage girls, embodied in the prototypical teenage girl *Seventeen* named "Teena," were a viable economic market, "Teena is a copycat—what a break for you! . . . She and her teen-mates speak the same language . . . wear the same clothes . . . use the same brand of lipstick." Some girls proudly admitted such peer loyalty. As girls grew older, though, they began to emphasize individuality. A seventeen-year-old OGS participant wrote that the girl she most admired "is not like the mob. She stands out in front, comparatively original. She is admired and isn't like Susie and Janie." Ironically, she used the language of teenage advice literature, including the ubiquitous "Susie" and "Janie," to describe this unique girl.[17]

What was new by the 1940s was the keen awareness of age-appropriate sizes and styles designed for teenage girls. Manufacturers, retailers, and advertisers played an important role in developing this awareness and the teenage girls' clothing market, however unevenly. In the 1920s, a few companies began to realize the needs of—and potential profits from—high school girls. Throughout the 1930s, attempts to reach high school girls intensified, but not in a coordinated, linear way. By the early 1940s, the teenage market was in full swing. High school girls themselves played an important role in shaping this market as they began creating fads, expressing style preferences, shopping with peers, and refashioning available clothes to create desired looks. Conflict generally occurred at home and in school, between girls and their parents or between girls and school officials. In the world of consumption, girls purchased or rejected styles, sizes, and designs, but on the whole they met these efforts eagerly.

Production and Marketing of Teenage Fashions

Advertising developed into a large-scale industry in the 1920s. As ready-to-wear clothing spread, manufacturers and retailers established their role as creators and distributors of fashion. Department stores sold clothing for men, women, or children. This led to "teen" sections for high school girls and targeted advertising, strategies that expanded in the 1930s. Manufacturers caught on more slowly as recognition of high school sizes translated into an understanding of girls as a separate culture with distinct styles.

Fredonia Ringo, author of a retail sales manual published in 1924, advised stores that mothers wanted daughters to look young as long as possible. She further recommended that styles for girls and juniors be changed infrequently. Ringo's description provides a benchmark for the consumer world that disregarded styles and sold girls' clothes to their mothers. Yet many high school girls already aspired to the fashion trends of college students or flappers in the 1920s, bobbing their hair and raising their hemlines. These styles promised the sexy sophistication and independence of an adult but not a matronly sort. High school girls did not have the freedoms of older "youth" but were nevertheless willing to struggle against families, schools, and even their own bodies for desired fashions. And a few stores were beginning to recognize their clothing challenges, willpower, and influence.[18]

Hutzler Brothers, a successful department store in Baltimore, Maryland, exemplified this early recognition in May 1926 with an advertising flyer entitled "Dressing the 'Difficult Age' of Thirteen to Seventeen." It sympathized with mothers: "When one's long-legged daughters have out grown childish garb, but have not yet attained the dignity of the debutante era, dressing them appropriately—and becomingly—is frequently a problem." Hutzler Brothers offered a solution with "smartly youthful styles" in a special section. This concept, a separate physical space with distinct styles and sizes, became a central theme for retailers interested in selling to teenage girls.[19]

Hutzler's remained in the forefront of the developing teenage market, advertising regularly in high school yearbooks in the 1920s, as shown in figure 2.1. These simple, text-based ads implied recognition of youth not only as a category but as one with special needs for clothing and service. Although "youth" in the 1920s often referred to late teens and early twenties and the ads referred to Junior and Misses departments, placing ads in high school yearbooks demonstrated awareness of the high school market. By 1930, Hutzler's ads mentioned clothes specifically for the "High School Age."[20]

Hutzler's was not the only Baltimore department store to notice high school girls. In a 1923 yearbook advertisement, Hochschild, Kohn & Company promised, "Whatever the High School Girl needs—in apparel and accessories," seen in figure 2.1. An article in the company's internal bulletin in 1930 recommended laying a foundation for the "alert modern miss of fifteen or sixteen" who would become the shopper for herself and her future family. According to this article, the store should promote "confidence in our merchandise values and style-sense" in the girl who shops with her mother, as well as the girl who, "in these days of feminine independence, comes alone." The bulletin advised salespeople to foster friendship with teenage girls: "whether the junior shopper comes to

*Whatever the High School
Girl needs---in apparel
and accessories---will
be found at*

HOCHSCHILD.KOHN & CO.

Baltimore's Best Store
Howard and Lexington

SMART APPAREL FOR SPRING

- - - - in the Hutzler Shops for Boys and
Girls. And service based on the understanding of youth.

HUTZLER BROTHERS C

2.1   Department Store Advertisements, High School Yearbooks, 1920s

your department to buy toothpaste, tennis shoes, gym suit or roller skates, always visualize her as Miss Baltimore of 1935 or Mrs. Baltimore of 1940 and make that contact
count. . . . She is a most important young person."[21]

This article combines several important messages. The reference to girls shopping
without adult supervision demonstrates that store personnel noticed teen shopping
habits. And although these girls were more likely to purchase inexpensive items, store
loyalty was extremely valuable. The article overlooked the clothes high school girls were
already buying but showed remarkable foresight and established a recurring theme in the
development of teenage girls' consumer culture—promoting brand loyalty in young
consumers to ensure future sales. By 1930, Hochschild Kohn had been advertising in
high school yearbooks for more than a decade.

Many stores experimented with language and strategies for attracting high school
consumers. The Hub, a major department store in Baltimore, announced an entire
"High School Floor" in 1926. Smaller stores emphasized "schoolgirl" messages, such
as "Priced Within One's Allowance," addressing a recurring theme in teenage girls'
fashion marketing—budget limitations—and acknowledging some autonomy in
clothing decisions. The language throughout these ads, however, demonstrates the
instability of the category "teenager." Some addressed schoolgirls, others "youth" or
"young moderns." Despite their presence in high school yearbooks and concerted efforts to attract high school business, advertisers did not yet conceive of teenage girls
as a discrete market.[22]

These yearbook advertisements come from a broad range of high schools in and
around Baltimore, Maryland, and Washington, D.C., including female and coed,
parochial and secular, white and African American, large and small, public and private,

and day and evening high schools. Some stores targeted exclusive schools; others technical schools. Many advertised intermittently. Why would a department store create the text for a high school ad but place it in only one local yearbook? Most likely, department stores responded to inquiries from yearbook editors seeking sponsors, but did not seek out this venue and did not consider local yearbooks a standard advertising medium. Nevertheless, they saw some value in reaching high school audiences and experimented with language and selling strategies.

These advertisements demonstrate industry awareness of teenage girls in the 1920s, yet the clothing advertised was still primarily made for children, "juniors," or older women. Although notoriously inconsistent, the industry worked to develop uniform size ranges. The term "junior," however, had a different meaning in the 1920s, 1930s, and 1940s than in the twenty-first century. In the loosely standardized terminology, "juniors" referred to women in their early twenties. These styles were distinct from "misses," more conservative clothes for older women. Little girls' clothes remained a separate category altogether. Further demonstrating the transitional nature of the teen market, Joel Gutman and Company in 1925 advertised The Twixteen Shop, where "the particular needs of Miss Fourteen-to-Twenty are carefully studied and intelligently provided for." This early use of "Twixteen," shown in figure 2.2, seemed to imply special sizing, but 14 to 20 was a common age-size range for "juniors," not teenage girls. The language, however, demonstrates an awareness as early as the mid-1920s that teenage girls were "in-between" sizes and styles as well as an attempt to sell them on older cloth-

2.2   Department Store Advertisements, High School Yearbooks, 1920s

ing rather than younger. Teen sizes appeared by 1930. The age-size range, 10 to 16, became the standard for teen sizes by the mid-1930s.[23]

The Sears catalog offers a valuable case study because of its semi-annual presentation of advertising campaigns and fashions. Sears worked hard to reshape its image in the 1920s from a farm catalog to a marketer of fashionable clothing at economical prices, creating inexpensive imitations of styles from New York or Paris and increasingly from Hollywood. It emphasized clothing acceptable to the broadest range of consumers: rural, small town, and urban. Relevant categories for teenage girls shifted within and between catalogs and, as the catalog frequently reminded buyers, age-sizes did not correspond with actual ages. The tone and targeted audience also shifted. In fall 1929, the catalog offered high school sizes for boys, but high school references reappeared in the 1930s only for girls. Much of this confusion was shared throughout the industry, as well as among parents and professionals. Few could define "appropriate" clothes for this group that would please the range of high school girls, moving between "childish" and "sophisticated" with only a vague conception of high school styles.

Perhaps counterintuitively, the 1930s proved to be a critical period of experimentation. The Depression bred innovation as traditional strategies failed to bring desired profit, leading some manufacturers to look to the margins for new markets. High unemployment added to the steady rise in high school enrollment leading young people to stay in school longer and fostering teenage culture. In addition, as competition for the college fashion market intensified, marked by the spread of college shops, fashion shows, and advisory boards, attention to high school girls increased. Marketers, retailers, and advertisers began to recognize the potential of the high school age group and tried, with varying degrees of success, to attract girls' attention. But their superficial understanding of teenage girls' consumer desires and purchasing power led to intermittent, often conflicting, efforts.

In July 1930, *Women's Wear Daily*, an industry newspaper, advertised a new line of clothing for the "growing girl"—Mary Lynn Frocks in half sizes, 10½ to 16½. The advertisement sympathized with retailers who tried "to satisfy the needs of your 'growing-girl' customer by *altering* your regular size dresses." In August 1930, Mary Lynn offered clothing "scientifically SIZED to FIT their PERSON and PERSONALITY." Appearing in time for the back-to-school season, these advertisements identified two important clothing issues for teenage girls—size and style. Successful teenage clothes had to fit both the bodies and the lifestyles of teenage girls. Yet Mary Lynn Frocks disappeared by 1931. The depressed economy could explain the fall of any new clothing line, but other factors contributed. No "teen" infrastructure existed in the early 1930s. Department stores advertised in yearbooks, but there was no large-scale advertising or manufacturing network. There was no accepted way of reaching girls, no recognized language for addressing girls, and no research on whether mothers or girls made purchasing decisions. And teenage girls in the early 1930s were still just beginning to see themselves as a cohesive, influential group.[24]

In the early 1930s, *Ladies' Home Journal* began to recognize high school students as distinct in size, if not yet in style. As seen in figure 2.3, this editorial advertisement from September 1932 grouped girls from kindergarten through high school under the heading "New Clothes for School." The drawings incorporate the elongated figures common in fashion illustrations in this period, but the patterns clearly differentiate "Junior High girls" in sizes 6 to 12 and 8 to 14 (patterns 1036, 1037, and 1039) from high school girls in sizes 10 to 16 (patterns 1038 and 1040). While there is some overlap in size

NEW CLOTHES FOR SCHOOL

1038. Use one of the new soft nubby woolens, and you'll have the smartest frock in school. That's not a bolero—it gives you a chance to use contrast in the blouse. Designed for ages 10 to 16.

1039. The square neckline is so becoming to Junior High girls—and those little white tabs at neck and wrists button on and off; easy to launder and keep fresh. Designed for ages 6 to 12.

8330. We'll not be outdone by our elders— we'll have suits too! The sleeveless frock has little bows to match the turnback revers and cuffs of the jacket. Designed for ages 6 to 14.

1043. Try a grown-up trick on your pudgy youngster and make her look taller and slimmer. Those plain-colored sections, front and back, make her look slender. Designed for ages 1 to 6.

1036. Whisk—and a change of blouse and Jane is ready to go off to school, fresh and clean! These jumper frocks are a time-saving help to mothers. Designed for ages 8 to 14.

1037. Five big buttons and a close-to-the-throat collar make this one of the sportiest of school dresses. It's an ideal design for the new soft wool fabrics. Designed for ages 8 to 14.

1040. The long lines of this dress will make your growing teen-age daughter look tall and slim. The kick pleats at the side of the skirt are comfortable. Designed for ages 10 to 16.

2.3   *Girls' Dress Patterns*, Ladies' Home Journal, *September 1932*

range, the "high school" models have more adult figures and appear older than sixteen or seventeen. The reference to "your growing teen-age daughter," however, addresses mothers. The drawings demonstrate both an awareness of graduated sizes and styles and how tenuous that awareness was.[25]

By 1933, in the depth of the Depression and with many years of experimentation ahead, teenage girls began to attract more attention. Notices mentioning teens or high school appeared frequently in the "Children's Wear" section of *Women's Wear Daily*. In

Detroit, the J. L. Hudson Company opened a High School Shop and decorated it in local high school colors with the goal, according to a company executive, of removing "the childish atmosphere for girls of high school age who are interested in shopping outside of children's sections and whose requirements cannot be filled properly in the misses departments." The same year, the L. Bamberger and Company department store in New Jersey held a "Justeen Fashion Show" using local high school girls as models. Bamberger successfully adapted this gimmick from college fashion promotions and celebrated the turnout, "a large number of girl[s] of the 'teen age who paid the closest attention to both the clothes and what was said about them." Teen fashion shows with models drawn from local high schools proved effective marketing tools, attracting the attention of shoppers and drawing friends of the models into the store. These examples also demonstrate the industry's growing concept of high school girls as teenagers, of the "teen age."[26]

The size range 10 to 16 appeared more frequently by the mid-1930s, as did mention of clothes designed for school and high school. Clothing advertisements included phrases such as "teeners," the "'teen' age," and "junior miss," but the size ranges, clothing styles, and marketing strategies remained far from uniform. Relevant articles in *Women's Wear Daily* appeared regularly in both the "Children's Wear" and "Junior Wear" sections of the paper. And the debate over size, style, and audience for teenage clothing and between "childish" styles and "grown-up" styles intensified.

Several manufacturers noted the popularity of teen-sized party dresses, but they approached the "sophistication" debate warily. Rainbow Children's Dress Company introduced black party dresses in moiré and taffeta because, "It is thought here that young girls in their teens have always coveted a black party frock as a symbol of the ultimate in sophistication." Others felt that party dress styles "should be selected with both childish and sophisticated customers in mind." The debate over sophistication in teenage clothes deepened as the market expanded. A *Women's Wear Daily* headline in 1937 proclaimed, "High School Girls Want to Dress Like College Girls," and asked, "Have You Followed Campus Trends in Your Teen Shop?" One buyer for girls' clothing asked, "'Sophistication' Is It a Teen Dept. Boomerang?" She blamed retailers and copywriters for "ma[king] so much of the fact that the teen girls must look sophisticated" that the "teen girl customer rejects merchandise in the teen shop as 'too young,'" and buys her clothes in the junior department.[27]

This issue, and its coverage in *Women's Wear Daily*, speaks to a larger question: teenage girls' agency in the development of the teenage market. The first headline stated that teenage girls had altered their tastes and asked if the industry kept pace. The second implied that copywriters and retailers wielded a heavy hand, creating the desire for sophistication where none existed and shifting market demands, leaving production lagging. This article assumed the existence of well-established teen shops as well as a growing tendency to watch teenage girls' consumer habits and argued that girls turned to the juniors department only when they could not find what they wanted in teen sizes. This debate demonstrates the strength of teenage girls' opinions, sometimes rejecting clothes newly designed to fit their bodies for the styles they desired. The styles and the question of "sophistication," a source of conflict with parents, schools, and adult advisors, often centered on sexuality and displaying the body.

Looking at the debate from the perspective of girls further highlights the fluidity of the market and the emerging strength of girls' fashion desires, especially in relation to the advice of parents and magazines. A yearbook picture from 1930, "Forest Park Girl

2.4   *Flapper Drawing, High School Yearbook, 1930*

as Others See Her," shown in figure 2.4, depicts a chic flapper, the symbol of youth, vi-
tality, and modernity, wearing a fitted black dress, a long string of pearls, and shoes with
exaggerated bows. The flapper fingers her pearls coyly and smiles seductively at the
reader with darkened eyelashes, thick lipstick, and stylishly bobbed hair. Similar images,
seen in figure 2.5, appeared throughout high school yearbooks in the 1920s and portrayed the artists' fantasies, how they wished to be seen. The drawings, however, had little in common with yearbook photographs of high school girls, shown in figure 2.6.
Although girls often imagined themselves as flappers, they rarely appeared so to others.
High school students dreamed about adult styles, but with the rise of teenage girls' fashions, they increasingly saw themselves as teenagers, too.[28]

2.5   Flapper Drawing, High School Yearbook, 1926

By the mid-1930s, there were enough clothes designed for the high school lifestyle and in teenage girls' sizes to create a middle ground. High school yearbooks began to depict the quest for sophistication with humor. Yearbook editors joked, "It seemed that our sagacious seniors forgot to look up the word 'sophisticated' in the dictionary before they voted" for the "most sophisticated girl." Commenting on a school-sponsored

2.6   *Photographs, High School Yearbooks, 1920s*

fashion show and tea, one OGS observer differentiated between "adult" and "appropriate" dresses.[29]

Similarly, advice literature discouraged high school girls from imitating glamorous debutantes and encouraged them to look clean, neat, and wholesome. This advice soon dominated all teenage media, from *Scholastic* to the *Ladies' Home Journal* "Sub-Deb Column" in the 1930s, and from *Calling All Girls* to the highly successful *Seventeen* magazine in the 1940s. Many girls by the mid-1930s willingly invested time and energy into being teenagers rather than sophisticates, at least for daily wear, and represented a growing trend supported by the fashion industry.

The Sears catalog, an example of that trend, continued experimenting to fill the gap between little girls' and women's clothing with a real, albeit awkward and inconsistent, interest in the teenage market. Sears had no clear understanding of the purchasing patterns of teenage girls, yet the company understood enough to vie for their business, altering age and size ranges as well as section names and demonstrating budding knowledge about teenage consumers. Sears used words such as "youth" exclusively for boys and "teen" exclusively for girls, defining high school boys and high school girls as separate groups of consumers and establishing girls as the first "teens." Gender remained a central framework for this market—teenage fashions were fashions for high school girls.

As shown in figure 2.7, Sears introduced a Collegiate Shop for the Junior Miss in spring 1933 that blended college and high school sizes. Yet the models described as "'Teen-Age' beauties" were tall and shapely with clinging, sophisticated dresses and high-heeled shoes—not high school girls. A year later, in spring 1934, a "High School Shop" appeared for the first time, seen in figure 2.8. The images displayed age-appropriate models, but sizes ranged from 6 to 16 years, not specific to high school. Copy read, "And Dad—Sears High School Shop is the place! All the girls buy there and save money, too!" This could have been a line for girls to use on their fathers, or an attempt to sell girls on the popularity they would gain by wearing Sears's clothing. It could also have been a safe way to imply male approval. These scattered efforts marked a significant change, but the High School Shop for girls disappeared by the next catalog.[30]

These experiments were inconsistent, but they were also purposeful efforts to understand and capture a new market. By the time consumers ordered from a fall catalog, the spring catalog was in production, so these radical changes were not immediate responses to consumer feedback. And market trends in the mid-1930s were analyzed inefficiently, if at all. Sears orchestrated schemes such as the High School Shop, advertised styles and sizes for teenage girls, and appealed to their desire for popularity and the "right" clothes. Yet Sears dropped these efforts as rapidly as it introduced them, sometimes overlooking high school girls completely. By the late 1930s, however, teenage styles had established a permanent place in the Sears catalog and throughout the fashion industry.

From 1936 to 1940, teen shops and fashion shows expanded while attention to teenage styles and sizes intensified. "Teen" remained a fluid category, however, and teen sizes did not always equal "teen" styles. An executive from Wieboldt department store praised the company's new high school advisory board, the first in Chicago, and stated the seemingly obvious "discovery" that "the volume possibilities in catering to high school and grade school girls are far greater than for college girls." In these years, Macy's and Stix, Baer & Fuller opened teen or high school shops, Saks Fifth Avenue expanded its teen section, and Hecht's declared its "'Teen Age' Shop" successful, claiming clothes "just grown up enough." The new 'Hy-Teen' shop in Lincoln, Nebraska, the "Twix-Teen

Presenting
THE COLLEGIATE SHOP
for the junior miss

IT'S A DAY AHEAD OF TOMOR-
ROW WITH ALL THE BRIGHT
NEW CLOTHES IDEAS YOU
YOUNG THINGS ARE "KEEN
FOR"...IT'S SETTING THE STYLE
PACE FOR YOU "TEEN-AGE"
BEAUTIES ALL OVER AMERICA!
GET ACQUAINTED WITH IT NOW!

1933's
gay new version
Bunny Ear
FROCK
has a bright
contrasting jacket
all its own!

2.7   "Teen-Age" Beauties, Sears Catalog, Spring 1933

"And Dad— Sears High School Shop is the place! all the girls buy there and save money. too!"

Dashing STYLE $6.98 Ⓒ

The Smart "SWAGGER" $4.98 Ⓑ

WITH CAPE FOR DRESSY WEAR
• • •
WITHOUT CAPE FOR EVERY DAY

New York Juniors love this "TWO-IN-ONE" $6.98

SIZE SCALE
Ages: 6- 7- 8- 9-10-12-14-16 years.
Chest: 25-26-27-28-29-31-33-35 inches.
Length: 27-28-30-32-34-37-39-42 inches.

JACKET-ADES
to happy days

2.8   "High School Shop," Sears Catalog, Spring 1934

Shop" in Knoxville, Tennessee, and reports of increased teen sales in Seattle further demonstrated the national extent of this phenomenon.[31]

By the second half of the 1930s, the consumer economy was well on its way to recovery. Sears expanded its definition of teenage girls in 1939 with the popular song, "Just an In-Between," sung by Judy Garland in the movie *Love Finds Andy Hardy* (1938), "Too old for dolls? . . . Too young for dates? YOU'RE JUST AN 'IN-BETWEEN-ER.'" Yet an attempt to explain juniors as "A Girl of Twelve and a Woman Aged Forty-Five," showed continued confusion. The sales pitch for teen sizes, however, was increasingly specific to high school culture, incorporating teen slang and fads, promoting a dress as the "Latest High School Rave!"[32]

Along with others trying to cultivate the teen market, Sears danced around specifics. Did the "in-between" stage begin at ten or thirteen? Did it end at fifteen or eighteen? When were junior styles and sizes appropriate? There were no concrete answers, in part because individual physical and emotional maturity varied, but more important, societal norms were dynamic and the category teen still highly elastic. These efforts marked a crossroads in the creation of teenage norms. The term "Teen-Age" first appeared in the Sears catalog index in 1940, referring exclusively to girls' clothes as it had throughout the 1930s. In the marketplace, teenagers were girls, preferably girls with some interest in clothing, autonomy, and money to spend.

Teenage girls' fashions started with haphazard and often local efforts, but by the early 1940s a large-scale, national market emerged. Despite war and shortages, the teenage market developed rapidly. Department stores experimented further with sizes, shop configurations, and ads for high school students. By 1940, Hutzler's divided girls' clothes into "Girls' Wear" and a "High School Shop—Girls." By 1944, "Teen-Age Wear" and the "Teen Shop" replaced references to high school. Manufacturers of teenage clothing still appeared and disappeared, but never again would there be a void. The uncertain means of communicating with teenage girls—watching their trends and reaching them with advertising—did not dampen industry efforts.[33]

Teenage clothing sizes nevertheless remained inconsistent. An editorial advertisement in *Parents* in January 1942, entitled "Be True To Your Type," recommended styles for different body types. The article introduced a company named Teenette that offered a new size range, 10 to 14: "She's too grown-up for [children's] 7 to 14 dresses, but too small for Teen sizes." It also recommended Chubbette frocks for the girl who was "Still a Chubby / In another year she'll be a slender teen." And finally, dresses by Tailored Girl, sizes 10 to 16, for the "Full Fledged Teen . . . perfect for a long torso." The teen size was not only out of the novelty category, it was worthy of three subcategories.[34]

In April 1945, Maidenform printed an article by *Calling All Girls'* fashion editor Betty Green, under the pen name Nancy Pepper, in its internal newsletter, the *Maiden Form Mirror*. The article celebrated the importance of teenage girls in the marketplace. "Don't call 'em 'Sweater Girls,'" she advised, "They like it even less than they like being called 'Bobby Sockers'—and that's very little, indeed. We're referring to those fabulous, sought after leading ladies of the day—the Teen Agers of America." Once again, female equaled teenager. Green warned Maidenform not to "underestimate the power of the Teens. If they can make a national idol out of a Cadaverous Crooner; if they can transform a pair of bobby socks into a national symbol; if they're the targets for millions of dollars worth of advertising of every type of product from cokes to curlers—then they're the new customers to go after." She emphasized girls' enormous impact as consumers and their role in shaping the market.[35]

By the end of the war, the teenage market was firmly established. Bobby sox, saddle shoes, rolled jeans, and baggy sweaters, while not new, had become entrenched teenage fashion staples. Teen sizes and styles, as well as slogans designed to reach high school girls, played an integral role in the teenage girls' fashion market. Marshall Field & Company's High School Shop was not exceptional in 1946. What was remarkable was the recurring claim to novelty. In 1946, J. J. Teen Type declared its girdle, "The Very First Girdle Ever Designed only for Teens . . . [to] firmly but oh so gently correct that sway-back tendency, that protruding derriere, and that too-round tummy." Yet Sears had introduced a girdle for teenage girls a decade earlier. By 1946, manufacturers, retailers, and advertisers respected the buying power of teenage girls, paid attention to their shopping trends, and tried to follow teen fads.[36]

The story of the fashion industry and teenage girls from the 1920s to the end of World War II is one of negotiation, confusion, and experimentation. Social scientists, educators, writers, and other professionals began to notice and encourage girls' growing interest in and anxiety over fashion in the late-nineteenth and early-twentieth centuries. This intensified as manufacturers, marketers, and retailers began to recognize teenage girls as potentially valuable consumers as early as the 1920s. But with only an emerging teenage culture and no sure avenue for reaching girls, a great deal of confusion ensued. Teen sizes began to appear, but understanding of a separate consumer identity lagged with a slower development of distinct teen styles designed for high school, dating, dances, and leisure time. There was no market research to track teen fashions or even formally to aggregate consumer response.

This is a story of group formation, as well as of the difficulty of identifying and shaping a new market. Manufacturers tried not only to shape teenage fashions but also to imitate teenage fads. High school girls were beginning to conceive of themselves as teenagers, as members of a distinct cultural and consumer group. Advertisers attempted to understand teenage girls and how to reach them, alternating frequently between sophisticated and girlish designs, imitation adult clothes and distinct styles, as well as between slang use and "straight" copy. As girls themselves became aware of their distinct status, they became a major force in negotiations over styles, sizes, age categories, appellations, and advertising messages. Girls' agency manifested in consumer choices was celebrated by the industry because it almost always meant sales, even if those sales were not exactly predictable. It was not always celebrated in homes and in schools, though, as girls encountered conflict from parents and educators over what styles were considered age-appropriate, modest, and respectable.

Shopping

Access to money and parental control defined the parameters of girls' clothing decisions, but girls exhibited amazing creativity when negotiating fashion. Throughout the rise in commercial production and consumption of clothing, clothes were still made and "made over" in the home, especially during the 1930s. Sewing was part of the commercialized teenage market from its inception, as were dreams of fashion careers. Dress design contests allowed manufacturers to solicit teen opinions while profiting from teen dress designs and promoting brand names. Sewing offered one way to engage with the teenage market, but shopping held special allure.

Shopping presented a world of possibilities—of new fashions, elegant outfits, and silky lingerie—for fantasy if not always for purchase. Shopping offered an entrée into the adult world, especially in the 1920s before teen departments were established. Purchasing some items or even imagining owning them opened a doorway into that world. Shopping brought female consumers into the public sphere, and as girls began to shop more frequently with friends or alone, it also became an activity filled with excitement and a hint of danger.

In the 1920s, girls' references to shopping often included mothers, especially when they purchased clothing. The situation varied with age and the type of item sought— older girls shopped more frequently without parental supervision, especially for small purchases. As department stores opened teen divisions filled with high school themes and eventually "Coke bars" that sold sodas and encouraged girls to linger and socialize, shopping with siblings or friends displaced shopping with mothers. Expensive items still required adult accompaniment, but as illustrated in figure 2.9, peer opinions played an important role. In this picture, drawn for the *Ladies' Home Journal* "Sub-Deb" column in 1936, one girl, wearing folded socks and flat shoes, tries on full-length evening dresses. Her friend leans forward actively admiring and discussing the dress. The sales clerk displays the dress quietly, offering no advice. Mothers are noticeably absent.[37]

By 1939, Frances Coleman wrote in the *Journal of Home Economics* that high school girls usually shopped for clothing alone, although mothers participated in buying clothing more than other purchases made by girls. Coleman saw a great need for education, however, because she found that for high school girls, "Appearance seemed the quality most frequently considered." Retailers also found this to be true, although they celebrated it.[38]

For those with limited finances, shopping could be less pleasurable. Helen, the protagonist in a high school student's short story, gazed longingly into a department store window. When she finally entered, the "stately and luxurious" store stared at her and "Its shining counters and its crazy mirrors showed her a dozen drab Helens." As she stood,

THE SUB-DEB · EDITED BY
ELIZABETH WOODWARD

"GEE, SUE, COULD YOU SWOOSH IN THAT! UNDO THE LONG DRINK OF BLACK COFFEE AND TRY IT ON"

2.9   *Shopping with Friends,* Ladies' Home Journal, *February 1936* frozen, "A clerk, very manicured and very blonde . . . appraised her, from slush-soaked shoes to shapeless hat." Holding money in her hand did not lessen the store's ability to intimidate.[39]

In the 1930s, references to buying one's own clothing increased. Girls without this freedom found ways to scrape together money for desired clothes. In addition to borrowed clothes and gifts, some girls saved money by skipping lunch or limiting discretionary spending. In the OGS, sixteen-year-old Edna enjoyed "buying her own clothes, and had saved from her lunch money enough to buy herself a pair of stockings and a gold belt." Historian Natsuki Aruga found that teenagers in Berkeley, California, during World War II worked primarily out of desire for spending money rather than patriotism. Some believed in the "intrinsic value of hard work," but desire to participate in the growing teenage consumer culture predominated.[40]

Teenage Girls and "Fads"

By the 1930s, teenage girls had clear notions of how to negotiate shopping trips and shape their wardrobes. As high school girls' culture developed alongside the teenage fashion market, clothing became an important site for the development and manifestation of teenage fads. Fads were significant in high school culture, marking separation from adults and distinguishing among teens. Fads bound teenage girls together, visually marking their participation in and loyalty to various peer groups. High school youth experienced strong peer pressures and valued peer approval. And almost as quickly as high school girls invented fads, manufacturers attempted to reproduce and profit from them.[41]

For example, teenagers often personalized belongings, writing on shoes, books, cars, and especially clothing. To proclaim friendship, interests, and devotion to idols, girls wrote autographs or names of favorite stars on everything from skirts to hats, as illustrated in figure 2.10. Some girls signed each other's shirts in bright colors; others used nail polish to paint their names on glasses or jackets. Any surface teens could control was fair game, and the bigger and brighter the display of friendship or adoration, the better.

Manufacturers picked up on this trend quickly and marketed it back to teenagers. A yearbook advertisement for "The New 'Slickersoll' Umbrella" in 1926 offered predesigned products, "or plain if you prefer to paint them yourself." A Women's Wear Daily column in 1937 describing teen trends noted that high school girls wore jackets "embellished with fantastic or collegiate decorations." Shortly thereafter, Moistureproof Fabrics, Inc., introduced a Deanna Durbin "Stormy Weather Ensemble," including an umbrella "plastered with college pennant stick-ons. These are sold separately, and the customer can stick them on to her heart's content. She may even paste them on her raincoat, if she likes."[42]

By the 1940s, media characterized high school girls almost exclusively by their fads, emphasizing conformity. A Life magazine article on "Teen-Age Girls" began with the sentence, "There is a time in the life of every American girl when the most important thing in the world is to be one of a crowd of other girls and to act and speak and dress exactly as they do." Similarly, The March of Time newsreel Teenage Girls portrayed girls who cared primarily about clothing, soda shops, and telephones. But high school girls did not quietly accept this dismissal of their intelligence or their efforts to experiment with peer conformity and individual expression through fads. A number of girls wrote to Scholastic magazine's "Jam Session" column to protest: "Certainly my life is far from

Many a fair co-ed
sports Oxford Bags,
— When she dons
her painted slicker.

Headliners — "Everybody's wearing white sailor caps, covered with friends' autographs or teen jabberwacky." —

—*Shirley Young, Skillington High, Reading, Pa.* (Shirley is president of a Tricks for Teens Club in Reading. Club dues go toward buying materials for Tricks. Recently the Club exhibited its Tricks for Teens at a school arts and crafts show.

2.10   *Personalizing, High School Yearbooks and* Parents' Magazine, *1925-1945*

the ecstasy of carefree existence which *Life Magazine* would have me believe." Another wrote that the depictions "of us as frivolous, flippant morons is not in the least accurate. . . . The average teen-ager discusses world affairs as well as the latest crooner."[43]

Teenage girls as a group responded favorably to contests, promotions, clubs, and invitations to write for advice in part because they craved an outlet for communication with other teens. In February 1941, *Parents* introduced, "Tricks for Teens." This column was the outgrowth of a Gimbel's department store promotion featuring an essay contest, "What are the Fashion Fads in your school?" The initial column addressed mothers, sympathizing with those who could not understand their high school daughters' "fashion language." The column offered prizes for the best "Teen Tricks" submitted by either "you" [the mother] or "your teen-age daughter." It also encouraged mothers to accept fads because they promoted beauty culture and kept daughters interested in appearance. The column editor, however, received hundreds of entries from teenage girls thanking the magazine for the opportunity "'to compare notes with other high-school girls.'" Addressing teenage girls directly by the second column, the editor promised the establishment of a monthly feature. By April, the column declared, "TEEN-AGE high-schoolers, this is *your* feature. Urge mother to read it, too." *Parents* continued the column for three years and then transferred it to *Calling All Girls,* a magazine designed for "girls and sub-debs," also published by Parents Institute.[44]

Parents extended its national design contest in 1941 to include "Hi Style Scouts," a teen fashion advisory board connected to department stores across the country. Editorial advertisements promoted fashions and used the "teen approved" slogan frequently. A column in February 1942 introduced "Tricks for Teens" clubs and Saks–34th Street held its first official meeting in May 1942. Local newspapers ran the syndicated "Tricks for Teens" column and fashion shows, contests, and clubs spread rapidly.[45]

The outpouring of enthusiastic letters, rich with descriptions of teenage fads from high schools around the country, demonstrated teenagers' involvement in consuming and creating fashion. Through clothing selections and alterations, girls identified themselves as teenagers and as members of specific peer groups. This phenomenon was not new in 1944, as writers at *Life* and *The March of Time* claimed. Nor was it new in 1941 when *Parents* announced, "Your ideas are making the designers of teen fashions sit up and take notice. After all, your Fad-shions are the *real* source of teen fashions." With the rise of the teenage fashion market in the 1920s and 1930s, high school girls gained new understanding of their power as consumers. In February 1936, "Sub-Deb" column editor Elizabeth Woodward criticized fads such as "Beer jackets, saddle shoes, baggy skirts and hair ribbons" and encouraged girls to "Dare to be Different. . . . Look new and everyone will look twice!" But Woodward missed the point that sometimes the goal was to look alike, to blend with the group rather than attract individual attention and to highlight friendships with certain girls and not others.[46]

Fads did not spread evenly. Small groups adopted some fads, while other fashions moved rapidly across the country. Yearbooks identified successful trendsetters as well as girls whose styles remained unique. One senior was remembered for "coming to school in the most astounding 'get-ups' and with the strangest hair styles." She wore clothes in unique ways, but because others did not copy them, they remained "strange." Another girl wielded "considerable influence on the school," installing "'The Era of Short Hair, Socks, and a New Tomboyish Attitude.' Never before has a senior class been so comfortably dressed." The often unspoken guidelines were inherently inconsistent, varying by region, subgroup, or even by day: wooden spoon necklaces replaced pearls, saddle shoes were favored over moccasins or loafers. When *Parents* launched "Tricks for Teens," it relied on the established presence of fads while providing a venue for national communication. Recurring themes included wearing boys' clothing and altering clothes.[47]

References to cross-dressing, almost exclusively girls borrowing boys' or men's clothing, appear throughout the sources on teenage girls' lives. As shown in figures 2.11 and 2.12, girls wore men's neckties as belts, necklaces, collars, bow ties, or even—sewn together—as

Bedtime Story — "We *borrow* **our fathers' pajama tops and wear them over skirts for school. The giddier the better."** —*Marcia Bowlley, Alexander Hamilton High, Los Angeles, Calif.* **"Some of the boys are coming to school in striped pajama coats over their slacks, and tassel caps that look like night caps."** —*Rosalie Lomanto, Grover Cleveland High School, Buffalo, N. Y.*

2.11 *Male Clothing,* Parents' Magazine, *1941*

skirts. Some girls wore their fathers' pajama tops; others large sweatshirts that "hung down practically to our knees." Girls similarly wore boys' plaid shirts "long and sloppy." Yearbooks highlighted girls in boys' clothing in text and drawings. One caption read, "We borrowed (ahem) the shirts and ties from our brothers." Dressing in men's clothing and borrowing or shopping for men's clothes was exciting, a form of rebellion against the prescriptions of femininity. Wearing baggy pajama tops or oversized sweaters minimized one's sexuality, hiding new curves from uninvited glances or stares. It did not preclude wearing a fitted sweater the next day, but it presented an option, allowing girls more freedom to control their emerging sexual identities. Borrowed clothing also allowed for gender play as girls "borrowed" or at least imagined themselves having male privileges.[48]

Girls may have encountered consumer culture in ways unintended by manufacturers or retailers, but those selling clothing and accessories celebrated all indicators of girls' active interest. Parents, however, had more concerns about the daily use of such items and about girls' clothing selections. At age sixteen, Irene, a Berkeley Guidance Study participant, told an interviewer, "I want to buy a boy's sweater and [mother] won't let me. Can you see anything wrong with that? Boys' sweaters are better made and they last longer and they don't cost as much money." Her plea was partially a rational assessment of the marketing situation—boys' clothes were generally sturdier and less expensive—and partially a wish to be fashionable. The mother's opposition was also noteworthy. She asso-

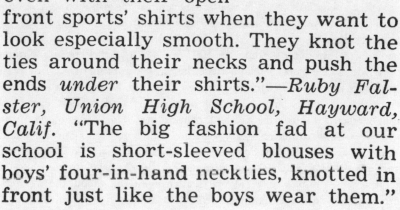

All Tied Up — ''Men's neckties for belts are the password. We knot them in front, four-in-hand fashion, and let the ends hang down.'' —*Charlotte Bennighof, Marshall High School, Minneapolis, Minn.* "Boys now wear ties even with their open-front sports' shirts when they want to look especially smooth. They knot the ties around their necks and push the ends *under* their shirts."—*Ruby Falster, Union High School, Hayward, Calif.* "The big fashion fad at our school is short-sleeved blouses with boys' four-in-hand neckties, knotted in front just like the boys wear them."

2.12   *Male Clothing,* Parents' Magazine, *1941*

ciated clothing so closely with gender that she was unwilling to allow her daughter to wear a sweater "made" for boys.[49]

Although some fads appeared annoying or silly to adults, they served the important work of defining group boundaries, visually identifying those in a group and those outside it. Fads reflected girls' efforts to bond with friends, exclude others, define and participate in high school society, and broadcast cultural preferences. Through media such as the "Tricks for Teens" column, fads provided a focus for national group formation and dialogue. As manufacturers appropriated these styles and marketed them back to teenage girls, fads helped forge a new relationship between mass culture and the fashion industry, between consumer culture and an emerging group identity.

Shaping Bodies

In other cases, the industry more explicitly attempted to shape, rather than follow, teen trends. The support garment industry watched high school consumers with growing interest. By the 1920s, girdles replaced corsets, allowing greater freedom of movement. The brassiere was a well-established foundation piece by the late 1920s, further modified by the mid-1930s with new material, padded cups, underwires, and cup sizes. For teenage girls, bras and girdles became symbols of growing up and sometimes of resistance, inspiring anxiety, debate, and humor.

Although the industry primarily emphasized college girls during the early 1930s, references to high school girls increased. An article in the *Maiden Form Mirror,* written in 1931, quoted Alice Dowd, the associate editor of the *Corset and Underwear Review.* Dowd heralded high-school girls as overlooked consumers "'who are just ripe to fall into the lap of the store that, by clever advertising and by selective merchandising, shakes the bough.'" High school girls were becoming aware of fashions and their figures, Dowd wrote, but "it is up to your Advertising Department to let them know their urgent need of the proper foundation garments in order to fit into the new fall 1931 fashion picture.'" Sears joined the effort in 1934, promoting "High School NEWS!" of girdles for junior figures. By spring 1935, Sears dedicated an entire Junior Miss underwear department to "the *teen-age smart set.*" This battle between teenage girls who were not eager to wear girdles and the industry, often supported by mothers, that wanted them to continued for decades.[50]

Maidenform introduced "Etude" in 1937 to "Preserve the Precious Firmness of Youth." Made for the "smaller-than-average" breast, it was primarily "a 'first' brassiere" marketed with the slogan "'Catch 'em Young.'" In 1939, Maidenform introduced the Adagio bra for girls and women with small breasts at a "'Coming Out' Party," and aggressively marketed it to teenage girls and their mothers. The *Maiden Form Mirror* recommended a strong educational campaign for high school girls and their mothers, including tie-ins with clothing departments, "'clubby' or diary-like advertising," and presentations at Mothers' Clubs and Parent Teacher Association meetings. *Parents* adopted this cause during weekly radio talks, advising mothers about the importance of support for girls whose "teen fashions" demanded "a good figure. Waistlines and hips have to be controlled to complement the fitted silhouette of the season. A schoolgirl slouch is distinctly out of place." This assumption that all girls had some figure problem to be controlled was at the core of teenage girls' consumer culture.[51]

The industry recognized reluctance among girls to wear girdles and occasionally acknowledged that many high school girls had little "need" to reshape their bodies. Marketing strategists therefore recommended fostering insecurity and inventing desire to convince the "slim young girl" in her teens that she needed "figure restraining" garments. In 1935, a *Maiden Form Mirror* article advised salespeople to suggest to girls as they tried on clothes how "marvelously well-bosomed they would look in their new evening dresses if they would only get 'Masquerade' brassieres." Maidenform did not design the Masquerade bra, with pads to enhance the bust, only for high school girls, but they appeared to be targets. Audience remained an important issue, yet marketers were still unsure whether to address girls or parents. These Maidenform marketing strategies presented the teenage girl as self-conscious and tractable, but they also imagined her as the "shopper." Fostering her insecurity would lead to better sales. The article did not recommend selling the mother on the idea; in fact, mothers were often unsuccessful in encouraging teenage daughters to wear girdles and support garments.[52]

In 1943, Maidenform marketers celebrated the opportunity to reach a younger audience directly through the magazine *Calling All Girls* and attempted to imitate teen language: "Simply Super for A Smooth Figger! . . . You'll cut a neater figure in sweaters and in date dresses if you [make sure] you're well stacked by wearing a brassiere Maidenform designed for *your* type of bosom." The *Maiden Form Mirror* celebrated the results of a *Calling All Girls* survey, announcing "Yes! 'Teen-Agers' DO Wear Brassieres!" More than 65 percent of the responding readers wore them and purchased their first bra between the ages of thirteen and fifteen.[53]

Teenage girls explored and struggled with ways to shape and display their bodies. They discussed bras, especially the appropriate age for wearing a first bra. At ages thirteen and fourteen, OGS participants debated this topic as they dressed for study physicals while observers secretly recorded their conversations. In 1933, Judy said, "I don't mind wearing a brassiere in the summer time tho. . . . they are so nice and cool," but Edna responded, "I don't need one." In similar conversations, Rita said emphatically, "I don't need a brassiere I'm telling you that right now." When her friend responded that she wore one, the first girl hesitated and cautiously asked, "Do you think I do [need one]?" Wearing a bra too soon, however, could bring ridicule. When asked why she didn't wear a bra, Evelyn responded, "oh puleese," and Rose commented that Betty "wears brassieres and she doesn't need them any more than I do." The peer pressure and debate surrounding bras faded as girls matured physically and the majority began to wear bras regularly.[54]

Acceptance of girdles was less automatic. Manufacturers worked hard to expand their markets, trying to convince girls to "train" their figures with girdles, bras, and other items that promised to mold young bodies into adult silhouettes. Mothers as well as manufacturers often complained of teenage girls' refusal to wear girdles. Manufacturers were clearly interested in sales. Mothers' motives were less obvious and usually centered on ensuring that their daughters accepted certain norms of femininity and the necessity of shaping and controlling their bodies. Girls in the 1930s, however, were less willing to compromise comfort and wear uncomfortable undergarments than those of previous generations. Girls often resisted efforts by mothers, manufacturers, and advertisers to sell them on girdles, especially "preventative" girdles designed to "train" their growing bodies. A *Calling All Girls* survey in 1943 found that only 31.3 percent of respondents wore girdles. Similarly, a survey of sub-deb clubs by *Ladies' Home Journal* in 1944 found that 80.3 percent did not wear girdles, despite concerted industry efforts.[55]

The New Teenage Look

The twentieth century introduced dramatic changes in women's clothing, trading corsets and full-length dresses at the turn of the century for jeans and shorts by mid-century. New styles drew more attention to body shape and body parts, limiting the new freedom to some extent, but still offered a greater range of options. High school fashions reflected these changes, developing partially in response to these larger trends and partially in response to the rise in high school attendance, the creation of teenage girls' culture, and the development of a distinct teenage girls' fashion market. Teenage fads also shaped high school dress, especially when publicized by national media.[56]

High school girls in the 1920s wore formal clothes, including dresses and stockings, to school, as seen in figures 2.13 and 2.14. In the 1930s, girls' fashions became more casual and distinctly "teen," as blouses or sweaters and skirts, shown in figures 2.15 and 2.16, appeared alongside dresses in greater numbers. The transition to skirts marked a significant shift to less formal, more affordable school clothes. This move began in the

2.13   Photograph, High School Yearbook, 1926

1920s, strengthened in the 1930s, and culminated in the 1940s when, as illustrated in figures 2.17 and 2.18, high school girls frequently wore shorter skirts and blouses or sweaters interspersed with casual dresses.

By the early 1940s, the informal high school "uniform" included sweaters, skirts, ankle socks, and saddle shoes or loafers. These items, often embellished through teen fads such as decorated shoes or sweaters worn backwards, identified girls as teenagers. By the mid-1940s, high school juniors and seniors imagined themselves outgrowing this style into more "adult" clothes—longer skirts, fitted shirts, nylons, shoes with heels. A number of yearbooks included sketches of the transformation from early days in high school as "teens" to later days when girls imagined themselves looking older. Comparing these with yearbook photographs, though, shows that this transformation was rarely completed during the high school years.

One change girls eagerly adopted was the rising acceptance of pants for females. The 1930s proved an important period of transition. In the early 1930s, little girls wore pants or jeans, but prolonging the habit into the teenage years met resistance. Peers and observers considered high school girls in the OGS who wore jeans in these years "different." By 1938, however, observers found it normal that all of the girls on a field trip wore jeans "turned up so that about six inches showed between shoes and jeans."[57]

Some schools forbade girls from wearing pants, but resistance across the country also came from parents and male peers. In one school, "To show how they resent [slacks], the boys now think it's necessary to label themselves 'Male.'" These high school boys felt

2.14   *Photograph, High School Yearbook, 1929*

2.15   Photographs, High School Yearbooks, 1930s

2.16 *Photographs, High School Yearbook, 1939*

uncomfortable with the shifting boundaries of gendered clothing, perceiving a threat to their emerging masculinity by the erosion of fashion categories that designated pants as "male." Despite these protests, *Parents* fashion editors supported slacks and printed an editorial advertisement, "Our 'Hi' Style Scouts say 'Slacks are Slick,'" stating that teens, meaning girls, were "a Slack-Happy crowd," increasingly wearing pants to school as well as after school. Despite efforts by manufacturers to catch up, girls bought pants in various places, adopting these mass-produced clothes in personalized fashion, "we borrow our brother's pants" and tighten the legs "for that tapered effect." One girl wrote to the "Tricks for Teens" column that she and her friends pinned up the legs of their "Levis" with large blanket pins, an early mention of name brand jeans. Adopted quickly by teens, jeans became an important article of clothing that permanently changed societal norms of physical beauty for all ages.[58]

Age, gender, and sexuality merged with fashion and societal standards for feminine appearance in the mid-1930s around the issue of shorts. Shorts spread with the rise of leisure and sports clothing throughout the 1920s and were popular among teenage girls.

2.17   Photographs, High School Yearbook, 1940

2.18   Photograph, High School Yearbook, 1942

The "Sub-Deb" column displayed a group of girls wearing short shorts as standard as early as 1932. But in 1935, five "girl hikers" were cited for wearing "'scanty' attire" in Yonkers, New York. The alderman who led the battle against "abbreviated costumes on public thoroughfares" objected to girls over the age of sixteen wearing shorts. During the summers of 1935 and 1936, similar ordinances were passed in cities around the country. Sixteen seemed to mark an important age for these lawmakers, a point at which females stopped being little girls and became sexualized women. This demarcation did not coincide with physiological changes, such as the onset of puberty. Nor did it reflect the growing teenage fashion market in which twelve to seventeen or eighteen defined high school ages and teenage styles. Girls and manufacturers ignored these concerns, selling and wearing shorts and these highly publicized efforts to control the clothing of young women in public places proved futile.[59]

Sexuality can be a complicated topic for teenage girls. Girls were often eager to look attractive to gain peer approval, male and female, exploring their sexual appeal and energy. At the same time, many were wary of too much attention or negative attention. In 1927, as teenage styles were only beginning to emerge, Yvonne Blue was highly embarrassed by a friend's "adult" attire and behavior, "She wore a gray fur coat and high pumps . . . and millions of boys yelled 'Hi Teddy!' to her as she skipped along while I stalked at her side in torments of self-consciousness." Yvonne was acutely aware of her friend's successful efforts to attract attention through dress and action, yet did not see the attention as a compliment. More than two decades later, June Calender explored her emerging sexuality in her diary at age fifteen: "I also felt awful clothes wise because in haste, I put on my blouse with the plunging neckline. [A boy] began commenting and I started getting nervous." A few weeks later, she wore a similar shirt and again received male attention. She felt uncomfortable with the focus on her breasts, but she enjoyed one particular boy's attentiveness. She vowed not to "wear plunging" just to get his attention, yet she continued to experiment with necklines, simultaneously exploring her sexuality, welcome and unwelcome attention, objectification, and the limits to her freedom.[60]

Elizabeth Woodward furthered this confusion in her 1939 "Sub Deb" column, "It's All Your Fault." Woodward warned girls, "If the boys down at the corner leer and make you feel that your petticoat shows when you walk by—it's your fault. For walking by! There's always the other side of the street!" She further exonerated boys who "whistle through their teeth, catcall and hurl all too audible comments" by claiming that they were just "letting off steam." Girls should be cautious and not "get in the way." The accompanying drawing depicted two girls dressed modestly with skirts to their knees, kerchiefs on their heads, dark ankle socks, and saddle shoes. Unlike Yvonne's friend, these girls did not appear to solicit whistles and catcalls. Presuming, as Woodward did, that this attention was unwanted, her willingness to blame the girls unequivocally reflects a double standard of gender expectations for appearance, behavior, and use of public space.[61]

Sweaters could serve both of these purposes. High school girls wore sweaters regularly by the mid-1930s, and by the late 1930s they came to symbolize high school life. High school girls sometimes wore sweaters to highlight their emerging figures and at other times to conceal them. Tight sweaters offered an avenue for expressing sexuality, a "glamour girl" look; baggy or oversized tops made girls noticeable in different ways. Girls experimented with new ways of wearing sweaters in the 1940s. The "Tricks for Teens" column listed many sweater fads, such as wearing cardigan sweaters backwards. Pushing up sweater sleeves came into fashion by the late 1930s and symbolized teenagers nationally by the 1940s. Girls may not have worn sweaters as manufacturers intended, but they still bought them in large numbers. And when manufacturers noticed trends, they often sold them back to teens, advertising sweaters that buttoned up the back, sometimes fitted and sometimes loose.[62]

Bobby Sox: The Ultimate Teenage Symbol

As sweaters and skirts became the high school uniform, ankle socks and saddle shoes became the ultimate symbols of being a teenage girl. In the 1920s, most girls wore stockings with pumps, oxfords, or sandals to high school, prompting references to stockings as "abominations" that ran at inopportune moments. At the same time, female tennis players began to adopt a "stockingless mode," wearing only socks, and the trend spread. Girls slowly abandoned stockings for socks as the teenage fashion market emerged, bare legs gained acceptance, and high school fashions became more casual. By 1931, socks appeared in yearbooks as part of athletic uniforms. A yearbook essay in 1933 joked, "That's the third sock I have lost this term. I must have "sox" appeal." This reference to 'sox,' in addition to the pun on sex appeal, shows that ankle socks already merited their nickname but in the context of athletics rather than daily wear.[63]

2.19   Bobby Sox and Saddle Shoes, Photographs, High School Yearbooks, 1936 (above), 1942 (below)

2.20   Bobby Sox and Saddle Shoes, Photograph, High School Yearbook, 1940

Fashion historians often credit the wartime stocking shortage in the 1940s with the rise of ankle socks, but by the 1930s the practice was already widely accepted. Although little girls had worn socks for years, the trend grew among teens by the mid-1930s and ankle socks with saddle shoes or loafers appeared frequently in yearbooks, as illustrated in figures 2.19 and 2.20. Yearbooks still noted girls who loved "Rolled Stockings" or hated "Wrinkled" ones, but in smaller numbers. One senior dedicated "girls who don't wear socks" to a teacher who disapproved of their takeover. By 1936, OGS observers only noted girls with particularly "loud" socks. An observer wrote that fourteen-year-old

$1 44 Girls'

—Leather sole —1-inch heel; rubber lift
Girls' Sizes 12, 12½, 13, 13½, 1, 1½, 2,
2½, 3. Wide width. *State size.* Shipping
weight, 1 pound 2 ounces.
15 H 1332—White Elk-grained Leather
15 H 1333—Black Patent. Pair.$1.44
Women's Sizes 3½, 4, 4½, 5, 5½, 6, 6½,
7 in C (medium) width. *State size.* Shipping weight, 1 pound 4 ounces.
15 H 1334—White Elk-grained Leather
15 H 1335—Black Patent. Pair.$1.59

$1 49 Girls'

—Leather upper —Crepe rubber sole
Girls' Sizes 12, 12½, 13, 13½, 1, 1½, 2,
2½, 3. Wide width. *State size.* Shpg. wt., 1 lb. 5 oz.
15 H 1386—White and Brown.
15 H 1387—Two-Tone Brown.
Pair.....................................$1.49
Women's Sizes 3½, 4, 4½, 5, 5½, 6, 6½,
7 in C (medium) width. *State size.* Shipping weight, 1 pound 7 ounces.
15H1388—White and Brown.
15H1389—Two-Tone Brown. Pair.$1.69

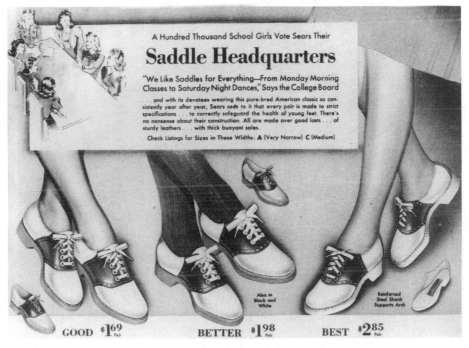

A Hundred Thousand School Girls Vote Sears Their

Saddle Headquarters

"We Like Saddles for Everything—From Monday Morning
Classes to Saturday Night Dances," Says the College Board

. . . and with its devotees wearing this pure-bred American classic so consistently year after year, Sears sees to it that every pair is made to strict
specifications . . . to correctly safeguard the health of young feet. There's
no nonsense about their construction. All are made over good lasts . . . of
sturdy leathers . . . with thick buoyant soles.

Check Listings for Sizes in These Widths: **A** (Very Narrow) **C** (Medium)

Also in
Black and
White

Reinforced
Steel Shank
Supports Arch

GOOD $1 69 Pair   BETTER $1 98 Pair   BEST $2 85 Pair

2.21   Advertisements, Sears Catalog, Spring 1938 (above), Fall 1940 (below)

Sandra wore "inappropriate Cuban heels with bobbie socks"—an early use of the term. She remarked on the heels, though, not the socks, indicating that ankle socks had become an established teenage accessory.[64]

Woodward advised girls in August 1935 to relax during the summer and let "glamour go by the boards" with "[a]nkle socks, freckles, and hair in their eyes." In 1936 she recommended wearing brightly colored socks to stand out, "Dare to be different! . . . Yellow [socks] with your brown sweater; blue ones with yellow." Woodward first recommended socks for lazy summer days, along with other carefree styles acceptable in summer. The following year, she seemed to accept ankle socks as status quo and tried to influence only which socks would be worn. By August 1938, however, Woodward expressed disapproval of girls' increased informality and advised, "legs look better covered in silk sheen than they do in just socks."[65]

By the mid-1930s, Sears advertised ankle socks and saddle shoes without fanfare. By 1938, Sears offered anklets for "School-Age Misses of 10 to 16 Years" and saddle shoes "For Fashion-Smart Teen-Agers." By this time, Sears recognized their popularity, "A Hundred Thousand School Girls Vote Sears Their Saddles Headquarters," as seen in figure 2.21. This second ad mentions the "College Board" showing showing awareness of the college trend high school students adopted.[66]

High school girls in socks and saddle shoes became the ultimate symbol of teenage girls' culture. Photographs from a broad range of yearbooks illustrated the popularity of ankle socks and saddle shoes by the mid-to late-1930s and text caught up by 1940: "Happy while . . . wearing dirty saddle shoes" or "just loves dirty saddles and bowling." Yearbooks saluted girls who wore the "loudest socks," and named one senior the "Queen of Bobby Socks" in 1944. Bobby socks and saddle shoes soon distinguished teenage girls from other age groups. As the trend spread among teens, college students lost interest.[67]

Saddle shoes and anklets also provided the perfect palette for teenage fads. Girls wore socks in bold or muted colors; folded, pulled up, or pushed down; decorated with gadgets and charms; over stockings; or held up with boys' garters. They decorated saddle shoes using nail polish, shoe polish, or paint, with everything from pictures of flowers to friends' names to favorite songs.

By the 1940s, girls in high school yearbooks wore ankle socks with saddle shoes or loafers almost exclusively and the term "sox" gained popularity. Media, not girls, however, largely used the phrase "bobby soxer"; many girls rejected the associated stereotype. A *Time* magazine article in 1943 described "hundreds of little long-haired, round faced girls in bobby socks" who sat "transfixed" as they worshiped Frank Sinatra, "crooner extraordinary." A *New York Times Magazine* article the following year claimed that a sock became a bobby sock only "on the retailers counter" when purchased by a "teen-age, high school girl or a croon-swooning adolescent. . . . The purchaser and her motives change an innocent pair of anklets into a sociological problem." This article asserted, however, that those who complained about the "bobby sox brigade" failed to distinguish between female juvenile delinquents and wholesome high school students. By the mid-1940s definitions of bobby soxers often referred to Frank Sinatra fans or to teenage girls "addicted to adolescent fads and crazes." But the rise of ankle socks and saddle shoes were first linked to the establishment of casual clothing as high school fashion years before Frank Sinatra's solo career.[68]

Dressing Up: Formal Dresses and High Heels

Skirts, sweaters, and saddle shoes were practical, not sexy. In contrast to the increasingly casual styles worn during school and after, dressing up in formal gowns and high heels marked a different teenage rite of passage, one more closely tied to sexuality. Girls frequently described the extended pleasure of imagining a dress, shopping, and preparing to wear it. The dress itself located girls on a continuum from child to teenager to woman: How long was the dress? What color? How fitted? How revealing? How high were the heels? These choices were culturally determined, class-based, and personal, yet they were also linked to peer pressure and parental approval. A diary entry, written by Katherine Rosner at age fourteen, illustrates the power of the evening dress in teenage mythology:

> Feb 16, 1929—Well, diary, in a few minutes I leave for the greatest event of my life, my first dance! . . . I love my dress. It's rose colored taffeta, with a fitted bodice, and a bouffant skirt. There's a ruffle of tulle along the bottom of the skirt, and tulle at the very top of the dress, and there are many-colored taffeta flowers on different parts of the gown. All I hope, diary, is that I can dance.

In fact, preparations were almost as significant as the date or the dance. Katherine hoped that she danced well as an afterthought.[69]

A "Sub-Deb" column in 1934 perpetuated the Cinderella myth, "Don't slither into your dress and run. Swish around in it in your room—practice your dress. This sounds terrifically artificial—and, of course, I've told you girls to be natural. But it's perfectly natural for every woman to be an actress. Glamour is being thrillingly alive, calm, gracious, poised, lovely." Woodward navigated her mixed messages awkwardly, cajoling readers simultaneously to be "natural" and "an actress." A provocative description in a short story written by a high school girl the same year extended these concepts, including sensual pleasure for the wearer and a desire to look sexually appealing: "Sydney shivered as she slipped the sheathing satin dress down over her cool, trembling body. As she smoothed it down over her lifting, young curves she glanced at herself in the mirror. She looked like a wet, young blade of grass." A girl could be clean and sweetly perfumed, with stockings and perfectly arranged hair, but only when she finally donned the dress did the fantasy come alive.[70]

Cinderella tales of transformation through clothing were not unique to teenage girls in the twentieth century. They did, however, develop certain teenage nuances through their constant re-telling, whether *by* girls in their diaries and short stories or *for* girls in magazines and fiction. A first dance magically symbolized a significant step on the path from girlhood to womanhood. Some versions introduced a tomboy who suddenly saw the benefits of formal gowns and high heels upon meeting "Mr. Right." Sometimes peers transformed a bookworm into a beauty, other times the girl changed on her own, and sometimes the boy was not worth winning in the end. But in every case, new clothing brought a complete transformation, creating a stunning Cinderella at the ball.

In a typical example, two "popular" girls transformed Margaret from "an old bookworm" into a beauty with new clothes, curled hair, and silver shoes in a story written by a high school student in 1926. Although the girls warned Margaret not to discuss anything substantive, she found when she danced with the class president that he appreciated her intelligent conversation over that of the "dummies. . . . You can paint them up and put pretty clothes on them, but you know that the first rain ruins them and nothing will be left but sawdust." Girls should not necessarily disguise their brains, the story moralized, yet the boy had never noticed Margaret in her ordinary clothes.[71]

The most frequent outcome of the Cinderella transformation was the attainment of sophistication. Clothing allowed girls to experiment with the highly coveted looks and privileges of adults, at least temporarily. The meaning of "sophistication," however, changed with the advent of teenage girls' fashion, leading to a wider range of options between girlish ruffles and adult styles, although the debate continued among manufacturers, retailers, advertisers, parents, and girls themselves. Compare figure 2.22 with figures 2.23 and 2.24. The advertisement in figure 2.22, located in the "Children's Wear" section of *Women's Wear Daily* in 1939, displays dresses supposedly designed for teenage girls. Despite the use of the word "teen," the heading emphasizes adult fashion terms such as "wasp waists" and "romantic silhouettes." On the far left, a man who is definitely not in high school gazes both at and past one of the "teens" as she looks straight ahead, either unaware or avoiding contact. These images are about glamour and sex appeal, not dancing or lighthearted fun. The images in figures 2.23 and 2.24 show high school girls at dances in the 1940s. Even dressed up, they appear as high school girls enjoying their peer environment. Advertisements for formal dresses portrayed idealized images that girls aspired to but rarely achieved. What girls did create was a teen version, rooted in high school and peer culture.[72]

At age fourteen, Yvonne Blue described her dream dress for "when I grow up." Made "of black satin, rather short and a trifle tight. The neck is quite low and V shaped." In addition, "round the neck is thrown a chiffon scarf, of brilliant scarlets, blues, and greens. . . . Tan silk stockings, black patent leather pumps and a string of pearl choker beads & earrings complete the costume." She concluded the entry with the note, "I never heard of such a dress, but I think it would be lovely. Mother says I can have one for best, next year. I can have one when I grow up too." In this diary entry, Yvonne revealed many things about teenage girls' relationship to fashion, consumer culture, and age. A creative young girl who loved reading and imaginary worlds, Yvonne toyed with femininity and "adult" themes through her dream dress. The elaborate detail in her de-

WOMEN'S WEAR DAILY, WEDNESDAY, SEPTEMBER 13, 1939 *Children's Wear* ——— 1r

Wasp Waists, Bustles, Romantic Silhouettes in Stiff Fabrics for the Teen Girl's Big Moments

2.22   *Advertisement,* Women's Wear Daily, *September 1939*

2.23 Photograph, High School Yearbook, 1941

scription demonstrated her interest in, as well as her knowledge of, fashion styles and accessories. While the dress appeared "grown-up" to Yvonne, her mother approved it for her at age fifteen. This was good news, but she still saw herself as a girl and wanted one when she "grew up."[73]

Mothers and daughters did not always agree so easily. When the main character in a high school girl's story, written in 1939, shopped for a dress, the salesclerk addressed only her mother: "'It looks so sweet on her.'" The girl thought it too frilly and looked longingly at a dress "they hadn't bothered to show her. It was without puffed sleeves, and

2.24   Photographs, High School Yearbooks, 1940s

its well-designed simplicity gave it the little air of sophistication that appealed to her. Somehow, she knew that this was the one [a boy she admired] would choose." She resigned herself to the dress selected by her mother and the salesclerk, "Anyway, the girls would like it." This further complicated the notion of peer approval—she longed primarily for approval from a young man; her girlfriends served as consolation. Other girls asserted their opinions more effectively. Adele Siegel attended a party at age fifteen in a "scarlet evening dress with a black velvet sash so's I could raise the devil."[74]

Formal dresses inspired fantasy and drama, but they were extravagant. Although they were hardly clothing necessities, demand for formal dresses rose as high schools sponsored dances more frequently. In 1935, 53 percent of ninth graders in the OGS wished to own a new evening dress; by twelfth grade that number reached 83 percent. Study observers used an increasingly standard language when discussing girls' clothing at a dance in 1936: "many transformed girls arrived in attractive low-back, heel-length dresses." At age seventeen, an observer described Linda's dress as having a "bodice slightly too large for her, and she had entwined some cheap gold ribbon around the shoulder straps—effective, but tawdry looking." OGS participants were frequently unaware of or uninterested in observers' disapproval, and as demonstrated by the recurring negative comments, they continued to wear the clothing they preferred. These comments displayed generational differences and to some degree class distinctions between observers and participants.[75]

Full-length dresses and high heels, borrowed from adult fashion, took on great significance in teenage life. As girls grew older, their disdain for ruffles as well as their interest in sleek lines and revealing cuts increased. These dresses held hope and promise for attracting attention from boys; they also offered the opportunity to feel sexy. But girls had to please parents (if only to obtain approval for purchase), girlfriends, and prospective dates—all of whom potentially had different standards.

999

Clothing and fashions were significant for high school girls during the emergence of a teenage culture in the 1920s, 1930s, and 1940s. Teenage girls often eagerly consumed fashion messages from women's magazines, advice literature, peers, and even mothers. There was not one cohesive culture to which all girls belonged, but the overall trends of the emerging teenage girls' culture were adopted and shaped by large numbers of high school girls across the country. High school girls incorporated the messages and language of fashion into their daily lives—sometimes to a remarkable degree.

But teenage girls also played an active role in this complicated interaction between individuals, a growing cultural and consumer market, mass media, and the fashion industry, shaping teenage styles and influencing market trends. Through fads, high school girls expressed individual preferences, yet also identified themselves with friends, a particular school, or, as seen in the response to the "Tricks for Teens" column, with a national, culturally defined age group. Fads, as *Parents* magazine editors quickly recognized, further promoted interest in dress and mass culture, not opposition to them. Interest in fads reflected girls' efforts to distinguish themselves as teenagers and as different from other teenagers and often met resistance from parents, schools, and occasionally peers.

OGS observers evaluated these trends, approving of girls' interest in fashion and appearance, yet judging them according to middle-class values of femininity, controlled sexuality, and shifting standards of age-appropriateness. Parents exerted more direct control over their daughters' appearances but struggled with similar concepts. Mothers in particular often wanted their daughters to make the transition from girls to young women as defined by the world of consumer goods. Conflicts arose not over the transition but over the guidelines—when heels were appropriate and ruffled dresses inappropriate.

With the rise of teen consumer culture and clothing designed specifically for teenage girls, dresses and silk stockings of the 1920s gave way to informal high school attire, and teenage girls created their own norms. Girls imitated some adult styles and desired sophistication in certain settings, but they also used clothing to strengthen peer bonds, define group membership, and separate themselves from adults.

As defined by manufacturers, retailers, and advertisers, girls were the first and the most important teenagers. The words "teen" and "teenage" referred, without clarification, exclusively to females. Industry attention to teenage girls' bodies and trends helped shape the emerging consumer culture, despite its uneven nature, but girls selected their clothing from a range of departments, including men's, when it fit their styles and interests. Some manufacturers failed because they did not realize that girls wanted to be sexy; others failed because their styles were too sophisticated for teenage bodies and tastes.

Similar issues arose regarding presentation of one's self beyond fashion. As hemlines rose, a new world of commercial beauty culture encouraged shorter hair, cosmetics, and a host of advice literature written to guide women, as well as girls, through these products and styles. During this period, high school girls actively sought out beauty and health products. As they experimented with fashion, girls explored sophisticated looks as well as decidedly teen looks. In contrast to the fashion industry, however, the commercial beauty industry paid little attention to teenage consumers.

"Good Looks"

Commercialized Beauty and Health

GIRL 1: Did your friend, Miss Beauty, get her good looks from her father or her mother?
GIRL 2: From her uncle; he keeps a drugstore.

—Joke, 1926 high school yearbook[1]

As this joke in a high school yearbook illustrates, teenage girls understood the commercialized nature of "good looks" and their significance for young women by the mid-1920s. Beauty, health, and cosmetics were bound up with the construction of high school girls' culture as was fashion. But teenage girls displayed interest in adult beauty culture long before manufacturers, retailers, and marketers recognized their potential as a distinct market. Girls negotiated messages and products designed for adult women, incorporated them into their habits and friendships, and explored the links between consumer goods, appearance, and femininity in an effort to participate in the growing commercial beauty culture. Makeup and permanent waves symbolized adult looks and privileges, yet girls integrated them into teenage rituals such as pajama parties and makeovers. Girls used beauty products to experiment with femininity and with their roles as teenage girls in the same way they adopted clothing styles, exploring various looks for private and sometimes public display. Consuming beauty products did not necessarily distinguish girls as teenagers, but teenage strategies for using them did.

By the 1920s, advice literature emphasized beauty routines for high school girls that incorporated commercial products. In the 1930s, a few manufacturers and retailers began to recognize age-specific concerns and tried to match products with teenage uses, further defining teenagers as female. Not until the 1940s and 1950s did companies begin to manufacture and market products *for* teenage girls on a large scale, with special colors, prices, and slogans. Teenage girls, sensitive to appearance and peer approval, proved a viable market for health and beauty products long before the industry understood their interests and spending habits. Girls' eager responses to messages designed for adult women indicated not only their interest in experimenting with femininity and commercial beauty, but also the effectiveness of mothers, advice literature, and women's magazines in shaping their values of beauty. Parents, especially mothers, often encouraged their daughters to participate in beauty culture, although they frequently disagreed over appropriate definitions of femininity, displays of sexuality, and use of cosmetics.

In the nineteenth century, writes historian Kathy Peiss, only prostitutes "painted" their faces. Although "respectable" women began to experiment with cosmetics in the early twentieth century, makeup did not became a commonly accepted "medium of self-expression" until after World War I. Identity increasingly became "a purchasable style," as seen in the yearbook joke. Conflict over cosmetics remained widespread, but makeup sales rose as American women began to accept the notion that they had not only the ability to improve their looks through consumer goods, but a responsibility to do so. High school girls were susceptible to this message. According to historian Joan Jacobs Brumberg, when girls in the nineteenth century discussed identity or improving themselves, they did not focus on their bodies. In contrast, by the late twentieth century, girls saw the body as a central focus, something to cultivate and shape, often through purchasing clothing or commercial beauty products.[2]

With the national spread of movies, magazines, and marketing, highly perfected images of beauty began to shape women's expectations and use of cosmetics. Young women, especially those in high school, college, factories, and offices, used the new beauty and health products more frequently than older women did. Influenced by promises of beauty and success, girls often mimicked, sometimes playfully, advertising slogans when describing their habits. High school girls' beauty rituals centered on cream and face powder in the early 1920s. They quickly expanded to include rouge, lipstick, and eyebrow pencil by the late 1920s and added eye shadow, eyeliner, and nail polish in the 1930s. Makeup did not have one uniform meaning for girls of all racial, ethnic, and class backgrounds, but for many high school girls it signified an opportunity to strengthen peer ties and to look older, offering a momentary entrée into the adult world.[3]

High school girls, increasingly self-conscious about their bodies and faces by the 1920s, expressed great interest in beauty advice. Girls did not absorb it unquestioningly, but many read it voraciously. Movie magazines and newspapers ran beauty columns in the early 1920s, but popular women's magazines, such as *Ladies' Home Journal, Delineator,* and *Good Housekeeping,* initially resisted. By the 1930s, all women's magazines regularly included beauty advice, often linked with specific products through editorial advertising.[4]

By the early 1930s, the *Ladies' Home Journal* "Sub-Deb" column offered booklets on a wide variety of topics, including health and beauty. A column in 1931 promoted "The Sub-Deb's Book of Beauty" for girls who "would like to have an exquisite complexion and glistening, healthy hair of which you can be proud." The booklet also offered advice for applying "make-up—if you use it—correctly and effectively." Column editor Elizabeth Woodward encouraged girls to send in photographs for personalized beauty advice and recommended that each girl examine herself carefully in a mirror using a bright light to appraise pores and search for facial flaws. Woodward then advised conservative makeup use and various beauty rituals to cover or improve upon the newly identified flaws.[5]

In August 1935, Woodward conceded that girls could relax briefly during the summer, letting freckles show and hair hang loose. The August issue a few years later discouraged even this short break from a beauty regimen with strict, militaristic language: "Summer's time out for rehearsal. A new hair-do . . . getting yourself set for fall conquests. Take time now for glamour." In November 1940, Woodward sympathized that "Being beautiful [was] such a struggle. A constant battle against eyebrows that won't stay out, curls that won't stay in, spots that won't stay off and powder that won't stay on." She further commiserated that all girls faced a lifetime of struggle with beauty since "any lad teethed on Garbo, Dietrich and Lamarr adds high." According to Woodward, boys' expectations—and, implicitly, girls' desire and duty to meet those expectations—were based on glamorized movie stars and necessitated strict beauty and health routines.[6]

By the 1920s, many high school girls understood the culturally constructed nature of beauty and internalized beauty advice, discussing the need for "beauty sleep" and aspiring to be fashion models or beauty queens. By the 1940s, cosmetic use was ubiquitous, encouraged by advice literature and often by parents, although the latter were not always pleased with the outcome. Girls eagerly experimented with cosmetics and beauty and health regimens gleaned from magazines, movies, and advice literature. Most of these experiments were fleeting, resolved in preparation for a dance or a pact with girlfriends. Attention to beauty, dieting, and cosmetics, however, remained prominent throughout high school girls' diaries, letters, stories, and yearbooks. And while girls often made independent judgments about products or rituals and frequently joked about advertisements or advice, commercial health and beauty culture fostered insecurity and sold solutions. High school girls challenged adult authority, in the form of parents and schools, over use of beauty products but rarely challenged the concept of commercial beauty. Initially targeted at adult women, the industry eventually capitalized on teenage girls' interest and desire for sophistication.

Dieting and Figures

In the 1920s, women's bodies became increasingly public. The rise of beauty pageants, bathing suit contests, and female athletes focused attention on physical attributes in a new way. In tandem with the growing commercial beauty culture, the body became central to prevailing definitions of beauty. Girls' attention to dieting and preoccupation with body shape began in this period, as magazines, advice columns, and stories increasingly equated thinness with popularity, fun, and dating. Teenage girls often accepted these messages, resulting in widespread attention to dieting and figures from the 1920s through the 1940s.[7]

Yvonne Blue wrote about dieting extensively in her diaries in 1926 and 1927. Yvonne determined to lose weight at age fifteen, but after fasting for several days she wrote, "I feel awfully weak and trembly." She resumed drinking water and using toothpaste, but continued to fast until her parents intervened. Yvonne remained focused on her weight, counting pounds and calories meticulously, and wrote the following year, "Good lord, but I made a fuss about not eating for two days last year! Now I think less than nothing about not eating for a day. I don't feel the slightest bit weak or hungry and I'd just as soon not eat as eat." She then described her routine: "I fast at least one day each week, and l[o]se two or three pounds. In between times I gorge, but I manage to keep my weight between 128 and 131."[8]

Beth Twiggar, tall and thin, also confided anxiety about body image to her diary. She wrote in 1928 that she wished to be, "Slim, short, slender." Although Beth longed to be short throughout her diaries, here she pined to be "slim" as well as "slender." A few months later, she wrote, "I intend to stay hungry. Tis good for the feegaire!" She joked about fasting and her interest in her body, but her preoccupation did not abate. She frequently wished for "less size and weight," as did many girls in their private and public writings, and wrote emphatically, "I must not get large! . . . I must control my appetite!" Although she occasionally indulged her desire for sweets, such as eating two sundaes in one afternoon, she and her friends remained conscious of consequences. One day they collectively decided that they "were getting fat" and "went out to jump rope."[9]

Yearbooks similarly demonstrated the growing centrality of dieting, weight, and body shape to teenage girls during these decades. In 1928, Lillian "willed" her "slender figure" to a younger girl and many seniors listed "Gaining weight" as their main "Abomination." In 1931, a senior received praise for her "fashion-plate figure," and in 1932 another left her "'Garboish' figure" to a junior. Yearbooks increasingly mentioned dieting as a "weakness," "pet peeve," or "ambition." One senior was "always found on a diet," while others aspired to "lose 20 pounds," "weigh 105 pounds," or "eat all day and lose weight."[10]

Magazines encouraged such attention. *Ladies' Home Journal* reported in 1937, for example, "There is no guesswork" for daughters "about their weight. They get on the scales frequently, and three out of four have dieted at one time or another." But magazines also unwittingly illustrated the negative impact of these messages. Girls' letters requesting advice from the magazine *Calling All Girls* conveyed low self-esteem and acceptance of the link between "thin" and "popular." Girls compared themselves, unfavorably, to an idealized "normal" portrayed in mass media and advice literature. One girl wrote that she did not have "enough" dates or party invitations, and included what she identified as the pertinent facts: she was "five 11, 132 lbs., curly hair—rather medium length and with big dark blue eyes and good complexion." She asked hopelessly, "Am I too tall? / Too thin? / Too fat? / Maybe it is my disposition? I've been trying to improve it." She doubted herself rather then the vague but ubiquitous notion of "popularity" and its relationship to beauty.[11]

The "ideal" body shape has changed throughout the twentieth century. The flapper of the 1920s replaced the Gibson Girl's curves with a straight, boyish figure; by the late 1940s, the "new look" exaggerated feminine curves once again. Girls in their teenage years experience rapid physical growth and emotional development, making them more prone to insecurity and confusion over body image. Although girls could control some aspects of body size and shape, they could not affect height or skeletal structure. This caused some girls to focus on seemingly tractable areas—at least according to advertisements—such as the newly emphasized concern with bodily functions and odors.

Sanitizing the Body

With increased attention to the body and commercial products for taking care of it, advertisers cultivated new anxieties. By the early twentieth century, medical professionals, media, and advice literature emphasized cleanliness and sanitation, creating new "needs" that manufacturers, retailers, and advertisers happily strove to fill. In addition, clothing that displayed arms and legs led American women to shave and purchase new products in search of smooth skin. Commercial deodorants, bathing products, shaving paraphernalia, toothpaste, and mouthwash multiplied and girls experimented with them widely. These products were marketed to adult women; the unsolicited interest by high school girls is particularly notable. Because of the lack of attention to distinct teenage needs, girls navigated these messages, imitating adult beauty rituals and inventing "teen" ways of using them.[12]

Sensitivity to body odors was a relatively new preoccupation in the twentieth century, as were products designed to eliminate them. Advertisements and advice literature discussed odor "scientifically" and always with a ready solution. Marketing transformed Listerine in the mid-1920s from a general antiseptic into a profitable mouthwash and multipurpose disinfectant. Ads imitated tabloid confessionals and personal-interest stories. Young men or women, attractive and wealthy, who failed socially because of "halitosis" recovered after using Listerine. Copywriters also heralded Listerine's virtues for curing dandruff, body odor, colds, and sore throats, further boosting sales. Advertisements for Odorono antiperspirant alternately appealed directly to personal fear, highlighting social rejection due to underarm perspiration, or touted scientific "evidence" and testimonials by physicians. One Odorono ad that frequently appeared next to "Sub-Deb" columns in 1928 included "high school girls" among the "reputable women" who considered Odorono "an absolutely essential part of an adequate toilette." Ruth Miller, an "Authority on Perspiration Problems," advised applying the product "after the bath a few times a week" to keep the underarm "perfectly dry and fresh in spite of heat, nervousness, and exercises making impossible the reproach of odor or stained dresses."[13]

Similarly, Lifebuoy soap advertised the "True 'B.O.' Experience" in which a beautiful, yet socially outcast, young woman is saved by a friend's honesty and Lifebuoy soap. Teenage girls were very susceptible to these fears. At age eleven, Oakland Growth Study (OGS) participant Barbara echoed the Lifebuoy advertising slogan, asking a friend while dressing, "I got B.O. . . . Do I stink?" Similarly, OGS participant Elizabeth complained to a friend in 1934, at age thirteen, "I got B.O." Her friend asked, "Didn't you have a bath last night?" The friend did not recommend a specific brand of soap as an advertising confidant would have, but the dialogue and solutions were remarkably similar. Adult women may have questioned their body odor, but they were less likely to discuss such personal matters openly or to imitate ads so closely.[14]

Beth Twiggar frequently mimicked advertising messages regarding personal cleanliness in her diary entries. In 1928, at age fourteen, she recorded her musings while walking home from school, "'Odorono would help you lots' to a fish store" and "'Even if your best friends won't tell you, you might guess it,' to someone who hasn't discovered listerine." Beth's commentaries revealed her fascination with advertising, as well as her awareness of marketing strategies. She was exceptionally articulate, but her relationship to consumer culture mirrored that of many teenage girls in this era. She absorbed advertising language and messages, and even when using irony, integrated them into her daily language and routine.[15]

Beth continued this trend by personalizing romantic advertising images, "I feel delightfully luxurious and sweet-smelling. Elisabeth Arden and I had a séance in the tub with bath salts and her wonderful soap. . . . Verily Elizabeth is a witch!" Bathing became part of an elaborate beauty ritual for teenage girls, offering pleasure as well as the promise of social success. In 1937, Ladies' Home Journal beauty editor Louise Paine Benjamin surveyed high school girls on their beauty habits and confirmed that ten years after Beth's diary entry, girls "jump[ed] in and out of the tub frequently" and used many accessories, including "talcum powder, bath salts, sponge, nail brush, back brush, Eau de Cologne and olive oil."[16]

Shaving also became an integral part of girls' beauty routines by 1930, as illustrated by Beth Twiggar's list of things "to do" before a dance: "Set hair; Use odorono; shave;

manicure nails." Shaving blended unremarkably with her regular beauty preparations. Beth was seventeen when she wrote this list, beyond the major changes of puberty. For girls in early adolescence, the important question became when to start shaving. Age twelve or thirteen generally marked the beginning of interest in shaving, but individual variation, as well as parental and peer influences, shaped the process.[17]

In November 1933, OGS participant Jean told a friend that the study doctor "asked me if I shaved myself under my arms and I wonder why she asked me that because I haven't got any [hair]." The doctor had asked in an effort to catalog the onset of puberty; at age twelve, Jean was puzzled not at the suggestion of shaving, but at the notion that she had already begun. The following year, girls in the OGS discussed shaving freely, although the idea was sometimes more prominent than the hair. Sharon told her friend Helen in 1934, "I shave under my arms. I don't need to but I did." When Helen responded, "I never have any at all under my arms," Sharon asked, "Haven't you any at all? Isn't that funny." Girls, therefore, learned about body hair and shaving from a multitude of sources: parents, doctors, advertisements, and each other. But they were most comfortable sharing information with diaries and friends.[18]

Teenage girls with white or light skin also frequently accepted sun tanning as a necessary skin ritual. By the mid-1920s, the growth of sports and outdoor recreation helped spread the suntan "craze" as a tan came to symbolize leisure time spent outdoors. A yearbook advertisement in 1926 promoted Dame Nature cream, a lotion that promised a suntan "without SORENESS or blisters." The ad reflected interest in high school girls as consumers, as well as awareness of the harmful effects of zealous sun tanning. Although the industry was slow to accept consumers' preference for darker skin, by the mid-to late-1920s, tanning products kept pace with interest. Throughout the 1930s, yearbooks increasingly mentioned suntans, teasing girls with a "Weakness" for "Sun-bathing" or praising the trendsetter who set the school "summer tanning to its heart's content."[19]

Only a bright smile could match the perfect tan, and that smile required the right brand of toothpaste. A Listerine advertising campaign, "When lovely women vote," claimed in 1932 that thousands of "charming, educated, well-to-do, prominent" women cast their ballots for Listerine toothpaste. The following year, the Forest Park high school yearbook mimicked the ad, presenting the results of their own "toothpaste vote. . . . The greatest election since the election of [Rutherford B.] Hayes." The article continued, "Ipana started out with a valiant spirit but was soon overhauled by Pepsodent. . . . Ipana's first spurt was evidently not in vain, however, for it passed Bon Ami and came out first." Despite the light tone, this "vote" showed that teenagers understood advertising campaigns, as well as competition for their toothpaste dollars, and demonstrated knowledge of competing brands. Marketing studies years later showed that by high school, teenagers had established strong brand and product preferences and influenced household purchasing decisions. Yearbooks further demonstrated the effectiveness of advertising images through frequent references to students with "a tooth paste ad smile" or, more specifically, a "Pepsodent smile."[20]

In contrast to toothpaste makers who did not target teens, manufacturers of feminine hygiene products, led by Kotex, began to recognize teenage girls as unique in the 1920s. Kotex acknowledged age-related biological changes in marketing campaigns long before most commercial beauty and health products, although advertisements did not incorporate references to teenage culture for another decade. The average age of menarche was fourteen in the late nineteenth century. By the mid-twentieth century, the average

age dropped to 12.8 for white girls and 12.2 for African American girls, in part because girls were healthier and taller than their predecessors. As teenage girls remained dependent upon their families longer, however, emotional age often lagged behind biological age. Menarche marks the ability to reproduce, traditionally linked with sexual maturity, but Americans in the twentieth century were not ready to accept teenage girls as sexually mature. The ways in which girls learn about menstruation and how they respond to it are historically and culturally constructed. American society in the twentieth century emphasized hygiene rather than sexuality or maturity during menstruation, focusing on cleanliness, sanitation, and consumer products.[21]

By the late nineteenth century, menstruation had been "medicalized," and many girls learned about it from doctors or hygiene manuals rather than mothers or other female relatives. With the rise of disposable sanitary napkins, the marketplace established its role in this process and the relationship between menstruation and consumer choice. The Cellucotton Company attempted the first public advertisement of feminine products in the 1920s with an ad campaign for Kotex sanitary napkins. Weary of negative backlash, ads cryptically mentioned that Kotex "completes" the "toilet essentials" of schoolgirls and assured timid consumers that nothing "except the name" appeared on the box. The campaign expanded after a positive response, introducing a professional nurse who advised mothers on how to educate their daughters. Kotex cornered the commercial sale of feminine hygiene products for many years, and girls frequently mentioned it by brand name. By the 1930s, education through schools, girls' organizations, and the marketplace increased access to information and made discussion of menstruation more acceptable.[22]

Girls in the OGS discussed sanitary products more easily than menstruation. In a dressing room conversation at age twelve, Anna asked a friend, "Do you like Kotex?" Barbara responded that her mother burned them, and Anna volunteered, "My mother washes the rags but the Kotex she don't." Barbara asked incredulously, "She does wash the Kotex?" but Anna replied that she washed only the rags. Then Barbara clarified, "I don't mean the cotton, I mean the other part," and Anna added, "Mine [sanitary belt] is a rubber one." The girls did not shy away from the discussion although it remained scattered. They also did not mention menstruation directly, but named the associated product—Kotex.[23]

Mary confided to a friend the same year, "When you are 13 you begin to wear that Kotex stuff." She had not yet begun to menstruate and perhaps did not understand the individual timing of puberty, but she linked thirteen with menstruation and a brand name product. Kotex was unequivocally equated with menstruation, a link between a product and a perceived need that every manufacturer dreamed of achieving. Anna's mother still occasionally used rags, presumably to save money, but Kotex dominated the commercial market. At age fifteen, two girls discussed their acquisition of knowledge about menstruation: "I was so surprised your mother didn't tell you anything [about menstruation] until you were so old." When the second girl asked how the first girl had learned, she replied, "Mother told me all—I saw the boxes around and you read the ads." The marketplace, mothers, and friends provided information, often brand specific.[24]

By the mid-1930s, manufacturers of sanitary napkins designed special sizes and expanded advertising campaigns for high school girls. As shown in figure 3.1, by 1935 Kotex offered "Junior Kotex" for "women of slight stature, and younger girls." The photograph for Junior Kotex shows a young girl, perhaps twelve or thirteen, although the

3.1   Kotex Advertisement, 1935

smaller pads are also marketed for "days when less protection is needed." By the early 1940s, some advertisements focused exclusively on girls and high school culture.[25]

By 1942, advertisements focused on girls as consumers who, if they purchased the right product, could tame the inconveniences of menstruation and avoid embarrassment such as bulky pads or stains. Ads that formerly stressed a mother's responsibility to provide information to her daughter now addressed girls directly, encouraging autonomy while cultivating high school anxieties such as fear of losing a boyfriend, attracting unwanted attention, or failing in the quest for popularity. For example, a Kotex ad that ran in *The Parents' Magazine* (hereafter *Parents*) in 1942, seen in figure 3.2, relied on the popularity of the "Tricks for Teens" column to attract young readers. Ad copy professed sympathy with high school girls, "What a day! Words with mother over that perfume you charged . . . late to your first class. . . . That blonde tigress had a gleam in her eye . . . what if she starts stalking your 'Mr. Big' in earnest?" The ad promised no "embarrassing, telltale bulges" on difficult days and offered a free

You're fit to be tied !...

WHAT A DAY! Words with mother over that perfume you charged ... late to your first class ... then at lunch, fudge sauce dribbled down your new dicky. You rushed home to change ... and now this! Actually, you're afraid to think of tonight!

That blonde tigress had a gleam in her eye last time ... what if she starts stalking your "Mr. Big" in earnest? Can you keep him interested? ... charm that prom bid out of him? ... *feeling the way you do?*

Well, calm yourself! In this day and age, there's little excuse for letting trying days of the month ruin a sunny disposition!

Why can't you be like the other girls?

Look around you ... other girls *always* seem to be carefree and gay, regardless of the days circled on their calendars.

But do you know *why?* Maybe you never realized ... *most* of them choose Kotex sanitary napkins!

For one thing, when you're comfortable, your troubles take a nosedive! And Kotex is *more comfortable* ... see if it isn't!

Kotex is made in soft folds that are naturally less bulky ... more comfortable ... made to stay soft while wearing! A lot different from pads that only "feel" soft at first touch.

As for your lingering doubts and fears ... with Kotex you can snap your fingers at worry ... not lose your confidence and poise for one precious minute.

Honestly! Because Kotex has flat, pressed ends to prevent embarrassing, telltale bulges ... to keep your secret safe. And a new moisture-resistant "safety shield" for extra protection.

Of course there's a moral ... let Kotex come to the aid of your party ... help you *sail* through "difficult days". After all, *millions* can't be wrong ... and Kotex is more popular than all other brands of pads put together! The best proof that Kotex stays soft!

Be confident ... comfortable ... carefree

—with Kotex*!

KOTEX

A GIRL'S PRIVATE LIFE is fully explained in the booklet, "As One Girl To Another". It gives tips on what to do and not to do on "difficult days". Send for it today! Mail your name and address: P.O. Box 3434, Dept. PM-2, Chicago, Ill., and get a copy FREE!

★ Trade Mark Reg. U.S. Pat. Off.

3.2   *Kotex Advertisement, 1942*

booklet, "As One Girl To Another," filled with tips for reducing the challenges of menstruation. Peer advice, or simulated peer advice, for overcoming teen problems replaced medical advice from a nurse.[26]

Throughout these decades, girls grew increasingly knowledgeable about the consumer world of health and beauty—aware of the products, benefits, and drawbacks. Beth Twiggar discussed her most intimate hopes, fears, and sexual experiences in her diaries, but she never mentioned menstruation explicitly. Other diarists in the 1920s and 1930s similarly avoided specific references, referring instead to "the curse," being "sick," or having "my friend." Barbara and Anna awkwardly shared information in what they thought was a private conversation in the OGS dressing room in the early 1930s. Twenty years later, partly as a result of the public nature of advertising campaigns for sanitary products, Ruth Teischman wrote freely about menstruation in her diary at age twelve, "Today I got my period for the third time," and shared details with friends.[27]

"That Schoolgirl Complexion"—Beauty Rituals

While high school girls from the 1920s through the 1940s spoke little about menstruation, they spent considerable time discussing their complexions. In 1931, a yearbook satirically defined a "Schoolgirl Complexion" as "A 'natural' complexion acquired by a careful use of cosmetics." This high school author adapted a well-known advertising slogan for Palmolive soap, "Keep That Schoolgirl Complexion," assuming it was common knowledge. She joked about the effort and commercial products required to attain what was supposedly "natural," but she did not address the irony that they were schoolgirls working hard to achieve a "schoolgirl complexion." If they did not already possess such a complexion, did it exist? Or were beauty products marketed so effectively that even high school students joined the ever-elusive quest for "young" skin? If the ads were intended to target older women who had lost their youthful skin, why were teenage girls attracted to them?[28]

Yearbooks frequently mentioned faces and related beauty products as well as the term "schoolgirl complexion." Some yearbook editors admired girls graced with a "peaches-and-cream" complexion but more commonly they referred to the effort required: "That school-girl complexion we wash and we sun; And a lip-stick will help." One yearbook proclaimed in 1933, "Things We Were Paid to Tell: Nonie's schoolgirl complexion is entirely natural, obtained by outdoor exercise." The tone implied that Nonie created her looks inside with the help of commercial products.[29]

Emphasis on skin and complexion was not novel in the twentieth century, but it was qualitatively different from earlier times. In the nineteenth century, complexion was viewed as a window to the soul and blemishes as a sign of moral corruption. Solutions ranged from tonics to soap and water. By the turn of the century, germs and poverty were blamed for acne, designating it as a lower-class problem, and solutions emphasized cleanliness and grooming. When middle- and upper-class adolescents continued to suffer skin problems, medical professionals reclassified acne as an equal-opportunity affliction and offered remedies including special diets and cleansing rituals.[30]

The medicalization and commercialization of acne allowed girls to speak more freely about pimples and remedies by the late 1920s. Beth Twiggar wrote to her diary in 1928, "There is a stubborn, ugly repulsive blackhead on one side of my nose." Beth named it Marjory after a girl she disliked. In the mid-1930s, when Fleischmann's Yeast promoted its use to cure acne during the "Rudy Vallee Hour," a music show popular with high school students, a concerned father complained to the president of NBC. He accused the network of "sinking to a new 'low'" by "mentally torturing children's minds." An NBC editor replied that other listeners supported the ad, "on the ground that yeast has proven helpful in many cases of skin troubles during adolescence."[31]

By the 1940s, discussion of acne appeared publicly. In 1941, a *Ladies' Home Journal* article, "Young Skin Needs Watching," espoused the contemporary notion that "teen-age skin trouble" was common and "as likely as not to happen to young people of irreproachable background, blood and behavior." The author recommended washing one's face with grain alcohol and avoiding greasy or spicy foods, including chocolate, pickles, and mustard. An advertisement for Poslam, a concentrated ointment designed to "Treat 'Teen-Age' Skin," in *Scholastic* magazine in 1942 claimed thirty-five years of experience fighting pimples.[32]

Face creams, sometimes offered as acne remedies (albeit not very effective ones), also gained popularity in the early twentieth century. The manufacturers of Pond's, originally a nineteenth-century elixir, began producing cold cream to capitalize on the growing demand for skin products. Noxzema, developed by a Baltimore druggist, was sold locally to "soothe sunburn and 'knock eczema'" for years before its national promotion as a cleansing and moisturizing cream. In 1916, Ponds introduced a two-part beauty "system": cold cream at night for cleansing and vanishing cream during the day for protection. This ritual became so popular that face cream sales tripled between 1916 and 1920.[33]

Teenage girls actively participated in this expanding beauty culture by the 1920s, despite the marketing emphasis on adult women. Although they often had limited resources, many high school girls had free time and some discretionary spending money, and they enjoyed exploring various products. Beth Twiggar exemplified this interaction with her rich, illustrative diary entries. At age fourteen, she wrote, "I do love beauty preparations though. I think I could spend hours applying and experimenting with them!" She kept a running commentary, analyzing the beauty messages she read yet remaining intimately engaged with them. After reading an article on "beauty plus cosmetics," Beth wrote, "It moved me so I long to purchase all the cleansing creams and astringent lotions, and vanishing concoctions and shades of beauty mud, and rouges and perfumes and powders on the market." Beth then joked that the author should "willingly donate the money concerned in following her advice!"[34]

Nevertheless, Beth proceeded to experiment with and dramatize "the fatal issue of what cold cream to use next." She listed her requirements, "They must be indorsed by my [friends], Mrs. Reginald Vanderbilt, 500 young women from prominent colleges or Vilma Banky! They must be done up attractively and not cost over a dollar." Beth demonstrated media savvy, making fun of advertising efforts to impress readers with endorsements by famous people or glamorous images of college life. Attractiveness and cost were also important—these remained prominent features as the teenage market expanded—as were packaging and design. Beth evaluated multiple creams and wrote, "I think I shall go back to Mr. Woodbury. . . . Wowy what a sheik he is on the soap!" The entry did not comment on product effectiveness. Beth's histrionics notwithstanding, she demonstrated a strong knowledge of product design and claims yet retained a sense of humor about their excesses.[35]

When Beth wrote these diary entries, her exposure to cosmetic advertising was limited to movie magazines, women's magazines, and newspapers. In the 1930s, creams and cosmetics began to advertise more directly to teenage girls, even appearing in high school yearbooks, as shown in figures 3.3 and 3.4. Yearbook advertisements promoted creams for girls who "desire[d] that schoolgirl complexion." Noxzema advertised "New Beauty Because It Corrects Skin Faults" in its "Famous Jar," and promised to correct

> If you desire that beautiful
> schoolgirl complexion use:
>
> # Pacquin's . . . .
> # HAND and FACE CREAM
>
> It can be purchased at any
> Druggist or Department Store

3.3   Skin Cream Advertisement, High School Yearbook, 1932

"large pores, blackheads, surface pimples, oiliness!" Although these advertisements were not significantly modified for a younger audience and many did not address high school students directly, girls paid close attention and product messages began to appear in yearbook texts. One student wrote satirically of a mystery product, merging advertising slogans from soap to cigarettes: "It is taken from contented cows with that skin you'll love to touch. If you would be healthy and have that school-girl complexion, reach for our product instead of a sweet." Yearbook editors mentioned girls "with 'Palmolive' skin" or "that Camay complexion." Presumably, these girls had naturally beautiful skin. In the intertextual world of twentieth-century advertising, product claims established reference points for describing real people.[36]

The notion that time and effort could transform an average woman into a beauty was well established by the 1920s. The message that society demanded "natural beauty" created by commercial products was clear as well. Mass marketing of beauty products established ideal features as well as a common vocabulary. Girls read beauty advice and advertisements primarily written for adult women and incorporated their ideas and language. But this did not always translate into brand loyalty or even product loyalty. Many girls, exemplified by Beth, tried new products frequently and abandoned them just as often. With the emergence of products designed for teens, such as acne remedies, advertisements began to address high school girls directly and manufacturers began to emphasize teenage culture. By that point in the mid-1940s, though, girls had already established a close relationship with commercial beauty culture.

Cosmetics

Beauty rituals generally took place privately—in bedrooms and bathrooms. Cosmetics were more public, visible on the face and even applied openly. After World War I, the

IN THIS FAMOUS JAR
You Will Find

NEW BEAUTY
BECAUSE IT CORRECTS SKIN FAULTS

Already over 6,000,000 women have learned the value of Noxzema in correcting skin faults like large pores, blackheads, surface pimples, oiliness!

Try Noxzema for two weeks and see what wonderful results *you* get! Apply Noxzema every night after make-up has been removed. Wash off in the morning with warm water, followed by cold water or ice. Apply a little Noxzema again as a protective powder base. It's *greaseless—vanishing —stainless!* Get a jar of Noxzema at your druggist's today.

NOXZEMA CREAM
10,000,000 JARS SOLD YEARLY

3.4   *Skin Cream Advertisement, High School Yearbook, 1935*

mass market for cosmetics flourished. Production expanded rapidly and commercial beauty products became widely available for the first time. The number of American manufacturers of perfume and cosmetics doubled between 1909 and 1929 and production value grew from $14.2 million to nearly $141 million. By the 1930s, cosmetics were well established and widely used, but controversy continued regarding how much makeup was appropriate, at what age, and in what situations. Out of this debate grew an extensive literature of how-to manuals and advice articles, all of which increased focus on external, commercial beauty.[37]

Although many schools in the 1920s and 1930s forbade girls from wearing makeup or applying it publicly, schools increasingly played a role in consumer and beauty education. Primarily through home economics courses, girls learned general care for their bodies, clothes, and faces. Cosmetic manufacturers and retailers worked with magazines and schools to promote habits as well as product loyalty through lectures, booklets, and free samples. An OGS observer casually mentioned a "demonstration 'facial'" at the clubhouse and wrote about "the Beechnut girl" who entered the Clubhouse "in gay costume, presenting free samples of coughdrops."[38]

Experimenting with cosmetics became an important part of teen culture. Although makeup was not manufactured specifically for teenage girls in the 1920s, 1930s, and 1940s, they purchased it, received it as gifts, used it, and shared it. Some parents banned all use of makeup while others bemoaned it. But many girls wore it anyway, applying it secretly at school, dances, or friends' houses when necessary. Girls avidly read beauty literature for women as well as for high school students. Hand and bathroom mirrors became common in the early twentieth century, and by the 1920s, with the new cultural mirrors of motion pictures and close-up photography, girls began analyzing their faces carefully. Two yearbook drawings from 1925, seen in figure 3.5, illustrate the established presence of mirrors and concern with appearance in high school life.[39]

The "Sub-Deb" column encouraged detailed analysis of oneself and other females with articles entitled "Look Into Your Mirror" or "Blonde, Brunette or Redhead?" Articles posed pointed questions: "Do you have 'particular problems' with your complexion" or "millions and billions of blackheads? Are the pores on your face so large you're afraid your powder puff will get lost in them?" As seen in figure 3.6, the accompanying drawings further encouraged girls to make beauty and cosmetics part of their daily lives, advising each reader of her duty to "Do Your Part." In May 1932, Woodward asked, "Do you know what colors you should wear? How to make a pug nose look long and distinguished?" and offered solutions in her booklet, "Let Make-Up Make You Over." Girls incorporated this language into their writings and peer relationships. Yvonne Blue described classmates in her diary by writing, "E. is neither a blonde nor a brunette; she has brown hair and eyes, wears gold rimmed glasses all the time (which look good on her as her face is broad)." She described another girl as "slender and fair with big blue eyes and cute little mannerisms. She has a slightly turned up nose, a few freckles, a rosy complexion."[40]

Beth Twiggar's diary entries similarly illuminate how the presence of vast quantities of consumer goods, accompanied by myriad advice columns explaining appropriate use, furthered girls' use of commercial beauty products and attention to looks. In 1928, she copied the directions from a jar of cream, "Leave for two minutes and then wipe off with soft cloth." She then wrote, "Armand's cold cream! I have been cheating you! Your good effects have been diluted because, oh woe! I leave your pure oils in my pores for only one minute and a half!" Beth's facetiousness notwithstanding, she demonstrated a strong knowledge of product design and strategy, yet retained a sense of humor about the extravagant claims and absolutes conveyed by advertising copy. Even skepticism, though, could promote further product use. Beth wrote at age fourteen that she returned to washing her face with soap and water, but she specified that she used "Ivory soap (99$^{44}/_{100}$% pure) and at present am like unto a healthy country Miss!"[41]

The rising commercial industry shaped girls' understanding of beauty, but some girls, such as Beth, continued to read advertisements with a critical eye. A high school student who wrote a poem entitled "Sonnet to the Lady of the Sign-Board," published in 1933, recognized the lack of connection between reality and a billboard model. Despite her hair "glinting gold, exactly curled" and eyebrows "graceful, thin, correctly smooth," she could "never soothe / the folk who look into [her] eyes." Similarly, OGS participant Rita told an interviewer during a drawing session in 1938 that her art was "too natural" for advertising: "If you look at the figures in magazines. They're always thin, and their eyes

3.5   Drawings, High School Yearbook, 1925

are always big and their lips just perfect—and I don't make mine that way." Rita never drew "the awful sophisticated girl—with drooping eyes—and perfect teeth and every hair in place."[42]

Most teenage girls still thought too much about cosmetics according to educators and parents. Yearbooks throughout these decades are filled with memories of girls who used cosmetics regularly, "wills" leaving future classes more space for storing beauty

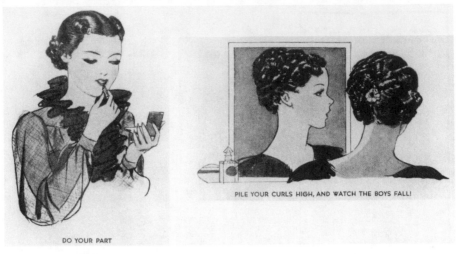

DO YOUR PART

PILE YOUR CURLS HIGH, AND WATCH THE BOYS FALL!

3.6   Ladies' Home Journal, *July 1935*

products or "the right to powder their noses," and frequent references to confiscated goods, such as mirrors, powder, and lipstick. Teachers who frequently reminded girls to use less "powder and paint" appeared as well, alongside the talents of Dorothy, who "gets out her mirror and makes eyes in it at Lou."[43]

Dorothy used the tools of cosmetics to flirt directly. For many other girls, makeup allowed them to explore adult status, privileges, and sexuality, often before parents were prepared for such a transition. And although mothers frequently encouraged their daughters' entrance into commercial beauty culture, conflicts arose over how and when girls could wear cosmetics. Beth Twiggar spent several years in the late 1920s in an intricate dance with her parents over the topic of makeup. By age fifteen, Beth felt she was old enough to graduate from creams and powders to lipstick and rouge. Her mother complimented her "color," but her father was firmly opposed. After several confrontations, Beth wrote in 1929, "Daddy saw me with lipstick on last night and said if he saw me with it again, he would turn me out of the house." A few months later, she "shocked and horrified daddy into a fit of silence this noon. A pair of earrings, a good deal of lipstick and some rouge did the trick."[44]

Beth continued to experiment with makeup, wearing it for dances and dates. She also confided to her diary that what her father witnessed was far milder than what she did outside of his view: "I wonder what he would have thought if he could have been at the girls gathering at the L's this afternoon. We were all sitting around, skirts to neck, minus stockings, and of course, smoking. We were embazzened [*sic*] with lipstick, discussing the time Betty and Alla went to a speakeasy in New York." The afternoon was about bonding, sharing information, and flirting with danger as much as it was about putting on cosmetics. The conflicts subsided by the time she was sixteen; her father either accepted her use of cosmetics or accepted the futility of resistance as she grew older. But this negotiation repeated endlessly in the decades to come as inexpensive products proliferated and granted girls easier access to cosmetics promising instant beauty and popularity.[45]

OGS participants related similar conflicts, although acceptable standards varied greatly with age and family circumstances. At age thirteen, Judith's father ordered her not to leave the house with lipstick or rouge. In contrast, Lillian reported to a friend, "[My mother] asked, 'is that lipstick' and I said 'yes' and she said 'Do you put it on all the time' and I said 'no.'" As long as she wore makeup responsibly, Lillian's mother chose not to interfere. Thirteen-year-old Jean and her mother crafted an unspoken agreement. Jean was not allowed to leave the house wearing lipstick, but her mother knew she wore it at school. An interviewer noted that the mother tolerated this as long as Jean did not confront her directly with her disobedience.[46]

Makeup had even greater significance for immigrant girls, offering a way to participate in American culture and assimilate with peers. The parents of recent immigrants, though, were even more likely to protest. OGS participant Margaret was born in Europe. An observer wrote that Margaret's mother had "very European" standards. The mother reported feeling "bewildered by American life" and "shocked at the amount of time Margaret spends on her clothes and her appearance. It is news to her that this behavior is quite general among girls of that age." This comment revealed the mother's cultural assumptions as well as those of the observer who expected makeup and fashion consciousness among American teenage girls in 1936.[47]

While anticipated by some adults, all makeup use was not equal. OGS observers frequently commented on the use of cosmetics by study participants, expressing interest in girls' early experimentation and makeup trends. As with fashion, however, OGS observers had strong opinions regarding the acceptable use of cosmetics. Comments by observers regarding makeup, similar to many parental responses, illustrate that adults often assisted in girls' induction into commercial beauty culture by encouraging attention to appearance and beauty "flaws" and purchasing gifts such as perfume and compact cases for their daughters. Yet these adults wanted girls to use makeup and perfume sparingly, to present a clean "wholesome" look eschewing blatant sexuality. Teenage girls often welcomed cosmetics, but they viewed them as a tool for exploring adult looks and sexuality.

Although OGS observers could not control cosmetic use by girls, their comments provide a window into middle-class views on teenage girls, beauty, sexuality, and femininity. References to cosmetics among OGS participants first appeared in fall 1933 when twelve-year-old girls shared lipstick and discussed colors. Over the following year, observers praised girls' budding interest in makeup and appearance, "Elizabeth has suddenly become quite the young lady; constant hair-combing and lipstick." OGS observers commended cosmetic use, a positive sign of appropriate maturation from girlhood to teenage years. One observer complimented Olivia's "improved appearance due to artistic use of lipstick, rouge, eyebrow pencil, curlers." Another wrote that Meredith "bloomed completely and successfully: hair waved, nails polished, lips painted, very aware of her femininity . . . looks quite sophisticated."[48]

As participants grew older, observers made special note of girls who did not use makeup. Comments about thirteen-year-olds were fairly neutral: "No sign of make-up" or "Never saw her primp." Observers grew more emphatic and disparaging when commenting on older girls. Dorothy, at age fourteen, "would be improved by a little makeup," wrote one observer, as would fifteen-year-old Beverly who wore "*no makeup*." Approval from adult observers, however, was not as simple as "using makeup." The "Sub-Deb" column and other advice literature warned girls to use makeup carefully, to follow prescriptions for looking natural rather than painted, pretty rather than sexual, and the observers agreed.[49]

Observers censored girls who wore "heavy" or "extreme" cosmetics, including dark colors, as well as those who applied makeup in public. They characterized girls with "excessive eyebrow plucking" as "cheap." Deborah wore "her adolescence somewhat extravagantly" at age thirteen, with dark lipstick and red nail polish. A note on Anna, at age fifteen, read, "She looked like a cheap edition of Mae West, only coarser." Another observer wrote that fourteen-year-old Rita, "has done strange and terrible things to her appearance—eye shadow, mascara, lipstick—blobs of it." The observers continued to praise girls who used makeup "judiciously" and "tastefully," with special notice for those who reformed beauty habits and became "less flamboyant." A note on Eloise at age fourteen read, "Marked improvement in appearance. Hair and make-up less extravagant." As summarized by an interviewer, adult feedback had influenced Eloise's decision: "she was tired of being told she was common or wild because she wore lipstick."[50]

This conflict between teenage girls and parents, advisors, and educators over "appropriate" makeup use continued as beauty products and messages for teenage girls expanded. *Seventeen* magazine heavily promoted its version of the "wholesome" teenage girl, based on standards for fashion, cosmetics, and hair, when creating a booklet for advertisers in 1944 entitled "Who is Teena? Judy Jeckyll [*sic*] or Formalda Hyde?" The cover, seen in figure 3.7, pictured a girl split in half. The left side shows a teenage girl in a sweater and skirt with straight hair and no cosmetics. The right side depicts a girl in a slinky evening gown and fishnet stockings with lipstick, rouge, large earrings, and hair piled on her head. Copy promotes the left half as age appropriate and advises on how to reach "Teena" through *Seventeen.* Copy chastises marketers who try to sell girls on the "other" half.[51]

Girls began to understand their place in this growing beauty culture and to negotiate relationships with images, products, parents, and peers as the industry grew. Yearbook photographs recorded interest in makeup, primarily powder and lipstick, in the 1920s and diaries, yearbooks, and stories frequently mentioned face powder. A packaging revolution in the 1920s furthered the debate on public application of makeup as attractive, portable containers replaced plain, heavy jars. Frances Turner thrilled to receive a small powder box for Christmas in the early 1920s, "to carry to a dance, you know." In 1926, a yearbook description of a typical day included "some tall and magnificent senior who has chosen the middle of the first floor hall as just the spot to powder her nose."[52]

Face powder was no longer a novelty by the late 1920s, but it still warranted discussion among girls. In 1927, at age sixteen, Yvonne Blue wrote at length about purchasing "a compact" while shopping with her mother. Beth Twiggar joked about surviving a day without powder at age fourteen and imagined the headline, "'Young girl by splendid endurance refrains whole day from powdering nose. Wins $20,000.'" That same year, Beth returned from a friend's house "loaded with cosmetics. It is so seldom I see any, I fairly jump and grab when I do. Three kinds of lipsticks upon my nature's cupid bow, blacking upon my lustrous lashes, a dash of color brightening my cheek and the whole dusted over with powder. And I was quite, quite stunning."[53]

By the 1930s, makeup use had increased among adult women as well as teenage girls. When Beth dressed for a dance in 1930, at age seventeen, she wrote "I made up my face with the utmost care, a slight shadow on the eyelids, just so much rouge on the cheeks & chin, lipstick, powder, carefully & thoughtfully—eyebrow & lashes smoothed black." Beth paused in her preparations to reflect on the process, enjoying the drama and anticipation, but her rhetoric mimicked beauty advice, "just so much rouge," "carefully"

WHO IS TEENA ?
Judy Jeckyll
or Formalda Hyde ?

3.7   Seventeen Magazine *Promotional Material*

applied powder, and "smooth" lashes. By the early 1930s, yearbooks listed "Cosmetics" in senior "want" columns and lamented misplaced lipsticks. In 1933, a yearbook remembered one senior's "weakness" for powder while other girls found "shiny" noses an "abomination." And by the late 1930s, editors joked about the "Daily Drama" of girls "adding war paint to their lovely faces" or "putting on final touches of makeup, trying their hardest where nature has failed."[54]

In addition to the plethora of advice from parents and the beauty industry, girls depended heavily on peer opinions. As girls learned to judge themselves—and their bodies and faces—critically, they also learned to judge each other. OGS participants frequently discussed appropriate, or inappropriate, use of cosmetics, although their standards and strategies differed from those of OGS observers. At age twelve, Virginia jokingly delivered a serious message to a friend, "Oh kid—you got . . . way too much [rouge] on." Grace used makeup to assert control at age fifteen, purposely making interviewers wait, "I'm going to take my time. I'm going to powder my face too." Her friend Lillian agreed, "[Me] too. Got any lipstick[?]" In 1936, one girl who chose not to wear makeup elicited ire from her peers. An observer reported, "I heard some of the girls expressing outrage that Elizabeth should affect no make-up. The implication was that she thought it only detracted from her natural beauty etc. but was necessary for others."[55]

Cosmetic use also signified growing up. A senior described her journey through high school according to landmark changes in appearance, as well as emotional maturity: "we passed through the transitional stage, gradually dropping crushes as a pastime and adopting long hair and lipstick." Editors of one yearbook commented favorably on the increasing maturity of sophomores, again marked by cosmetic use: "Could it be that the children of yesteryear are growing up? It's hard to find one of the native belles who doesn't use make-up." Yearbooks complimented seniors who wore cosmetics effectively and cheered girls who achieved glamour, characterizing them as "our 'It' girl" or a "modern Venus." References to glamour, actresses, and models increased throughout the 1930s, as Hollywood influence spread, and appeared regularly by the early 1940s.[56]

Praise often centered on specific attributes: "we are glad to report that Fran still wears her own eyelashes—and are we jealous!" One girl's eyes carried her "a long way on the road to vampdom." Other girls were remembered for having "long, thick, black eyelashes, the envy of the senior class" or for never being caught with a "shiny nose." Cosmetics played an important role in the lives of high school girls. Girls noticed who wore makeup and who did not, whether they wore too much or not enough, and whether the color was appropriate. They were conscious of the commercial and constructed nature of the beauty culture in which they participated, as one poem by a high school student joked, "And on her lips a little lipstick slaps / Its name is 'Rosy Future' (color fast) / Although it looks more like the shady past." Yet they reflected the anxiety and insecurity promoted through advice literature and cosmetics advertising, judging themselves and each other with a critical eye.[57]

Cosmetic Accoutrements: Nail Polish, Perfume, and Jewelry

Middle-class women considered nail polish, introduced in the early 1920s, "vulgar" well into the 1930s. Despite disapproval, its use expanded, as did close attention to hands and nails. A "Sub-Deb" column in 1930 announced, "Fingers Tell Tales." A sketch of two hands accompanied a drawing of a manicure set and advice about appropriate nail shape and polish color for each hand type. Revlon was created in 1932 and expanded rapidly, introducing new shades every season with extensive advertising campaigns and creative color names. In 1933, at age twelve, OGS participants experimented with nail polish with or without adult approval. Sally remarked to a friend, "You know what [an interviewer] said to me. She looked at my finger and she said—what do you put that old red stuff on for—the old poop. She gives me a pain."[58]

OGS observers noted which girls wore nail polish, criticizing those using "bright" or dark colors. One observer wrote in 1935 that Sharon painted her nails too "obviously." Girls in the OGS continued to discuss nail polish with friends, but its novelty decreased as girls grew older and nail polish gained broader acceptance. Similarly, by the mid-to-late-1930s, yearbooks commonly referred to "[p]eeling polish from finger nails" or girls with an "aversion" to "[b]reaking a carefully cultivated fingernail," although adult approval lagged. Elizabeth "willed" her red nail polish to Sadie in her 1939 "Last Will and Testament," while Edith willed "a class of girls without glaring nail polish" to a teacher fighting an uphill battle.[59]

In contrast, girls began using perfume in the 1920s at younger ages and with less conflict. Across class lines, women purchased perfumes and fragrances. Although some perfumers sought an exclusive clientele, others saw profit in an expanded market and sold inexpensive French imitations. In the 1920s, many girls received perfume for birthdays or holidays from parents, relatives, and friends. At age twelve, Yvonne Blue received "a dear little perfume bottle . . . shaped like a watch [and] gold-plated. Where you wind a watch it unscrews. I love it." This type of clever bottling was extremely popular with girls who reveled in the pleasures of receiving, opening, and using such gifts.[60]

An advertisement for "Seventeen Perfume" in 1930 promised "Youth itself . . . a mood which stole from a perfume bottle and entered my heart." Although this ad capitalized on the nation's passion for "youth" and addressed older readers, its placement next to the "Sub-Deb" column in Ladies' Home Journal ensured younger viewers. Its dramatic language, "I'm a helpless prisoner . . . captive to a lilting mood!" illustrated the flowing, passionate style Beth Twiggar frequently imitated. In the 1930s and 1940s, yearbooks identified girls who donned scents regularly, including the senior who could "discourse upon her favorite Kipling as lengthily as upon Chanel."[61]

Despite this devotion, cosmetics and perfumes were manufactured for adult women during these years. Although teenage girls often used them creatively, the basic products remained uniform, symbols of maturity. Jewelry, however, quickly became a site for expressing teen creativity, a medium for expression of teen styles. Some high school girls thought themselves beyond the "stage" of big earrings and loud makeup, but many welcomed the opportunities homemade jewelry provided. In contrast to expensive jewelry of gold, silver, or precious stones that symbolized maturity and required caution, girls made jewelry out of everyday materials, from macaroni to Life Savers, nail polish brushes to sugar cubes. A yearbook asked in 1939 "Do you remember—Or how could you forget . . . the M. girls' 'junk' bracelets? (Are you listenin' Miss Ruhe?)." A teacher had obviously tried unsuccessfully to stem the tide.[62]

By the early 1940s, teen jewelry flourished, and "Tricks for Teens" column editors added a section called "Jitterbug Jewelry," as illustrated in figure 3.8. Manufacturers also tried to capitalize on the high school jewelry trend. In June 1941, Parents "High School Fashion Board" endorsed commercial teen jewelry, such as "Nut, shell and wood gadgeteers" by "Tween-Age." In March 1942, "Beau Belle Jewelry" by Coro, shown in figure 3.9, claimed to offer the "[l]atest craze of the high school set. Dainty pearlized bows"

More Jitterbug Jewelry—Corks, macaroni, rubber bands, paper clips, dog collars, dog biscuits, powder puffs and many, many more Tricks pour in about Jitterbug Jewelry. Here are some of the newest inspirations: "Make a necklace of Life Saver candies, strung together on a velvet ribbon. The assorted fruit flavors are the prettiest."—*Esther Winter, Clarinda High School, Hepburn, Ia.* "We make necklaces of chewing gum sticks, assorted flavors, strung together in their wrappers by making a hole through the top of each one."—*Mary Neetz, New Trier High School, Winnetka, Ill.*

3.8   *High School Jewelry Fads,* Parents' Magazine, *1941*

in multiple forms and colors. The ad promised a product that proved "Smooth with dress-up clothes; solid with sweaters," demonstrating awareness of teen slang and of the newly emerged distinction between teen "dress-up" clothes and daily wear, characterized by sweaters and skirts.[63]

Girls continued to make jewelry, however, and daintiness was rarely a goal. In 1941, girls in New York City wore dog collars as bracelets or bent spoons around their wrists, initialing them with "bright red nail polish." A girl from Detroit, Michigan, proudly wrote that she and her friends sought attention by wearing "school and gadget pins" on their skirt hems: "It might seem an out-of-the-way place for jewelry, but it's very conspicuous." To ensure notice, a girl from Bethlehem, Pennsylvania, wrote, "We wear little

3.9   Jewelry Advertisement, Parents' Magazine, *1942*

bells on our shoelaces and make necklaces of about fifty bells on a chain. Noisy but cute." Costume jewelry companies, such as Coro, capitalized on and fostered this interest by sponsoring jitterbug jewelry contests and fundraisers.[64]

Jewelry also provided a vehicle for expressing peer group affiliation or identifying boyfriends, music preferences, and favorite movie stars. Girls pasted photographs of friends or boyfriends into milk bottle tops and wore them as necklaces. A girl from Fort Thomas, Kentucky, wrote, "Everybody's making Carmen Miranda lapel pins out of whole pecan nuts with painted faces, top-knot turbans and curtain-ring earrings." In 1944, a letter from Toledo, Ohio, read, "We're decorating our cedar-wood heart lockets with cutout pictures of our best friends, favorite crooner (guess who?) or movie star." Yearbooks similarly listed popular jewelry fads as well as girls known for particularly tasteful or outlandish adaptations. High school girls transformed jewelry into an important signifier of teen culture, an inexpensive avenue for expressing their interests and peer loyalties as well as their creativity and resourcefulness. Marketers tried to catch up with this trend, but making jewelry proved an important part of the fun and many girls continued to create their own.[65]

Hair

Homemade jewelry provided an inexpensive, fun outlet for girls, a realm for controlling fashion and establishing peer connections. Hair proved another arena, albeit a more contentious one, in which girls could assert independence and explore mature looks. In the 1910s and 1920s, bobbed hair made national headlines. By the 1930s, Hollywood hairstyles influenced women of all ages, from Shirley Temple's curls to Jean Harlow's platinum blond locks to Greta Garbo's waves. Teenage girls' relationship with hair illustrates the complexity of commercial beauty culture and teenage girls' roles as consumers. Girls often experimented with hairstyles in an effort to look older and respond to media directed at adult women, but they also used hair to distinguish themselves from adults and incorporated hair grooming into teenage rituals.

Bobbed hair marked a significant change for women in the first decades of the twentieth century. Ballroom dancer Irene Castle was reportedly the first American celebrity to bob her hair, just below her ears, in 1913 in order to dance more freely and prevent flying hairpins. A media uproar followed, and the American debate was underway. Betty Smith characterized the debate in her poignant, semi-autobiographical coming-of-age novel, *A Tree Grows in Brooklyn*. In the book, thirteen-year-old Francie Nolan asks her mother in 1914 if she can "get a Castle Clip." When her mother refuses because "hair was a woman's crowning beauty," Francie confides to her diary, "I want to be my own boss and get my hair cut off. . . ." At age fourteen, she again requests permission to bob her hair, arguing that she would "look just like Irene Castle" with short hair and that it would be easier to care for. Her mother does not relent.[66]

Heated debates about bobbed hair ensued. Opposition remained strong among churches, businesses, and some media. Front-page stories warned of young women losing jobs or being expelled from school after cutting their hair. Yet the freedom short hair offered, as well as the image of modernity and youth, attracted more women every year. A teenage girl wrote to her friend Frances in 1918, "I have bobbed my hair. Mrs. I[rene] Castle Style. Oh Boy. It has come out real curly and everybody down here likes it. I am not a bit sorry I cut it." Over the next decade, friends wrote to Frances regularly about their fantasies of and reactions to bobbed hair.[67]

Bobbed hair remained controversial into the 1920s. In 1924, at age thirteen, Yvonne Blue's friend cut her own hair while spending the night: "She would cut a curl off on each side and comb her bobbed hair and we would dance around and squeal." In the end, the friend, fearing parental disapproval, cut the bottom layer of her hair and covered it with longer top hair. The following year, Yvonne and several other friends had their "hair cut in a 'boyish bob,' just like a boy's only longer." Yvonne enjoyed testing gender boundaries, as did many girls in their teens. She "had a boyish bob, (Or Eaton crop as I prefer to call it)" before traveling and "to make the train trip more novel and adventurous . . . took a pair of Dad's old blue pajamas." Yvonne wrote excitedly about briefly being mistaken for a boy.[68]

Yearbooks continued to mention bobbed hair as a topic of debate and deliberation. By the second half of the 1920s, girls began growing their hair long again, "I've decided to grow up. I think I'll let my hair grow. Everyone thinks I'm at least three years younger than I am so I must become dignified and aged." The "Sub-Deb" column rushed to sell booklets entitled, "Letting the Bob Grow Gracefully" and "Bobs or Long Hair." "It's a serious question," the accompanying article confirmed, "for just the right coiffure can often make a plain girl pretty, and it can always make any girl both charming and smart."[69]

High school girls across race and class admired bobs and the freedom they personified. Girls sometimes bobbed their hair, despite parental disapproval, to imitate "adult" women's styles, but they wanted to emulate women in their twenties, not their mothers. Imitation of Hollywood styles in the 1930s and 1940s further demonstrates girls' desire for glamour and sex appeal—potential sources of conflict with parents and schools. Although these styles were not distinctly "teen," as with other trends, products, and styles circulating in the commercial world of health and beauty culture, girls often incorporated hair styling into high school culture and friendships.

The widespread popularity of bobbed hair waned by the late 1920s, but the era of fleeting hairstyles had arrived. Yearbooks praised long hair as "the envy of the whole class" and seniors "willed" it to juniors. Teenage girls continued to cut their hair, but haircuts were no longer central to their letters, diaries, and stories. One yearbook teased a senior in 1929 who "tried to please every beau / She spent half the time getting her hair cut / And the other half letting it grow." For the first time, girls had many options and changed styles frequently.[70]

Bobbed hair was not the only innovation of the 1920s to transform hairstyles and hair care. Women in the nineteenth century usually cared for their hair at home. The wealthy had in-home assistance, but hairdressing still took place privately. This began to change at the end of the nineteenth century as a rising commercial beauty culture cultivated hair salons and the desire for bobbed hair attracted women to professional hair cutters in large numbers.[71]

With the rise of permanent waves and hair dyeing, beauty parlors for women became a lucrative business by the mid-1920s. Charles Nessler invented the first permanent-wave machine in 1906. A combination of heat and chemicals broke down the hair structure, and a practitioner wound the hair around rods to create a lasting curl. The procedure was expensive, dangerous, and time consuming, requiring up to eight hours. By the 1920s, improvements made the system cheaper and faster but did not guarantee safety or lasting curls. A yearbook listed a "Permanent Wave" under the heading "Greatest Need" in 1922, and another in 1926 teased the girl whose greatest ambition was to "have a permanent *permanent*." A newsletter the same year contained a poem entitled,

"Boo Hoo! I'm So Blue!" that read: "I get a wave, a nice marcel / My locks look curled and neat / I think I look just simply 'swell' / But it only lasts a week."[72]

By the late 1920s and early 1930s, references to permanents increased. *Ladies' Home Journal* ran an ad for Gerardine waving lotion next to the "Sub-Deb" column in 1931. Beauty parlors regularly advertised in high school yearbooks, promising a range of permanent wave techniques. Girls complained about unattractive permanents or those that did not last. Others "willed" their curly hair to the less fortunate in yearbooks. OGS participants in the mid-1930s frequently discussed permanent waves, asking if curls looked natural or complaining about "need[ing] a permanent 'just terribly.'" Parents did not always approve, as the OGS mother who forbade her thirteen-year-old daughter to have one. But conflicts over hair were generally less dramatic than those about cosmetics or fashion. OGS observers occasionally applauded waved or curled hair—"Doris had a permanent, which improves her appearance"—but more often criticized the quality, describing the effects as "very unattractive," "fuzzy," or "frizzed."[73]

Words such as "fuzzy" and "frizzed" were commonly used to describe unattractive hair. These words also referred to "non-white" hair, especially the hair of African Americans. Although a certain amount of curl was desired, an undertone of racism was intertwined with the new language surrounding permanents, sometimes quite explicitly. In 1926, at age fifteen, Yvonne Blue described a "horrible" permanent as "fuzzy, kinky and unmanageable as a nigger's wool." This image was pervasive. A yearbook essay from 1941 remarked on girls who "appeared with their hair curled as tightly as African savages." African American girls were affected by these commercial definitions of "beauty" as well. Peiss writes that the "contradictory rejection and embrace of Euro-American aesthetic standards surfaced repeatedly as black writers, reformers, and educators responded to the new beauty culture." Beauty parlor advertisements in African American high school yearbooks offered waving, but also offered chemicals to "control your hair as you wish."[74]

Hair dyes also became big business. High school girls who imitated movie stars envied their glamour and sex appeal. As with cosmetics, mothers often encouraged hair grooming, but not the manipulation of hair to express sexuality or rebellion. A few commercial hair bleaches promised platinum blond hair in the 1920s, but popularity soared in the 1930s as movies promoted "blonde bombshells." Home remedies, such as peroxide, ammonia, and Ivory soap flakes, remained popular as references to dyed hair in yearbooks increased. Stereotypes of blond hair and envy toward girls with natural blond coloring increased simultaneously. By the early 1930s, yearbooks joked about whether Betty "peroxides her hair" or asked "What would happen" if a certain girl's hair was "'au naturelle'?"[75]

OGS observers usually mentioned hair dye pejoratively in the mid-1930s. An observer described fourteen-year-old Virginia as "quite disfigured" by hair dye and another participant's hair as "badly streaked" from "dye or peroxide." One observer described Anna as a "natural blonde" in 1936, at age sixteen, but another mentioned her "artificial appearance" heightened by "a new extreme blonde bleach" in 1937. An observer unquestioningly wrote that Betty "was a 'good-looking but dumb' blond" in 1938. Yearbooks mirrored these themes, with references to the only girl to graduate with "natural blonde hair" or a weakness for "ammonia and peroxide." The "blonde" craze spread even further by the 1940s and the phrase "Gentlemen prefer blondes" appeared throughout yearbooks. Only occasionally was a girl with blond hair exonerated from association with stupidity, "for underneath those golden locks is a gem of a brain."[76]

Whether teenage girls transformed their hair at home or in commercial beauty parlors, hairstyles remained important. Beyond the issue of whether or not to bob one's hair, hair care could require significant investment of time and money. OGS observers commented on girls' devotion to their hairstyles. Louise reported spending more than two hours "trying to fix my hair on some new kind of curler." Joyce arrived at the study center one day with "three carefully arranged curls at the front of her head that looked like coiled snakes," and Sally only half-jokingly warned the doctor during a physical, "You wreck that wave up there and I'll wreck you."[77]

Some high school girls remained near the forefront of hair trends, behind young women in their twenties but ahead of their mothers. They experimented with permanents, hair dyes, lengths, and styles, although even peers did not always approve of the outcomes. One yearbook pointed out the first girl to wear a "Veronica Lake hair-do," a controversial hairstyle. A girl from Chester, Pennsylvania, wrote to "Tricks for Teens" that the boys at her school were "'so annoyed about our Veronica Lake hair-do's that they have let their own hair grow long and now wear a wave down over one eye, just to ridicule us.'" Or perhaps the boys were also experimenting with gender boundaries. Teen years were a time for exploration, and the girl who was "usually found . . . changing her hair-do" took full advantage.[78]

The recurring theme of growing up motivated some of this attention because hair proved yet another marker of age. Hair styled in certain ways could help one look, or at least feel, older or more glamorous. Yvonne Blue wrote excitedly in her diary at age fourteen that an aunt had curled her hair: "it improved my looks 100% and made me look seventeen or eighteen years old. . . . I wish I had a perm[a]nent wave. I didn't know that it would change my looks so." Yearbooks also captured girls' enthusiasm for "adult" hair practices. A freshman remembered how "completely and wonderfully old" she felt in the seventh grade with a permanent wave. Seventh or eighth grade was a popular time to begin curling hair or having permanent waves and OGS observers often interpreted new hairstyles as interest in growing up. An observer saw Maria's permanent wave as "an obvious attempt at a sophisticated hair style that did not quite look 'smooth.'" Observers also began to expect girls to show this interest, noting as remarkable that Cynthia did not start waving her hair until 1937, at age sixteen.[79]

A high school newsletter essay characterized these sentiments in 1942, highlighting seventh grade as "the great beginning of the great change. One by one we would come to school with our first permanents, and our whole class would stand around us and jeer and squeal and stare at the dreadful looking fuzz that stuck out like poodle hair." In the eighth and ninth grades "we got the urge to be glamorous. Our frizzy permanents were cut off and our hair hung down over our eyes." As girls grew older, they experimented with individual styles, ranging from "sophisticated pompadours, sweeping up in the front and towering upwards, topped by mammoth bows" to bangs that "bob[bed] with every move and [fell] with every shake," or were "brushed aside and curled into a little mop of wiggles that flop[ped] around over one eye." As with fads, hairstyles could signify teen efforts to belong to a group as well as express individuality. But unlike fads, the styles high school girls imitated came from models and actresses as well as from other teens.[80]

Yet even when imitating Irene Castle or Veronica Lake, hair rituals linked high school girls, marking stages within adolescence characterized first by uniformity and later by decided efforts to express individuality. Teenage girls actively participated in the growing market of commercial hair services and products, as well as many other aspects of beauty culture targeted at adult women, incorporating them into teen culture. Fifteen-year-old Grace Watson, from Idaho, mocked adult criticism for teenage experimentation, "I tinted my hair a too bright shade / Folks thought that I was bold / But I caught a beau who kissed me / Before I grew too old."[81]

⑨⑨⑨

By the early twentieth century, manufacturers, retailers, and advertisers began to create and market mass-produced, commercial beauty and health products and advice, as well as professional haircuts and treatments. Many teenage girls avidly participated in this consumer culture, seeking out and often accepting commercial beauty products and messages aimed at adult women. In the realm of commercial beauty culture, as with fashion, teenage girls navigated advice and products—experimenting with various looks, pushing adult-approved boundaries and occasionally gender boundaries, and cementing friendships—before mass marketers sought their attention. As a result of teenage girls' efforts and, eventually, industry interest, the intensity, investment of time and money, and resulting insecurity increased dramatically. Commercialized beauty and health products and rituals helped girls identify themselves as a group, but they also indoctrinated teenagers into the world of appearance and consumption where girls learned to subdue nature in order to appear "natural."

High school girls demonstrated the extent of that insecurity through their writings. It manifested itself in concern with dieting and figures that centered on idealized body parts or popularity based solely on appearance. Girls accepted the need to sanitize their bodies, removing odor and hair whenever possible, often with commercial products. Girls were surrounded by messages aimed at adult women, and they desired cosmetics and cosmetic accoutrements long before the industry noticed their interest. Yet girls found avenues for defining high school culture, such as experimenting with cosmetics in groups or creating homemade jewelry. Through experiments with new hairstyles and treatments, girls imitated adult styles but also brought them into high school culture.

Parents and teachers did not shelter high school girls from anxiety and self-consciousness. They pushed girls into a commercial beauty culture while trying to direct it and to prevent unconventional experimentation. Teenage girls typically had less discretionary income than adult women, but they had heightened interest in appearance, time to experiment with a wide range of products, and strong peer feedback to inspire, critique, and shape their efforts. Fashion and beauty culture were central to the way girls represented themselves in public, which increasingly meant participation in commercial popular culture.

"Damn Good Jazz"

Music, Radio, and Dance

Don't forget that father may pay for the phonograph, but sons and daughters are the ones who seem to spend money most freely for the latest records.

—*Printers' Ink,* 1922[1]

Music is similar to beauty products and clothing in many ways—a cultural commodity, mass-produced and consumed in a primarily segmented market. In common with other cultural forms previously discussed, music simultaneously marks teen identity and incorporates teens into the adult world of consumption. But it is also different in important ways. A man's button-down shirt may be intended for wear over a T-shirt, under a suit, and with a tie to reflect a certain business status. But a teenage girl might purchase that same shirt in the men's department or borrow it from her father's closet with an entirely different purpose in mind. If she writes the name of her favorite singer or song lyrics on the shirt, embroiders it with brightly colored thread, and then wears the shirt untucked, unbuttoned at the neck, and over her jeans, she redefines the meaning of that shirt. Music, especially recorded music, is a more fixed entity.[2]

Consumers have less ability to alter recorded music, although there are ways in which they can alter its significance. Philosopher and cultural critic Theodor Adorno wrote in the early 1940s that consumers of music accept the "pseudo-individualization" of mass-produced, "patterned and pre-digested" music designed to be familiar and marketed to present the illusion of free choice. According to Adorno, music provides catharsis, "but catharsis which keeps [listeners] all the more firmly in line" and causes them to accept social dependence. Although listeners are limited commercially to available music options, this argument overlooks the ability of music consumers to incorporate music into their lives and create meanings. Listeners are able to use music in multiple ways, due in part to the variety of formats in which they encounter it: records, radio, jukeboxes, live orchestras, singing, and musical instruments. Teenagers in the 1920s, 1930s, and 1940s integrated commercial music into their lives through singing, dancing with friends or at formal dances, teaching each other dance steps, or discussing favorite bands, songs, radio shows, and records. Music reinforced messages of beauty, femininity, and romance, but it also fostered free expression and release of sexual energy, and it led teenage girls to question the links between popular culture and society.[3]

Teenage girls' interactions with popular music are noteworthy because, as with commercial beauty products, high school students pursued their interests long before they were recognized as a viable market. The common view is that rock 'n' roll created the teenage market, especially for music, although a few historians cite swing as influential in the early 1940s. Swing marked an important shift, but a relationship between teenagers and music began much earlier. While high school students in the 1920s listened to music created for a multi-generational audience, they often consumed it in teen-centered ways. The relationship of teens to jazz and swing in the 1920s, 1930s, and 1940s evoked negative attention from media and adults and demonstrates that music helped high school students develop a distinct teenage culture. After 1945, music created specifically for teenage audiences established a new dynamic, but music was central to teen lives long before.

Teenage girls actively engaged with popular music, pursuing heated debates over favorite singers, bands, or songs. They linked songs and music with dates and friendships, constructed memories out of song titles or lyrics in high school yearbooks, and sang or danced as they walked down school hallways, finished homework, or completed household chores. Dance and dance music were integral to teenage culture from the 1920s through the 1940s, playing an important role in leisure time activities, peer group formation, and individual friendships. In the realm of music even more than in fashion or beauty, teenage girls constructed their own age-specific culture out of commercial popular music before marketers and the music industry figured out their value as an audience and consumer group. As the *Printers' Ink* quotation implied with remarkable foresight, small investments in records by individual teens made high school students a valuable market in the aggregate.

Fashion and beauty are primarily gender-specific. The shift to popular culture, including music and movies, marks a change to products with male and female consumers. Historians of youth in the 1920s write that the most prescient symbols of "modernity" related to changes in women's behavior, including wearing shorter skirts, smoking cigarettes in public, and abandoning long hair. In some ways, these freedoms brought more equality between the actions of young men and women, making acceptable for women behavior once reserved for men. Although teenage boys and girls often shared their interest in music and movies and enjoyed them together, popular culture did not always have the same meaning for both. This is especially true for dancing, including public display of the body, and fan culture. The relationship between mass-produced music and the everyday practices of teenage girls from 1920 to 1945 addresses the power of commercial popular culture, but also of teenage girls' independence, creativity, and ability to find age-specific pleasures in unintended places.

Swinging Teens and the Music Industry

Ross Firestone, biographer of "King of Swing" Benny Goodman, writes that on August 21, 1935, "the Swing Era was born." Swing as a musical genre was not created that night, but Goodman's performance at the Palomar Ballroom in Los Angeles drew media attention and heralded the "era" of swing. By the end of 1935, swing's popularity was rising, but it was still loosely defined. Bands played swing music, but few played it exclusively. The "swing era," roughly from 1935 to 1945, describes the market rather than the invention; this was the period in which swing reached the height of its popularity, swing bands were in great demand, and swing records became top sellers.[4]

Swing music is difficult to define. It evolved from jazz, but music historians often characterize swing as a "gross commercialization of jazz" in part because of its wider audience and greater profits. Jazz, based loosely on African American musical traditions and gospel style interaction between soloist and chorus, featured individual improvisation within the group as well as rhythmic and harmonic effects not usually found in European and white American music. Swing built on basic elements of jazz, such as playing a melody outside of a structured rhythm while retaining the beat. Any music can be "swung," creating a freer, more relaxed feeling, but "swing" as a phenomenon generally refers to big band jazz, music arranged for large bands and played with a steady beat for dancing.[5]

Fans of swing first gained national attention in March 1937 when Benny Goodman's orchestra played at the Paramount movie theater. The Paramount successfully added live musical performances between movie screenings during the Depression to increase ticket sales. When Goodman appeared, offering many teenage swing fans an inexpensive opportunity to see him perform live, the turnout was unexpected and unprecedented. When Goodman played, fans danced in the rows, aisles, and on their seats—wherever they could find room to enjoy the music and express themselves through movement. A few celebratory media reports credited young people with the new energy and enthusiasm for swing. Although "young people" often included college as well as high school students, with the advent of swing, perceptive music industry forecasters began to view high school students as a profitable audience and record market.[6]

Most contemporary critics described the Paramount event as a "'near riot.'" *Variety* reported a "roar of handclapping, whistling, stamping, and ardent hallooing . . . tradition shattering in its spontaneity, its unanimity, its sincerity, its volume, in the child-like violence of its manifestations." When Goodman returned the following year, the *New York Times* headline read, "1,500 Storm Theatre to Receive Goodman," and the article described the audience as "composed in the main of high school students." One *New York Times* movie critic decried this violation of movie theater etiquette, claiming incredulously, "Anyone would have to give way before Mr. Goodman. Even Shirley Temple." He continued, writing that to the "legion of 'teenish admirers,'" acceptable behavior was as simple as "jump[ing] up and down." Goodman fans talked during the movie and when Goodman played, according to another reporter, they "danced in the aisles, clambered upon the stage, waggled their hands, shook their shoulders, whinnied, whistled, clapped and sang. It was a savage exhibition, as animalistic as a monkey's or an elephant's rhythmic swaying to the beat of a tom-tom." This strong language invoked a host of negative, non-human, and "non-white" images—young people highly sexualized and out of control. In similar rhetorical style, journalists described teenage fans as "locusts" who "swarmed . . . and then spread themselves on the ground." Critics claimed that Goodman's press agent hired the first group of unorthodox dancers, but whether true or not, dancing in the aisles spread quickly among unpaid fans.[7]

Swing evoked deep emotions among fans and non-fans alike. Media descriptions of teenage fans as animalistic, couched in racist language and images, illustrate the strong, visceral response it evoked. Although some writers praised swing as a celebration of the individual, even claiming that "Dictators should be suspicious of swing," others labeled it "'Musical Hitlerism'" because of the "mass sense of 'letting one's self go.'" Religious leaders warned that the "cannibalistic rhythmic orgies" were "wooing our youth along the primrose path to hell!" Journalists rushed to photograph "jitterbugs" in action, define the terms of swing, and convey the excitement of fans. In their rush to publicize, journalists helped spread the behavior nationally. Some reports claimed that "youngsters in their teens" dominated audiences, while others recorded mixed ages. But journalists, and to some extent the music industry, could not ignore the power of high school students and teenage musical preferences.[8]

Some writers credited teenage swing fans with a rise in record sales. Record sales did not skyrocket until the advent of rock 'n' roll, but they grew steadily during the swing era from their all-time low in the early 1930s. Record sales fell sharply after the stock market crash in 1929, but with economic recovery, the rise in dance music, and the growing popularity of swing, sales in 1938 surpassed 25 million records, almost five times the number sold in 1933. By 1938, fans bought an estimated 700,000 swing records every month. A *Printers' Ink* analysis of the music industry in 1938 attributed the growth in record sales to the "average swivel-heeled young person" and concluded, "the jitterbug must be given his measure of credit for the growth of the record business."[9]

This writer defined jitterbug as male or as the "generic" male, meaning not specifically female. The 1922 *Printers' Ink* analyst was more astute, crediting "sons and daughters" as notable record consumers. From 1920 to 1945, teenage girls bought records for themselves and friends and requested them as gifts, as seen in stories, private writings, and yearbooks. In 1938, a doomsayer predicted the decline of swing because it attracted "a young crowd with not too much money to spend," while older music fans with discretionary income disliked "the high jinks of hot jazz." This author referred to losses reported by prestigious hotels that booked swing bands, but he discounted the huge volume of sales from records, jukeboxes, instruments, music lessons, and radio sponsorship—the venues in which teen dollars had their largest impact.[10]

Teenage girls influenced the music industry in several ways. By the 1920s, records had become widely accessible. They carried great significance for teenage girls and played an important role in peer group activities. One girl wrote in 1925 that she and her friends spent a good deal of time during a trip "in the baggage car. I wonder why! We got Q's victrola and took it in & danced. Something new in the way of entertainment on a train. You felt like a stewed [drunk] person trying to dance, but it gave us pleasure." Katherine Rosner, a high school sophomore in 1929 living in Glens Falls, New York, conveyed her excitement about buying records to her diary. She bought two records from the show *Whoopee* and wrote that they were "the first new records we have had for ages, as we don't use our victrola much." Although she used "we" twice to identify the records and the player as belonging to the entire family, she asserted that she purposely bought records with only a vocal chorus because "I wanted dance records."[11]

Over the next few months, Katherine bought more records and listened to them frequently, "This evening I stayed home and played the victrola. I'm wild about that record I got." She later wrote of playing a new record up to four times a day, "I'm crazy about it." By the mid-1930s, yearbooks similarly cited deep passions for records. One yearbook portrayed a senior's "greatest need" as the "latest victrola records" and another senior as "addicted to records." In 1941, as depicted in figure 4.1, teenage girls in Walla

High-School Headlines—"Those copper- 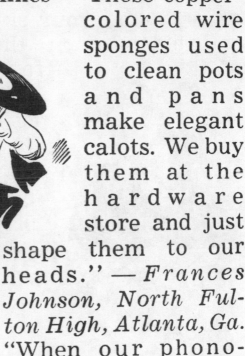 colored wire sponges used to clean pots and pans make elegant calots. We buy them at the hardware store and just shape them to our heads." — *Frances Johnson, North Fulton High, Atlanta, Ga.* "When our phonograph records are out of date we drill holes in the sides, pull ribbons through and wear them on our heads with the ribbons tied demurely under our chins."—*Ruby Holwager, Walla Walla High School, Walla Walla, Wash.*

4.1 Parents' Magazine, 1941

Walla, Washington, transformed "out of date" records into fashion accessories: "'we drill holes in the sides, pull ribbons through and wear them on our heads with the ribbons tied demurely under our chins.'" Girls in Omaha, Nebraska, embroidered the notes of their favorite songs on their skirts, shown in figure 4.2.[12]

Records were inextricably linked to teenage girls' lives as well as to icons of teenage girls. In 1942, a senior left school knowing "her three R's: Records, Rhythm, [and] Red Polish" while another "count[ed] her platters by the score." And in 1945, the *Britannica Book of the Year* defined "bobby soxers" as teenage girls who listened "for hours on end to recordings." Kranz Music Company advertised sheet music and "Victor Records" in a 1926 high school yearbook, as seen in figure 4.3. Hammann's record store advertised

Sew What?—Sew five rows of bias tape around your skirt hem and then embroider on it the notes of your favorite song."—*Ann Peterson, Omaha Technical High, Omaha, Nebr.*

4.2   Parents' *Magazine, 1941*

in yearbooks by the late 1930s, also seen in figure 4.3. Yearbook editors teased record fans, such as the girl who "wanted to be the owner of all [Artie] Shaw recordings" but "would end up broke." Others were "always found" or "addicted to" collecting "solid platters," whether by Tommy Dorsey, Benny Goodman, or later, Frank Sinatra.[13]

Teenagers also fed the music industry and affected song popularity through jukeboxes, which spread in the early 1930s and offered an inexpensive yet public and social alternative to radio or live music. In 1939, more than two hundred thousand jukeboxes in the United States played almost 13 million records; by 1942 the number of machines had doubled to four hundred thousand. Jukeboxes provided affordable, popular music in public places, and teenage memoirs and yearbooks verified their importance long before rock 'n' roll. June Goyne, a high school student in the early 1940s, danced at Candyland "to the 'Big Band' music . . . on the jukebox." June and her friends rarely had the opportunity to hear one of the "big names" in person, so their social lives centered on jukebox sessions. Students at Cambridge High School, as seen in figure 4.4, felt that "the most cherished spot in the whole school" was "the section around the jukebox" where songs played every lunch period, "giving out music fast or slow, sweet and low—whatever the young heart desires."[14]

The Radio Is Democratic

Teenagers found the easiest and least expensive access to music through radios and often structured their social lives around favorite programs for listening or dancing. One senior always sat "by the radio at four" and another "rushes into the Senior room, throw-

4.3   *Advertisements, High School Yearbooks, 1924 (above), 1939 (below)*

ing her books and car keys down, and then runs to turn on WBAL so as not to miss Sinatra singing *Stardust*." Teenage girls listened to the radio frequently and actively from its beginning, and it proved an important symbol of high school life.[15]

Radio grew from a static-filled toy for garage inventors to a national pastime in the 1920s. Production of radio sets increased from 2 million in 1925 to more than 6 million in 1935 and almost 30 million in 1940. The number of households with radios increased from 39 percent in 1930 to 73 percent in 1940 and 91 percent by 1950. By 1930, analysts estimated that music filled roughly 75 percent of all airtime, popularizing new genres, as well as traditional music such as classical and opera, by making them accessible. By the mid-1930s, radio programming regularly provided news, music, and entertainment to many Americans. And despite initial fears, radio promoted record sales rather than destroying them.[16]

By the late 1920s, teenage girls were attached to radios, such as the high school senior who "willed" her "love for radios" in 1928. But radio also became a site of contention

4.4   *Photograph, High School Yearbook, 1944*

between teenagers and parents—news versus music, classical versus jazz. Beth Twiggar, a high school student in the late 1920s, passionately loved jazz and dancing. Her parents did not. One evening as she sang "I Want to Be Loved By You," Beth angrily wrote in her diary, "there was some damn good jazz on the radio, I was enjoying it thoroughly" until her father complained, "What a racket!" and her mother turned off the radio, adding, "and they call that music."[17]

By the early 1930s, yearbooks listed "radio" as a "hobby." One girl searched for desired programming so frequently that her friends asked, "What Would Happen If . . . [she] ever left the radio dial at one station?" Radio provided ample entertainment when alone, but it also came to serve an important social role among high school students. Thirteen-year-old Eleanor wrote excitedly in a letter to her friend, "Without anyone saying anything to anybody else . . . everyone had congregated at the lovely drugstore . . . to hear Amos and Andy!!" Even when a show did not provide dance music, listening together in a public place provided inexpensive entertainment and peer interaction, both important to the development of teenage culture.[18]

In an effort to study the impact of radio, researchers catalogued teenagers' listening habits in the 1930s and 1940s. Paul Witty and his associates found in 1941 that 96 percent of high school students enjoyed listening to the radio and preferred "stories," followed by music, variety shows, and comedy. Swing was teenagers' favorite music, though slightly less for white girls than for white boys or African American girls or boys. Witty concluded that high school students did not learn anything of value from the radio: "immature interests are too frequently exploited and young people are offered a variety of emotional thrills *via* the air." He recommended that schools should train young people to listen intelligently. Alice Sterner also found in 1941 that interest in dance music increased as high school students aged, but concluded that intelligence was not a significant factor, "One cannot condemn a medium by sneering at its followers. All adolescents use these activities to a considerable degree."[19]

Statistics detailing the popularity of radio among teenagers, though, did not address the most important questions of how they listened and responded to it, how they integrated radio into their daily lives, and with whom they shared their listening experiences. In a high school discussion on radio listening in 1937, one student argued that radio "has a great effect on you although you may not realize it. If it hadn't been for the radio we might never have had this craze for popular music."[20]

Oakland Growth Study (OGS) participants also shared the details of their listening experiences. At least 70 percent reported discussing what happened on radio programs with friends "sometimes" or "often" during their high school years. For seniors, that number reached 80 percent. A conversation between OGS participant Margery and a friend about radio preferences exemplified this interest and the strong feelings attached, "Don't you *love* [Henry King's orchestra]?" Margery did not like Manhattan Merry-Go-Round, a popular music show, "I can't stand it, it's awful . . . they sing American songs with a French accent! Horrors!"[21]

Your Hit Parade first aired in 1935, and listening became a weekly ritual for many high school students. The show gained widespread popularity, but teenagers proved the most dedicated audience. *Your Hit Parade* initially presented the top fifteen songs of the week, later the top ten, based on record and sheet music sales. Despite allegations of inappropriate influence and a secret nomination process, *Your Hit Parade* promoted popular songs and older favorites. For June Goyne and a girlfriend in the 1940s, the show became a Saturday night ritual: "we listened in bed to the Hit Parade on the radio, the top ten songs of the week." Similarly, Betsy Hughes remembered well *Your Hit Parade* and its popularity from her teenage years in the early 1940s: "There was this huge market for records. The songs that the teenagers were buying were always on the *Hit Parade*." When Frank Sinatra sang for *Your Hit Parade,* from February 1943 through December 1944, the show became a "weekly media event." *Your Hit Parade* moved to television in 1950 and ended in 1959 due to music industry changes and the rise of rock 'n' roll. During its long tenure it proved a staple for many teenage listeners, promoting popular songs, record sales, and social interaction.[22]

As radio advertising through program sponsorship evolved in the 1930s, high school students evinced their ability to listen critically. An OGS participant stated in 1937, "I've heard a fifteen-minute program with three minutes of advertising at the beginning and three minutes at the end. The advertising took up nearly half the time. . . . students build up a dislike for it." Another student noted that companies should vary advertising slogans rather than "use the same line all the time. When they say the same thing over and over again most people don't believe it. They take it all with a grain of salt." *Your Hit Parade,* sponsored by American Tobacco Company Lucky Strike cigarettes, promised its young listeners "a cigarette that is genuinely easy on your throat" and that "leaves a clean taste." When OGS participants answered an open-ended advertising questionnaire in 1937, at age sixteen, they demonstrated teenagers' ability to recognize brand names and hinted at the influence of advertising. Fifty percent paired Lucky Strike with its slogan, "It's toasted," and many more guessed other cigarette brands or simply wrote "cigarette." Despite awareness of advertising and efforts by a few parents to protect their children from it within their homes, no one protested *Your Hit Parade*'s targeted advertising of tobacco products directly to high school students.[23]

Some high school students rarely turned off their radios. One senior admitted her "Woeful Weakness" for "Doing homework with the radio on"—a constant source of friction with parents. Another senior warned incoming freshman not to merge the two: "Just take, for example / That history preamble / Can you really get it down pat / If you do it while listening / To Ennis' whispering / Or a band of [Bob] Crosby's 'Bob-Cats.'" Beyond its influence on homework, critics warned that hours of radio listening harmed teenagers. Fearful of negative influences and underdeveloped critical thinking skills, these social critics decried the media-saturated world in which teens lived.[24]

Many of these studies presented the number of hours spent listening to the radio as though each teenager sat alone and listened intently for the length of every program. Teenagers did not passively accept all radio messages; they had strong preferences and did not listen to all things equally. Some radio shows, such as mysteries or dramas, demanded undivided attention. But many provided background entertainment for other activities, such as dancing, talking with friends, doing homework, or washing dishes. One high school student asked, "What do you mean by 'listening'? You can, of course, just listen to the radio. Or you can read the newspaper with the radio going some place in the house. . . . and barely listen to what's on the radio." Although radio influenced high school students' lives, many proved to be discriminating consumers and analysts of radio broadcasting and advertising.[25]

In 1936, one high school student imagined a fictional crooner's radio broadcast from multiple perspectives in an essay entitled "Impressions." She described the singer, introduced as "the idol of the air waves," as "a rather nondescript individual" with "small watery blue eyes which were concealed by huge tortoise-shelled rimmed glasses." She then described the listeners: a business man "murmured about the stupidity of a world which allowed crooners to survive" while a "spinster" thought "of her youth as the lyric cadences . . . bore her back in memory." A girl reading a movie fan magazine imagined "the tenor as a handsome young lover, while in her dreams she resembled Gloria Gorgeous, her latest screen idol." This author humorously envisioned the many ways that one song could affect various listeners, ending with the radio technician, who mused on the "funny faces [the singer] makes when he sings!'" She perceptively recognized the multiple meanings embedded in popular culture—each listener interpreted the broadcast according to his or her life while the actual production occurred in a removed setting and represented a different reality.[26]

Another student defined the radio as "democratic," offering itself equally to all wherever and however they listened:

> The radio is democratic.
> It drips
> glamour, and long slow songs of moonlit waters
> and tall boys and girls
> who are by courtesy of the copyright owners
> musically, lyrically and perennially in love.
> The music doesn't care if it comes into
> a long black car with an old lady in it
> who doesn't listen;
> the music doesn't mind a gray Ford with no love,
> only a foursome with nothing to say

except throw me the cigarettes and switch on the radio;
the music doesn't sound any more excited
when it is turned on in a bright yellow roadster
with a boy and a girl with bright yellow hair,
and a sky overhead with a bright yellow moon,
and it doesn't make the music any more wonderful;
    . . .
the music doesn't mind a little roadhouse with a hard wood floor
and sad waiters,
and no cover charge,
and girls in short dresses
shagging to the down beat;
the music doesn't get any more swanky in a tremendous
white terraced penthouse apartment near the stars
than in a little hot one-room with the rug rolled up for dancing;
it doesn't care what race is listening,
and I tell you it doesn't matter
whether you talk to it,
dance to it, die to it,
fight to it, or
love each other to it,
whether you listen or forget to listen,
it's always a certain program between ten and ten-thirty,
guaranteed to drip
glamour
and long slow songs of moonlit waters
and tall boys and girls
who are by courtesy of the copyright owners
musically, lyrically
and perennially in love.

This poet understands the mass and commercial nature of popular culture, the illusory promises of beauty presented by advertisers and mass media and the complex ways that people consume radio programming. The radio plays its music whether anyone listens or not, but the images "of moonlit waters" and "tall boys and girls" are constructed precisely to entice listeners, boost audience ratings, and sell sponsorships or advertising slots.[27]

All of these expressive students conveyed what other high school girls perhaps understood but articulated less clearly—the mechanical, commercial, and constructed nature of radio and popular culture. Teenage girls could simultaneously recognize pleasure in radio broadcasts and question the structure that produced them.

Music in Teenage Girls' Culture

Music, increasingly affordable and portable in the 1930s, became even more central in teenage girls' lives. They alternately loved or hated new forms of music, bands, or songs, defending their preferences vociferously. They argued with parents over access in the home and with teachers and administrators over access in schools. But music provided an important popular outlet—a forum for group activity, a background for dancing, and a way to express feelings within the realm of popular culture—that could not be suppressed.

Jazz spread somewhat unevenly in the 1920s, attacked by critics and staunchly defended by aficionados. Older youth had more access to "speakeasies" and clubs where they might hear jazz, but teenagers had already laid claim to dancing as a favorite pastime. Sixteen-year-old diarist Arvilla Scholfield, a high school student in northern California in the mid-1920s, loved to dance and took every opportunity to listen to music with friends. She recorded locations, orchestras, bands, and brief analyses in her diary, as illustrated in figure 4.5: "Went to the dance at Richfield not a very large crowd there" or "a chic orchestra played. Didn't have such a wonderful time."[28]

4.5   Diary Entries, Arvilla Scholfield, 1926

4.6   Photograph, Arvilla Scholfield, 1927.

Many high school students in the 1920s and 1930s loved music for its own sake. Katherine Rosner wrote in her diary about her newest record, "'Button Up Your Overcoat," and the flip side that played the "especially marvelous—and quite hot" song "'I Want to Be Bad." Yearbooks noted girls who loved jazz, labeling one "our greatest jazz-devotee" and another "the most jazz-conscious girl in the class." School administrators could feel differently, as demonstrated by the 1925 class will leaving orchestra members "the privilege of playing jazz." Some girls opposed jazz and popular songs with equal fervor. In 1923, at age twelve, Yvonne Blue wrote in her diary, "I hate it [jazz]," and referred to the loose morals of jazz listeners.[29]

Either way, music proved a popular topic in high school life. Jazz provided an emotional outlet for the frustrations of being "in-between" childhood and adulthood. One Saturday night in 1929, at age fifteen, Beth Twiggar listened to jazz on the radio: "I was stirred and thrilled, dancing alone." She eventually expressed frustration that she sat home alone rather than "razing whoopee." Two years later, Beth still cared deeply for jazz, "it did to me what jazz invariably does to me. Pulled me up from . . . whatever mood I was in and set me dancing alone—e[c]statically." She continued, "even the silence of the telephone did not irk me. . . . There's something about jazz. Something past and future generations ought to recognize." Other high school students jokingly defined jazz as "Music adapted to high school intelligence" or "a collection of saxophones with a hiccup."[30]

By 1937, swing had replaced jazz in high school culture. Yearbooks described students as "swingsters" and everyone had an opinion—either an "addiction" to swing or an "aversion" to it. But whether students suffered from a "weakness for swing" or "barely tolerate[d]" it, swing influenced high school life deeply. A senior compared the high school graduate of 1940 to swing: "You are modern and gay / Like a new 'swing' ditty / Played by Benny Goodman. . . . the urge of your spirit / Is peppy and fresh / With the sparkle of youthful adventure / Your head is high." *Scholastic* magazine deemed swing "the preferred jazz of 1937–38. . . . the perfect reflection of a world with the jitters" due to its "apparent lack of organization and direction, its raucous and discordantly loose frenzy."[31]

As high school poetry and prose championed jazz and then swing in a structured way, girls sang popular songs out loud in more spontaneous moments. Yearbooks by the 1920s highlighted students who loved to sing or knew the latest hits. Yvonne Blue complained again in 1923 about such a friend, "I don't like Thekla at all. She keeps singing 'Barney Google,' 'Yes, We Have No Bananas,' and 'I Love Me.'" In 1928, a yearbook teased, "If you ever arrive at school late, and hear lusty songs drowning the timid piano accompaniment, you'll know it's 'Trip' . . . our infallible source of all modern dance-hits." Another senior knew "all the latest song hits . . . what would [she] do without the new 'Hit-of-the-Week?'" Singing ability presented no obstacle: "the fact that she is always slightly off key does not stop her from crooning the latest hits morning, noon, and night. . . . she can always supply us with the exact words to the song of the moment." Singing provided enjoyment for the singer or friends, despite the occasional annoyance for passers-by.[32]

One OGS study recorded how often participants discussed the "Latest song hit." In ninth grade, 84 percent responded "sometimes," "often," or "very often"; by eleventh grade, that number reached 99 percent. Only the most devoted regularly talked about the latest song hit "very often," but the vast majority found it a regular topic of conversation. One yearbook commended the swing fan who had not "Swung the Hymn (yet!)"

as well as the "red-haired jitterbug" who simply had to sing "whether dancing . . . or eating fried shrimp."[33]

Teenage girls also bemoaned, celebrated, or signified the events in their lives, such as dating, with song. Beth Twiggar, at age fifteen, reflected on the boys she had dated through song. For her "first love," she sang, "'Who, who, who stole my heart away?'" Another date sang, "'Girl of my dreams, I love you'" several times to her and "gaze[d] at me meaningfully from under his funny, short eye lashes." An interchange while dancing captured her memories of a third: the orchestra sang, "'She's got eyes of blue'" and he "sang the whole business with them" but Beth responded, "'Nope . . . Green.'" He then sang, "'She's got dimpled cheeks,'" and Beth responded, "'Nope, not a sign of a dimple!'" She played with the song as she teased her date, but the song still symbolized that evening in her diary and later memories.[34]

Similarly, yearbooks by the 1930s used titles of popular songs to evoke memories of habits, trends, and relationships. In 1932, one girl had the "Fraternity Blues" while another celebrated that "Nobody's Baby is Somebody's Baby Now." One girl wistfully sang "Come a Little Closer," while her classmate thrilled, "Ohh! That Kiss!" Songs chosen for this purpose ranged from Tin Pan Alley to jazz, from classical to recent hits. With the rise of swing, song use increased. The theme for an entire yearbook in 1939 centered on current songs: "The staff feels that the fleeting popularity of the melodies is comparable to the enjoyable but rapidly fading days" of high school. The foreword continued, "The significance of the titles will soon be lost and students who follow will not appreciate their subtleties. But to the class of 1939 each class lyric will bring back memories of never-to-be-forgotten names and personalities."[35]

These yearbook editors captured some of the significance that popular songs held for teenagers. They understood the ephemeral nature of commercial popular music and compared it to the high school years that often seemed fleeting as one prepared to leave. But the yearbook staff of 1939 also felt that the songs would remain forever linked with memories of their high school years. Songs assigned to individual seniors, such as "You Must Have Been a Beautiful Baby" and "Chatterbox" painted images of youthful qualities. Songs reminded high school girls of a special dance, friendship, fight, or date. And songs sometimes said what teenagers could not articulate. One yearbook characterized an entire class by the song "Just an In-Between," about a girl caught between grown-up desires and a world not ready to accept that one is growing up. The editors added, "This sad, sad person is without any doubt a sophomore. Who else would have such a mournful theme song?"[36]

High school girls also found unique ways to incorporate music and musical accoutrements into their daily lives. As a variation on personalized clothing, girls pasted pictures of their favorite singers or bandleaders into heart lockets and wore them faithfully. As shown in figure 4.7, when the song "Pistol Packin' Mama" topped hit lists, girls around the country wore "dime store pistol holsters on their belts." The Parents' Magazine "Tricks for Teens" column further reported that "another example of the music influence is the fad-shion for paper dolls on your lapel or on your O.A.O.'s [one and only's]" after the revival of the song "Paper Doll."[37]

Such creativity illustrates the ways in which girls incorporated popular music into their daily lives. It demonstrates girls' active role in navigating and shaping teen consumer culture and their ability to create multiple meanings through mass-produced items. Teenage girls did not control music production, nor did they challenge the fundamental industry desire to sell records. They did, however, create new meanings

TRICKS for TEENS
Title Reg. U. S. Pat. Off.

Fashion Fads That Hit High School Fancies

TRICKS for Teens grow more entertaining every month. Wouldn't you know that girls would be wearing dime store pistol holsters on their belts as cosmetic and change carryalls, just because "Pistol Packin' Mama" is one of their favorite tunes? And since lapel and sweater gadgets always reflect current teen interests, one of the great favorites now is a little wooden pistol in a miniature leather holster. It's more decorative when you embroider the holster in wood or glass beads.

4.7   *Pistol Packin' Mama,* Parents' Magazine *(above),* High School Yearbook *(below),* 1940s

wherein song lyrics or records became fashion statements, memories, or raw material for parodies. They incorporated favorite songs into their daily language and embedded meaning from their lives into the lyrics. During the interwar years, teenage girls re-shaped music produced for multi-generational audiences into an identifiable teen cul-ture. Music also led to dancing, an expression of the individual, a courtship ritual, and an outlet for sexual feelings—a social bond as well as an individual statement.

"Sing Me a Swing Song and Let Me Dance"[38]

By the 1920s, dance was an established and commercial leisure activity. It was also an important activity for teenage girls, an outlet for those with a passion for dancing as well as a social activity that emphasized peer and romantic relationships. Teenage girls faced many challenges finding appropriate places to dance outside homes, but as demon-strated by the teens who danced in a train baggage car, they found creative solutions. High school students participated in private, structured dances, such as school-sponsored events, dance classes, or community and family gatherings. Some ventured into the forbidden world of dance halls and speakeasies, while others danced to juke-boxes in local drug stores. Depending on their race, class, age, and peer group, teenagers took advantage of these escapes in different ways. The repeal of Prohibition in 1933 led to more public dance options, but high school students still struggled to find socially ac-ceptable places to dance with peers. Not until World War II did the heightened concern over juvenile delinquents lead to teen canteens, teen-centered yet adult-approved cen-ters for dancing and recreational activities.[39]

Even before the 1920s, letters, diaries, and yearbooks recorded the popularity of dancing among teenage girls despite conflict with parents or school officials. In 1914, Shasta Union High School in Redding, California, forbade students "to dance the soci-ety walk, that is, the up-to-date dances." School events were unsuccessful when admin-istrators forced dancers to comply with the formal, "old-fashioned" waltz, two-step, and quadrille. Students rebelled by holding their own events outside school property. They invited chaperones to convince parents that dances were "conducted properly," but they chose the steps.[40]

Arvilla Scholfield's descriptions of dancing in 1926 illustrate the integral role it played in her life. After a high school dance, she wrote that she "had a pretty good time" but would have preferred an open-air commercial dance club. She had many other op-portunities, though, because she danced weekly, "Gee Saturday came quick. Went to the dance as per usual." She added Sundays or weeknights whenever possible, and although she sometimes wrote, "not such a wonderful time," she usually "had a good time" and occasionally even a "swell time." One dance was ruined when a friend got "so durn cranky" after her "boy friend stepped out & she caught him"; Arvilla was more disturbed by the interrupted dancing than by the unfaithful boyfriend.[41]

Not all high school students danced weekly, but many loved to dance. One yearbook asked, "Can you imagine Juanita not dancing?" in 1932. In the mid-1930s, OGS ob-servers interpreted dancing alternately as a sign of maturity and of precocious sexuality, depending on the dancer, the clothing, and the dance steps. According to one observer, Virginia showed a great "shift into maturity" at age fourteen because she spoke "now about dance steps," boys, and clothes. Another major shift occurred around age fifteen when girls and boys danced together more frequently. An observer noted approvingly that "not more than 5 percent of the hundred or so couples dancing at a school dance consisted of girls dancing with girls." She added that girls still primarily invited boys to dance, but the observer interpreted this as a sign of girls' sophistication. The following year, though, sixteen-year-old Sharon pushed the boundaries of acceptable maturity: "Seems definitely brazen in her behavior—danced in a complicated but rather 'dance-hall' style . . . made references to going to Sweet's (dance hall) with her 'boy friend.'"[42]

Conflict between adults and teens over dancing continued. Towson High School prohibited dancing during lunch periods in the late 1930s, but students persisted. OGS participant Nancy argued that her school should offer night dances because teenagers were not "permitted to go to dance halls and they enjoy[ed] dancing to orchestra music rather than always using the radio." Some teenage girls did patronize dance halls, but many parents forbade it because of older crowds and lack of parental supervision.[43]

By the late 1930s, as seen in figure 4.8, bands placed advertisements in high school yearbooks. As acceptance for high school students' public dancing grew, yearbooks frequently reported seniors with a "passion" for dancing, as well as those who were happiest while "jitterbugging," "cutting rugs," or "Truckin.'" Students danced in high school gymnasiums, as seen in figure 4.9. One senior was described as "absolutely music-mad—the original jitterbug! Anything from high-brow Wagner to lowdown jive gets her." Similarly, Esther could never "Sit still in the same room with 'hot' music!"[44]

OGS quantitative data on dance confirms its centrality to teenage social life in the 1930s, years before teen canteens and rock 'n' roll. By age fourteen, 82 percent of OGS participants responded that they had "danced" during the previous week, whether at home, at school, or in a more formal setting. That number hovered around 83 percent throughout the high school years, but this is just part of the story. Only 16 percent "Went to a Dance" during the previous week at age fourteen, but 54 percent did so at age seventeen. Similarly, almost 95 percent of respondents said that they talked about dancing "sometimes," "often," or "very often" in ninth grade, and this number remained above 90 percent through the high school years. Roughly 60 percent talked about dancing "often" or "very often."[45]

Dancing was frequently a shared activity, and peer approval played an important role. An OGS observer noted at a clubhouse dance, "Many couples dancing in the style almost universally adopted by the group—a sort of blasé shuffle." At another dance, the teens self-segregated by age and "younger boys and girls" danced "the fast swing steps." Couples who danced well took turns in the spotlight. As described by an observer, Linda was "delighted when she and her partner were called upon by the leader to 'shine' in the 'Big Apple' (to do fancy steps alone in the center of the large circle of dancers)."[46]

Yearbooks commended skilled dancers in the 1920s and 1930s, most commonly those on the cutting edge. In 1928, Pinky danced "everything from the Minuet to (dare we mention it?) the Black Bottom." In 1929, Rae "could not be beaten when it came to dancing. 'Charleston,' 'Black Bottom,'—they were all '[easy as] pie' to her." By the late 1930s, yearbooks dubbed a girl who danced well a "jitterbug," a "swingster [who knew] all the new steps," or a "professional rug-cutter." Those who did not participate earned names as well, "I is for 'ickie', we've plenty of those / while we dance in swing-time, they just stand and pose."[47]

Blatant criticism rarely appeared in yearbooks, but OGS observations and recorded conversations between friends illustrated the extent of peer critique. A group of OGS boys nicknamed Caroline "Tail Light" because "she dances sticking out so far." At an after-school dance in 1936, "A good deal of comment was aroused by the 'Dime Jiggers,'" or those who danced the "hottest" steps. One of these dancers, Melinda, had a

SAMUEL OMANSKY, Director

PHONE: FOREST 8928

Belvedere Dance Orchestra

"Pep That Makes 'Em Step"

FRANKLIN KLEIN, Manager

PHONE: MADISON 8704

THE CRITERIONS

"BALTIMORE'S SWING ORCHESTRA"

FOREST PARK 1936 MID-YEAR PROM

AD LIEDER   WOlfe 4153

4.8   Advertisements, High School Yearbooks, 1924 (above), 1936 (below)

"strip of bare skin" on her back that showed while dancing and "Heads all around the room followed this patch of flesh as it moved about gracefully, necks craning around the corner of the door as it slid into the other room." When Melinda noticed the attention she hurriedly put on her jacket, "but this covered her back only momentarily and then the watching was resumed." The observer's language bordered on voyeurism, emphasizing her "bare skin" and "patch of flesh" while recording Melinda's passion for dancing and perhaps for attention.[48]

At a school dance shortly thereafter, another OGS observer recorded student intervention, "When some dime-jiggers got on the rampage . . . student vigilantes quietly

4.9   Photograph, High School Yearbook, 1944

but firmly insisted upon their dancing in a more conventional manner." This tension between the newest steps and more traditional dances symbolized deeper social issues often marked by class. Sarah criticized students who danced "the present version of the dime jig" although they danced among themselves in a corner. An observer noted that the girls in this group dressed alike, but in a style different from other girls at the dance. Frances, one of these dancers, wore a "flowered muslin short flared-skirted dress" and had dyed blond hair. This group "attracted some attention as their steps were very intricate, but from a social standpoint, they were 'out.' They danced on the fringe where there was more room and simply didn't seem to care—just thoroughly enjoying the activity." On the same dance floor, though, a yell leader and his girlfriend received peer approval for dancing similarly "strenuous intricate steps." Reception depended in part on the class, social status, and dress of the dancers.[49]

Historian Kathy Peiss writes that "dance is a form of structured, expressive movement that articulates and conveys cultural information to its participants, helping them to make sense of their world." Dance allowed teenagers to express joy, frustration, or desire, to enjoy songs actively as well as explore romance and sexuality. Dance proved to be an important ritual for teens who dated to have fun, and to experiment with physical contact. Dance was also an activity embedded within an institutional structure of race, class, and ethnicity. Many dances popularized by white professional dancers through movies, shows, and dance halls originated among African Americans. Middle-class or upper-class girls or their parents with access to supervised dances through schools and social clubs might not frequent dance halls available to working-class girls.[50]

Peer groups helped spread new dances further as experienced dancers picked up steps and taught them to friends. Learning and perfecting dances proved to be an important teenage peer activity. Practicing dance steps at home or school with friends served as entertainment as well as preparation for public display from the 1920s through the 1940s. Arvilla Scholfield mentioned this ritual repeatedly in 1926: "Gave Inez lessons in dancing the Charleston" or "Stayed home and studied my lessons like a good girl. Danced Charleston with Anna." Dancing provided a study break or at least a different kind of lesson.[51]

OGS participants spent a good deal of their free time at the study clubhouse learning and practicing new dances with friends in the 1930s. Virginia was "much sought as a partner," and frequently "[d]emonstrated some of the newer steps." Sarah credited movies as worthy dance instructors, "'Lillian is darling when she trucks. . . . She went and saw Broadway Melody of '38 and came home and did some steps from it.'" Yearbooks also praised those who kept the class updated, calling Ginny a "gate" [because she swings so well]: "if the rest of the seniors have not learned to jitterbug, it is not for the lack of a good teacher." Learning a new dance could also inspire confidence. Anna wrote to an OGS observer that she had a wonderful time at a recent dance, "I learned how to do the Lambeth Walk. It was quite thrilling to me. I'm usually afraid, or bashful at most dances, but everyone was so friendly towards me and I had every dance."[52]

Following closely on the heels of new trends, mass marketers scrambled to profit from the growing popularity of dance and swing music among teenage girls. For those without friends who danced well, dance instructors stood ready to capitalize. Arthur Murray, owner of a dance studio and growing national mail-order dance business, placed an advertisement in *Scholastic* magazine as early as 1929. The ad did not mention high school students and the picture depicted flappers with short hair and pearls, but someone suspected that young people might be interested and purchased advertising space in this high school magazine.[53]

Arthur Murray also advertised frequently in the *Ladies' Home Journal* "Sub-Deb" column by the early 1930s. "Sub-Deb" editor Elizabeth Woodward informed readers of the importance of dance and teen trends, "Everybody does the fox trot these days—in one variation or another. . . . Most schools have their own pet particular style." She also promoted her booklet, co-written with Murray, "Frolicking Feet—How to Dance." In 1934, Woodward advertised a booklet on how to tango, again with Murray. By the late 1930s, the waltz and fox trot did not attract much teenage interest.[54]

Woodward, with the help of Murray, watched young people and followed shifting dance trends. They began to market "teen" dances in 1938, as illustrated in figure 4.10. "Shaggin' On Down!" promised lessons from Arthur Murray on "how to shag—so put on comfy shoes and get hot!" Several months later, Woodward offered her booklet, "Come On and Dance." To authenticate her advice, Woodward claimed that she had "Packed [her] Dancing Slippers and trotted around the country to see what you are dancing. Hops, shags, hesitations, rhumbas—newer than new." The following year, Woodward's booklet, "Hi-Stepping Hi-Jinks," again guaranteed "All the crazy new dances everybody's doing—clap hands, boomps your partner, circle quickly and slap it hard. Here are photographs and directions for the latest swingeroos." Murray and Woodward capitalized on the dance craze, using slang and the promise of popularity to sell dance booklets.[55]

Clothing designers also saw opportunity for profit from the new dance craze. In 1937, *Women's Wear Daily* noted that "The girls' skirt business is swinging . . . 'Big

Shaggin' On Down!

THE SUB-DEB

Edited by Elizabeth Woodward

Arthur Murray tells you how to shag—so put on comfy shoes and get hot!

THE TIME SHAG

This is the main shag step. It's the boy's part—but the girl does the same, starting with her right foot when he starts with his left.

1. Step on left foot and hop with left, landing on left. In the photo notice the boy's right foot.
2. Step on right foot and hop with right, landing on right.
3. Shift weight quickly to left foot, lifting the right foot about two inches off the floor.
4. Shift weight quickly to right foot, lifting the left foot about two inches off the floor.

Steps 1 and 2 get time count of 1, 2 each; steps 3 and 4 get just 1. Do the Time Shag twice before you break into a Shag Dip or Side Break.

THE SHAG DIP

The rhythm of this step is the same as the Time Step—the whole thing is done pretty fast.

1. Shift weight backward onto left foot, extending right foot in front. (In photo notice bent left knee.)
2. Shift weight backward onto right foot, extending left foot in front.
3. This step is the same as 1.
4. This step is the same as 2.

Count 1, 2, for both steps 1 and 2; count just 1 for steps 3 and 4. Study the photographs.

THE SIDE BREAK

This movement is almost the same as the Shag Dip except that the dip is to the side.

1. Hop onto left foot and extend right foot to side.
2. Draw right foot up to left, extend left foot to side, as in the photograph.
3. Draw left foot up to right and extend right foot to side.
4. This step is the same as 2.

Count 1, 2, for steps 1 and 2; just 1 for 3 and 4. These three steps are the Shag. Yes, you bounce around a lot, but it's great fun! Get these steps down pat—then get hot! Assume the other angles—with frills and fancy flourishes!

4.10   Sub-Deb Column, Ladies' Home Journal, *February 1938*

Apple' is the new name that is being applied to swinging 'teen skirts, derived from the new dance of that name." The winners of the Harvest Moon Ball "shag contest" at Madison Square Garden in 1938 endorsed a costume by Touraine Company consisting of "a loose flannel jacket with colorful jitterbug buttons, a suspender skirt exactly to match, and a 'sharpie shirt' in contrasting color in wool jersey. Completing this is a beanie or 'prep hat.'" The dancers toured Loews movie theaters offering demonstrations and promoting the outfit, leading *Women's Wear Daily* to advise clothing buyers with "a big following of swing and shag customers" to prepare for large orders.[56]

Many teenage girls loved dancing—an individual activity and a highly social one. It represented freedom, energy, shared activity with friends, and physical contact with boys. High school girls learned traditional ballroom dances at school or in dance classes, but they also challenged adult censure and adopted the dances of African Americans, flappers, and movie stars. During World War II, teen canteens began to offer age-specific dance locales for high school students, but teens danced long before that time. Whether dancing alone in their rooms, sneaking into roadhouses, or entertaining friends on a train, teenage girls who wanted to dance found outlets. As with music, marketers were slow to notice teenagers' passion for dancing and ability to spend money on it. Dancing lessons were the first such commodity, beginning with ballroom dancing and by the late 1930s teaching newer dance styles. Fashion retailers, most aware of teenage girls and high school trends, followed suit.

Jitterbugs, Idols, and Crooners

Whether the "swing and shag customers" rushed to purchase outfits with "jitterbug buttons" or not, their definition by marketers as a distinctive consumer group was significant. Benny Goodman's Paramount appearance in 1937 did not create fans—the enthusiastic young people who lined up early and danced in the aisles did so because they were already fans. But the event and ensuing media attention brought swing and swing dance into the national spotlight. Cab Calloway introduced the term "jitterbug" in 1934, but his song "Jitter Bug" referred to a jittery or nervous person. By 1937, *Down Beat* magazine applied it to people who danced energetically to swing music, and by 1938, "jitterbugging" was a popular activity.[57]

Life magazine ran a photo spread in February 1938, seen in figure 4.11, entitled "Speaking of Pictures . . . Jitterbugs and Ickeys." The article, filled with definitions of swing lingo, stated that "a lover of this particular form of jazz is a 'cat.'" The author further clarified, "A jitterbug is a cat whose reaction to swing is always intellectual, often physical . . . cannot keep still even when sitting down. An ickey is a cat who is affected only emotionally by swing." Photographs depicted high school students so passionate about swing that they danced all the time—walking to class, eating lunch, and riding a streetcar. As news of popular dances, such as the Shag, Truckin', the Big Apple, the Little Peach, Kicking the Mule, and the Suzie Q, spread quickly, high school students received special media notice as enthusiastic dancers.[58]

By 1939, "jitterbug" and "jitterbugging" also appeared frequently in high school yearbooks, as an "ardent aversion" as well as a "talent." Some girls could "always [be] found" jitterbugging and one senior received the nickname "the original jitterbug!" By 1940, "jitterbug" was ubiquitous and remained so for most of the decade. Yearbooks described many students as "happy while" jitterbugging; others were "allergic" to it. But whether the "No. 1 jitterbug," "a jitterbug at heart," or a "temperamental jitterbug," few escaped high school by the early 1940s without forming an opinion. A yearbook record review, printed in 1941 and shown in figure 4.12, addressed "All you hepcats and alligators" directly, recommending "solid senders" by Tommy Dorsey, Gene Krupa, and Harry James as well as "sweet" music by Glenn Miller and Jimmy Dorsey.[59]

National and local media highlighted teenagers, primarily teenage girls, as dedicated fans of orchestras, bandleaders, and singers by the 1930s. Journalists and the

In Iowa City, Iowa, swing-struck high-school students (*above*) "truck" downstairs to classes. In Columbus, Ohio, high-school students (*above, right*) spend their noon recreation hour dancing to hot tunes from phonograph records.

BIRMINGHAM, ALA.: SORORITIES HOLD SWING PARTY ON STREETCAR

4.11   *Photographs,* Life Magazine, *1938*

RECORDS—AS YOU LIKE 'EM

BY CECILIA KOEHLER, '42

All you hepcats and alligators, stop tearing your hair and start shufflin' your feet to the tunes that are racking the nation. To those who gather round Tommy Doresy, to those who go in for solid senders, I suggest "Pale Moon" and "Halleluija." They've got that extra bit that Dorsey puts in, and believe me, all you swingsters, it's really away down there in the much-talked-about groove!

However, if you are prejudiced and prefer Mr. Krupa, try his super version of "Let Me Off Uptown" with "Flamingo" on the reverse; it's guaranteed! Two more of the hotter numbers are "Trumpet Rhapsody I" and "Trumpet Rhapsody II", made by the nation's best, the greatest valve plugger ever known, Harry James.

From the musical, "Jump For Joy", comes a cure-you-or-kill-you antidote for whatever ails you, entitled "Chocolate Shake"; on the back of which is *the* composition that's really hep, "I've Got It and That Ain't Good." It's as solid as the Rock of Gibraltar, and a true-blue arrangement. And then—for the piece that really burns, the one that actually sizzles, we give you "Up Jumped the Devil", backed by "Southside," which

Earl Hines and his orchestra do for Bluebird.

It seems that on the sweeter side Glenn Miller has produced for all his ardent fans a little stimulant, listed as "Below the Equator". It has Ray Eberle and the Modernaires giving their all for good ole Swing College. Another softie is Jimmy Dorsey's swell arrangement of "Jim". He definitely has something there. The vocals by Bob Eberlé and Helen O'Connell are something to tell your grandchildren about. Then, too, topping the list and walking away from all others, is "Tonight We Love". The words are the sentimental kind that the young folks are after, and the tune is taken from Tschaikowsky's "Concerto For Piano and Orchestra". You all remember this from the motion picture, "The Great Lie". The Concerto is also recorded in its classical form by Freddie Martin, on a Bluebird. If you don't already have it, get it, 'cause without it you're 'way behind.

A "sender" known to dancers as "Darkness" was recorded many moons ago. Though the rhythm is slow moving, this tune is getting there—but fast. It's by the McFarland Twins, on an OKEH—just

public initially expressed surprise at the behavior of Goodman fans and remained un-
prepared for Frank Sinatra's popularity as a solo singer in the 1940s. Many writers
proposed that passion for Sinatra was exceptional, surpassing any previous fan attention. The level of intensity and media attention may have been new, but idolizing
singers was not. Many vocalists denied the appellation "crooner," but the singing style
had gained popularity by the late 1920s. According to music scholar Peter Gammond,
crooning deviated from "straight singing by a modified jazz intonation and phrasing
and the employment of a deep, sensual, ululating tone from deep in the throat; slid-
ing up to notes rather than hitting them instantly." Derived from African American
slang for soft, mellow singing, "crooning" gained popularity with the rise of the microphone. Gene Austin first popularized the sound in the mid-1920s, followed by
Rudy Vallee, one of the first radio and movie entertainers to gain a large public following of devoted fans. Bing Crosby followed a similar path in the 1930s.[60]

Bing Crosby's popularity and influence spanned decades. He started his long recording career in the 1920s and began singing solo in the early 1930s. Crosby attracted devoted followers, including teenage girls. But despite the important contributions of
Austin, Vallee, Crosby, and popular bandleaders such as Benny Goodman, Frank Sinatra heralded a new era. Neil McCaffrey, a devoted swing fan, characterized the shift from
big bands to singers in a reflective essay "I Remember Frankeee." McCaffrey arrived at
the Paramount on December 30, 1942, expecting to hear Benny Goodman and was un-
pleasantly surprised by the ovation that greeted the "Extra Added Attraction," Frank
Sinatra.[61]

Sinatra reportedly wrote that when he entered the stage that night, "'The sound that
greeted me was absolutely deafening. It was a tremendous roar . . . I was scared stiff.'"
Many analysts argue that Sinatra carefully constructed this image: "the straggling lock of
hair calculatingly disarrayed on the forehead; the hands tightly gripping a microphone,
as if to sustain a body too frail to stand alone." They charge that although Sinatra presented himself "boyishly, unpretentiously, and often shyly" onstage, he affected none of
these characteristics offstage. Whether "real" or not, his image was effective. Fans flocked
to hear him live, listen to his radio broadcasts, and purchase his records.[62]

Articles highlighted fan devotion, noting that girls wrote essays on "Why I Like
Frank Sinatra," inscribed his name and songs on their sweaters and coats, and signed
their letters "Sinatraly yours" or "'Frankly yours.'" Girls waited in line for hours to buy
concert tickets or records and combed cities to catch a glimpse or photograph of Sinatra in person. As media coverage of Sinatra fans increased, the "bobby soxer" image
spread. Journalists characterized Sinatra fans as "plain, lonely girls from lower-middle-
class homes" or twelve- to sixteen-year-old "children of the poor." These descriptions
represented media stereotypes more than they did Sinatra fans. Fascination with Sinatra
appeared throughout high school yearbooks and writings, at exclusive prep schools as
well as vocational schools, although less frequently at African American high schools.
Perhaps the nation did not want to imagine "wholesome" white middle-class girls
screaming or fainting for their idol, so characterizing fans as poor and lonely provided
an alternate explanation. As shown at the top of figure 4.13, media presented unflatter-

4.13   (right) *Fan Images,* Hi There High School *and High School Yearbook, 1940s*

ing images of such fans. When compared to high school yearbook images, seen at the bottom of figure 4.13, though, a more favorable image appears, one of devoted fans who were attractive and respectable.[63]

George Evans, Sinatra's press agent, may have hired girls initially to "swoon" and scream, but according to journalist Bruce Bliven, this response quickly became a "genuine phenomenon." Girls across the country responded emotionally to seeing, hearing, or even mentioning Sinatra. Explanations for teenage girls' behavior covered almost as much media space as tales of fan antics. They included Sinatra as a father-figure; a hungry son needing to be mothered; the boy-next-door; a substitute for soldiers overseas; "the product of a shallow, hero-starved society"; "the desperate chemistry of adolescence"; and pure musical genius. Occasionally someone mentioned that "just plain sex may have a great deal to do with it."[64]

Adults preferred to imagine teenage girls as asexual during this era. As historian Grace Palladino writes, middle-class filters purified popular music, denying its African American roots as well as the sexuality inherent in the music and dance. Writer Martha Weinman Lear reflected on the importance of rebellion and sexual energy to her experience as a Sinatra fan. In the early 1940s, at age thirteen, she and her friends missed school one day "to shriek and swoon through four live [Sinatra] shows." They forged notes to excuse their school absences and returned home in time for dinner. Lear remembered how she "loved to swoon," practicing with friends in their bedrooms, "We would take off our saddle shoes, put on his records and stand around groaning for a while. Then the song would end and we would all fall down on the floor." Despite efforts to explain the Sinatra craze as platonic, Lear remembered, "Whatever he stirred beneath our barely budding breasts, it wasn't motherly. . . . the thing we had going with Frankie was *sexy.* It was exciting. It was terrific."[65]

Scholars did not study female fans until decades later, but their findings shed some light on the 1930s and 1940s. Social groups experiencing acute role or identity conflicts, such as adolescents, are most likely to engage in fan activity. This was especially true for teenage girls who encountered increasingly restrictive gender roles as they grew from childhood to adulthood. Female longing for male stars, such as Sinatra, was initially seen as an expression of heterosexual roles, either as "motherly" concern or as sexual desire. Yet it can also be understood as resistance to traditional gender roles. Stars idolized by teenage girls are often far from "masculine," presenting instead an androgynous persona, creating room for the female fan as pursuer or imitator.[66]

Female fans could explore sexual identity in a non-threatening way, challenging gender boundaries and exploring options. This also manifested itself through crossdressing. "Style imitation" was a popular expression of devotion to Sinatra. A high school yearbook drawing, seen at the bottom of figure 4.13, illustrates that girls imitated Sinatra, wearing his trademark polka-dot bow ties. One group of seniors fondly remembered the year 1943–1944, using the term "bobby-soxer" to identify a stage long since past: "There is one thing that alone could always mark our sophomore year. During this time someone who shook the world of bobby-soxers entered our lives. Most referred to him as the 'Voice.' It is said that our bows tied themselves when Frankie sang." Girls learned to express themselves through dress at a young age and style imitation built on this cultural mode of communication. Girls read fashion texts and appropriated various looks into their everyday lives. Bows that tied themselves could imply sexual energy or affinity with Sinatra; they could also symbolize being Sinatra.[67]

Girls responded enthusiastically to Sinatra's "helpless" stage presence. Lear described him as "that glorious shouldered spaghetti strand. . . . [whose] suits hung oddly on him." She remembered, "He used to make jokes about hanging on the microphone for support, Bob Hope-type jokes, badly delivered, which we found adorable." Another fan wrote that Sinatra "made us feel like we're something. He has given us understanding." Fans identified with his projected vulnerability, solicited his advice on personal problems, and wrote repeatedly that Sinatra understood them. Swooning for Frankie offered a safe outlet, a way to admire independence and sexuality, to imagine being the idol as well as being with the idol. Swooning in the form of screaming, fainting, and crying offered an opportunity to abandon control, to ignore societal pressure that girls should listen, show interest in others, and contain sexual feelings or public displays of sexuality. Girls screamed so loudly that they often could not hear the music; the screaming itself was central to the experience.[68]

Singers and musicians create texts, but fans interpret songs and often reassign meaning. Several articles published under Benny Goodman's name charted his increasing frustration with swing audiences. Goodman initially tried to foster public sympathy for swing fans in 1938, arguing that swing offered an "outlet for fear, inhibitions, dreams, hopes. . . . a release from the pressure of depression and war clouds" as well as "an outlet for the exhibitionism in every one." He wrote more critically the following year, lamenting that fans had acquired annoying habits antithetical to music appreciation as they grew more numerous. The music suffered, according to Goodman, "We played loud when we should have played soft . . . to drown out the emotional racket and make ourselves heard." The jitterbug had become, "part of the act—unbilled, services donated freely." Paul Whiteman defined their exuberance as "ten per cent pulse and five hundred per cent exhibitionism" perceptively recognizing that fan behavior was enacted in large part as a release and for other fans. Goodman advised that fans focus on dancing without crowding the musicians, but fans did not heed his suggestion.[69]

Contemporary teenage sources confirmed the explosion of feeling surrounding Sinatra in the early 1940s, but among teenage girls it demonstrated the expansion of an existing trend rather than a new phenomenon. In 1932, a yearbook asked, "What would happen if . . . There was no Bing Crosby?" OGS observers interpreted "crushes" as a passing phase for younger girls and criticized Kay, age fifteen, who maintained her passion for Nelson Eddy, "She seems quite immature in her attitude toward the opposite sex." A few months later, Kay had formed friendships with boys but retained her enthusiasm for the popular actor and singer. In 1937, she urged the observer to buy Eddy's records, and the following year, when she requested permission to take his photograph from a magazine, the observer commented, "most of the group have outgrown this stage."[70]

Although Kay's infatuation may have been exceptionally persistent, her peers did not find her behavior unusual. One yearbook listed Nelson Eddy as a "Hero" several times in 1938. Seniors imitated Bing Crosby, felt "happiest" while listening to Nelson Eddy, and collected pictures of Bob Crosby. One senior even earned the title, "Bing Crosby's most ardent admirer." Some girls listed Nelson Eddy and other popular singers as their most "Ardent Aversion," expressing individual taste and defining themselves in opposition to the majority. Girls did, however, recognize a progression from idols to boyfriends that the OGS observer alluded to, as illustrated in the yearbook entry for Gloria: "'Whee, I'm gonna see my 'Butchie' tonight? (Nelson Eddy is now running a poor second, we fear)."[71]

After Frank Sinatra's appearance at the Paramount Theater in December 1942, fan worship reached new heights. By spring 1943, only a few months after Sinatra's rapid rise to national fame, he had become a yearbook staple. One senior "named her cat 'Sin' after the esteemed Mr. F. S.," honoring and personalizing Sinatra but also toying with sexuality through fan worship. Another girl was remembered for her "'Frank' and honest opinions." One senior's "purple passion" for Sinatra extended beyond emotion: "she has in her possession practically every recording that 'the heartbeat of the downbeat' ever made. Every evening she can be found . . . listening to his melodious voice carried over the airwaves." These sentiments intensified as Sinatra's popularity soared. Some fans remained faithful to former favorites, debating the "finer virtues of 'The Voice' and a certain Mr. Crosby," but many idolized Sinatra above all others.[72]

Girls identified with solo singers as individuals, imagining friendship or romance. Bands, orchestras, and orchestra leaders also received devoted attention from adoring fans, but following a popular band provided a more collective experience. Goodman is the best-known example, but high school girls mentioned a range of popular bandleaders in their writings. As early as 1932, a senior received yearbook mention because there was "not a dance orchestra of which she has not heard, and she has danced to many of them." By 1937, such entries became common, and girls named their favorite bands freely. OGS participant Eloise "went into spontaneous, languishing enthusiasm about Duke Ellington's music" at age sixteen. Yearbooks noted those with a "passion" for Benny Goodman while other girls had a "weakness" for Artie Shaw or were classified as Glenn Miller "fanatics," faithful fans of Tommy Dorsey, or "Happy while listening to Kay Kyser." Cab Calloway, Xavier Cugat, and Harry James were also popular favorites. Girls responded enthusiastically to the presence of bandleaders, but the music rather than the individual leaders or musicians gave them a "thrill." This distance allowed middle-class white girls to express their devotion for Jewish, Latino, and African American bandleaders without evoking strong parental censure.[73]

Yearbooks also noted interest in musical vocations—seniors who wanted to be crooners, vocalists, orchestra leaders, or "boogie-woogie" piano players. Some analysts credited swing music and young people's enthusiasm for it with the rising interest in musical instruments as sales rose more than 75 percent from 1935 to 1938. An improving economy and high school attendance may partially explain this increase, but swing music played an important role. Some schools organized bands and orchestras for the first time in the 1930s, capturing teenage enthusiasm for music. In New York City, schools succumbed to student pressure and offered instruction in "jazz and other modern music" including "'swing.'" Paul Whiteman agreed to guest lecture in schools, and other famous musicians, such as José Iturbi and Benny Goodman, considered similar offers.[74]

Participation in music ranged from heated debates to shared admiration, from singing or dancing with records to seeing live performances to playing musical instruments. Yearbooks heralded talented musicians and praised student efforts to organize bands. A high school graduate in 1942, nicknamed the "Steinway caresser," was dubbed "a killer" whose "boogie-woogie beat" would be missed by "[a]ll the alligators" at the high school. In 1944, a senior was renowned for her "wicked boogie-woogie." Forest Park High School celebrated the addition of a school band, orchestra, and glee club in 1937.[75]

999

Despite the lack of attention from the music industry to teenage interests and tastes, music played an important role in the lives of teenage girls. From the 1920s through the 1940s, high school girls accessed music through records, radio, instruments, singing, dance, and live bands. They began to create age-specific, teen-oriented ways of enjoying music, often combined with dance. Teenagers purchased records and radios, attended dances and concerts, played instruments and took lessons, participating in the commercial world of music as active consumers. They integrated the tangible products of mass-produced music into their lives, but they also fully integrated the intangible aspects, such as nostalgic memories linked to specific songs. Marketers occasionally noted the potential profit from teenage interest in music, but the industry as a whole was slow to appreciate it. Artists, manufacturers, retailers, and marketers did not create a teen market for popular music as much as they responded to one.

By the mid-to-late-1930s, teenage enthusiasm for swing music and dance began to receive national attention and caused some industry analysts to take notice. Throughout the 1920s, 1930s, and 1940s, teenage girls identified music they liked and sought avenues for expressing their enthusiasm through singing, dancing, and fads while searching for acceptable public places to enjoy music with peers. And they sometimes reflected on how that music was produced and marketed. Despite lack of interest from the music industry, limited public venues for listening to music and dancing, conflict with parents and schools, and negative attention from media, teenage girls became active consumers of commercial popular music, creating teenage music from music intended for a wider audience. Music provided teenage girls with an avenue for exploring sexuality and romantic fantasy as well as the opportunity to experiment with gender boundaries. Movies offered similar avenues.

"A Guiding Factor in My Life"

Teenage Girls and Movies

I n the late 1920s, a college sophomore reflected on her movie experiences, "I cannot remember ever having been without a movie house so that this enterprise can be called a guiding factor in my life." Educators, social scientists, and parents feared this exact response, but the young woman did not explain how movies "guided" her. By the 1920s, teenage girls accepted movies as part of their everyday lives and mentioned them frequently in letters, diaries, and yearbooks. But teenagers, and especially teenage girls, did not always respond in ways prescribed by adults—moviemakers among them. They adapted movies and movie culture to their lives in unique, "teenage" ways.[1]

Movies played a crucial role in the development of teenage girls' culture in the 1920s, 1930s, and 1940s. They provided role models, influenced attitudes toward romance, and disseminated ideas of fashion, beauty, language, and behavior. Movies also offered an accessible social activity for teenagers, a topic of conversation, and opportunities for dating. Teenage girls used movies to escape daily life and build friendships as well as to explore fantasies of adulthood, independence, sexuality, and romance.

Movies, like music, reach consumers as a somewhat "fixed" product that could not, in the pre-digital era, be physically altered. They are, however, open to multiple interpretations. Movies represent the values of their creators, but viewers negotiate meanings. Although teenage girls were influenced by the messages movies spread, they challenged some of the values, selected movies not intended for them, and allowed movies into their lives in creative ways. As with music, high school students consumed movies, a commodity mass-produced for a general audience, in specifically "teen" ways, incorporating themes, dialogue, and interest in movie stars into their everyday lives, conversations, and friendships. And as with music, teenage girls and boys participated in an extended movie culture together and separately. But teenage girls still did so in gender-specific ways, such as creating a shared fan culture.

In this context, movie influence extended far beyond content. An entire movie experience could include many things: reading movie reviews; sharing recommendations; deciding what movie to see and with whom; getting to the theater; events inside the theater, such as seeing friends or sharing emotions; activities following the movie; and postmovie analysis. Attending movies became an important leisure activity for teenage girls, a relatively affordable place to meet friends or dates without parental supervision. As children matured, acting out favorite movie plots gave way to collecting photographs or autographs of favorite stars and imitating their fashions. These aspects of the movie experience begin to explain what movies meant to teenage girls and to the emerging teenage consumer culture.

During these same years, from 1920 to 1945, movie production changed dramatically. The industry blossomed from small and unstructured into one of the largest, most profitable creators of mass entertainment. Yet studios clung to the Hollywood ideal of a multi-generational audience—people of all ages enjoying movies together. In the late 1940s, faced with declining attendance, anti-trust legislation, and a massive cultural and political attack on Hollywood, moviemakers began to study audiences systematically for the first time and discovered that young people attended movies more frequently than adults did. Studios responded to this information in the 1950s, targeting teenagers as a distinct audience and producing low budget "teenpics" designed to attract teenage dollars. Long before these films, though, teenagers were important, if overlooked, consumers and characters in the world of movies.

While the motion picture industry was slow to notice teen interest in movies, others were not. From the advent of moving pictures, social scientists, educators, politicians, and parents expressed concern about their impact on society, especially on children and adolescents. Apprehension centered on young people's exposure to "adult" themes, such as violence and sex, and led to proposed solutions from censorship to education. The concern did not abate as studios increasingly portrayed adolescent characters and high school culture in the 1930s, appropriately enough, since teenagers remained more interested in watching and imitating adult stars and themes. Teenage actors achieved fame in the 1930s, promoted as role models and fashion leaders, but their fans were not always their peers. Marketers of movie fan culture did not understand teenage desires but eagerly sold photographs, whether of Douglas Fairbanks and Joan Crawford or of Mickey Rooney and Judy Garland. The various ways in which adults were involved with high school students and movies, from studying the impact of movies on teenagers to industry efforts to portray teenage characters and profit from teenage star endorsements, begin to illuminate the complicated interactions between Hollywood and teenage girls.

The Studies Begin

Hollywood did not study audiences before 1950, but others concerned with the influence of movies on young people did. Those with a strong interest in forms of entertainment and mass communication that influenced and educated viewers watched the film industry closely from its inception. Educators, community and religious leaders, parents, and social scientists had little control over movie content and feared harmful effects of exposure to morally suspect plots and characters, as well as unsupervised hours in dark theaters. The first step was research. By the early 1920s, researchers studying the impact of movies on the thoughts and actions of young people recorded movie attendance, tallied movie preferences, and collected countless questionnaires.[2]

While researchers studied the impact of movies on young people, social reformers sought to minimize their influence. The Chicago Motion Picture Commission held hearings in 1919, calling doctors who testified to increased "nervousness" and sleep deprivation among children who regularly attended movies. By the 1920s and 1930s, concern intensified. Religious educator Leora Blanchard blamed movies for turning a "silly girl" into one who is "dangerous to the moral fiber" of society because "she will pattern [herself] after cheap heroines." Similarly, sociologists Robert and Helen Lynd wrote in *Middletown* of the negative impact of movies on teenagers. A juvenile court judge, with whom the Lynds were sympathetic, explicitly blamed movies for juvenile delinquency: "the disregard of group mores by the young is definitely related to the witnessing week after week of fictitious behavior sequences that habitually link the taking of long chances and the happy ending." The problem was amplified, the Lynds argued in *Middletown in Transition,* during times of social change, such as the Depression.[3]

Clarence Perry conducted one of the earliest studies of student movie attendance in 1922. Although only one-third of fourteen- to seventeen-year olds attended high school in the early 1920s, the study provides an early measurement for understanding movie patterns among high school students. The findings remained fairly consistent throughout the 1920s and 1930s as high school attendance rose. Nationally, high school boys attended movies 1.23 times weekly and high school girls 1.05 times per week in 1922. Although freshmen and sophomores attended more frequently than juniors and seniors, only 15 percent attended no movie during the month surveyed and 70 percent attended one to two times per week. The remaining 15 percent saw more than two movies weekly. A decade later, Oakland Growth Study (OGS) calculations similarly found that roughly 80 percent of high school students attended movies at least once per week. This number peaked for sophomores, reaching a high of 95 percent in 1937, and then fell during the junior and senior years.[4]

Studies also focused on movie selection, although with controversial conclusions. Some echoed Perry's conclusion that high school students generally showed "intelligent and wholesome discrimination in preferences for photoplays and players." When Alice Sterner studied the motion picture interests of high school students in the early 1940s, she concluded that movies provided teenagers "a healthy emotional outlet." Moreover, she found that intelligence and socioeconomic status did not significantly affect movie attendance or selection. In contrast, other researchers conducted comparable studies and concluded that high school students made poor movie choices and suffered from them. Education professor Marion Edman argued in 1940 that movies could be "injurious as a form of entertainment for the young." He advocated standards taught through schools, including refusal to "patronize motion pictures of inferior quality." While some researchers collected data and compiled findings, others were anxious to act.[5]

Debates over censorship and protecting youth were well underway by the 1920s and intensified in the 1930s with the establishment of the Production Code Administration. Some researchers and reformers believed that education, a preventative method for controlling the influence of movies on children, was more effective than censorship. Written in 1933 as part of the Payne Fund Studies, Edgar Dale's bestseller, *How to Appreciate Motion Pictures,* helped to inspire a national movement to teach students movie appreciation skills.[6]

Scholastic magazine joined the call for movie education, co-publishing pamphlets in 1934 entitled "How to Judge Motion Pictures: A Pamphlet for High School Students" and "How to Organize A Photoplay Club." These booklets taught film analysis, including a

"Score Card For Rating Photoplays," seen in figure 5.1, and advised students to create clubs for discussing movies. *Scholastic* magazine's "Following the Films" column assisted by offering ratings, plot summaries, and recommendations. Success varied. Many high schools supported film clubs, such as the Cardozo High School "Moving Picture Appreciation Club" seen in figure 5.2. Yet studies showed that teenagers continued to rely primarily on their families and peers outside school for recommendations. And advice did not always achieve the desired results. One girl in a 1937 study commented that she "liked Don Juan because it was *not* recommended" in a list of approved films.[7]

Most studies focused on limited aspects of teenage movie experiences—what they saw, with whom, how frequently, and what influenced their movie selection. Sociologist Paul G. Cressey, a researcher in the Payne Fund studies, began to see these small questions as part of a larger whole that was consistently overlooked. He cautioned in 1938 that individual studies did not prove direct causality between movies and real life actions. He further argued that movies had their greatest influence "where prestige is attached to the acquisition of the 'latest thing,' as in fashion, popular songs, and slang." Cressey's approach to understanding the impact of movies holistically required studying how "a specific film, a specific personality, a specific social situation and a specific time and mood" worked together to create a movie experience. Cressey's contemporaries did not heed his recommendations, and only decades later did scholars attempt to understand the influence of movie behavior and messages on teenagers, as well as the impact of film education and censorship, comprehensively.[8]

Teenagers in Movies

Contemporary researchers emphasized the influence of adult themes in movies, especially crime and sex, paying little attention to portrayals of teenagers. Studios similarly exhibited scant interest in understanding how closely movie characters reflected the emerging high school culture or how teenagers responded. Studios, however, did begin to understand the box office draw of adolescent characters, and success bred repetition. In the 1920s, films about juvenile delinquents and the "road to ruin" of innocent girls sensationalized youth, crime, and sex, and proved highly profitable. Scattered throughout were early depictions of a separate teenage culture. Although these portrayals did not represent all teenagers, they began to establish the themes and images of high school life that would became standard in the 1930s as film characterizations of teenage culture increased.

This is not to say that the characterizations were realistic. In the adolescent genre, high school served as a background, a location for peer interaction and the ubiquitous school dance. Soda shops and old "jalopies" with provocative slogans were far more prevalent than classes or homework in movie depictions. Although these images appeared within the context of a wide range of movies, from drama to comedy, they quickly became the clichéd images of high school life and teenage culture that lasted for decades. From the flaming youth of the 1920s to the bobby-soxers of the 1940s, these images of youth attracted audiences of all ages. Teenagers watched these films, but not

5.1   (right) Photoplay Score Card, 1936

SCHOLASTIC SCORE CARD
For Rating Photoplays
By

Name _Syms C. Armstrong_ .... School and Club _Burn. H.S. Photoplay_

Name of Picture _I Dream Too Much_ .... Admission Paid _35 c._

Producer _R.K.O._

Director _John Cromwell_

	Multiply Score by Weight to get Weighted Score		
	Score	Weight	Weighted Score
[Item 1] ENTERTAINMENT VALUE +3 A first-class photoplay from beginning to end. An entirely satisfactory enter- tainment. No dull stretches. +2 As a whole, it was good entertainment, but there were one or two places where it lagged. +1 Fair enough, but not up to the standard I like. Second rate. 0 Poor entertainment. Not worth the price of admission.	+3	10	30
[Item 2] BASIC THEME (What the picture is about) +3 Significant and timely, consistently developed, challenging. +2 Significant, but being overworked in current photoplays, or not well developed. +1 Not made clear. 0 Of slight significance, or pointless. −1 Of no significance.	0	10	00
[Item 3A] STORY +3 Interesting throughout, vital, true to life, of wide appeal. +2 Interesting for the most part, good adaptation of story. +1 Lacks vital situations, ordinary in incident. 0 Trite, dull, lacks action. −1 Disgusting, boring, trashy.	+1	5	5
[Item 3B] TITLE (Name of picture) +3 Appropriate and attention-getting, novel. +2 Appropriate. +1 Commonplace. 0 Misleading. −1 No connection with the picture whatever, or sensational.	+3	5	15
[Item 4] DRAMATIC PLOT STRUCTURE +3 Flawless in development and continuity, inevitable ending. +2 Generally well developed, well-ordered sequence, good climax, sincere ending. +1 Apparent weaknesses, but manages to hang together; climax weak; ending unsuitable. 0 Many glaring inconsistencies; no conflict established. −1 Incoherent, lack of motivation.	+1	10	10
[Item 5]—SOCIAL VALUE +3 Makes definite contribution toward improving social outlook of audience. Makes audience more tolerant of other people (other races and religions). Shows horror of war. Exposes injustice, snobbery, greed, jingoism. Free from subtle propaganda for special interests. Avoids undue emphasis on sex or crime. Gives insight into real life. +2 Does not take fullest advantage of its opportunities to make above contribu- tion to society. +1 Makes some slight contribution. 0 Neutral, harmless. −1 Destructive, insidious, conducive to brutality, bigotry or irreverence, scoffs at law. Undue emphasis on sex, drinking.	+1	10	10
[Item 6] DIRECTION +3 Gives illusion of reality, well-balanced, clever touches, proper emphasis. +2 Convincing, varied, consistent, appropriate tempo. +1 All characters and materials made to function, but mechanical in effect; lacks individuality. 0 Irregular, spotty, incorrect emphasis; lacks unity. −1 Dull, loose ends not unified to fit; slow, stupid.	+2	10	20
[Item 7] CHARACTERIZATION (Acting and speech) +3 Sincere, convincing, at times rising to thrilling interpretation of characters, clarity and beauty of speech. +2 All acting adequate, some exceptional, consistent in speech and manner. +1 Poor acting by one or two, type casting evident, voices indifferent. 0 Whole cast below standard, stereotyped acting, voices displeasing. −1 Poor, ham acting, over-acting, incoherent speech.	+2	10	20
[Item 8] SETTINGS, COSTUMES, MAKE-UP, PROPERTIES +3 Noteworthy for beauty, authenticity, and contribution to interpretation. +2 Appropriate, consistent with characterization and plot. +1 Acceptable, little individuality. 0 Inappropriate, inaccurate, artificial. −1 Crude, hackneyed, flagrantly wrong, overdone, omission of key details.	+3	10	30
[Item 9] LIGHTING AND PHOTOGRAPHY +3 Of high artistic merit, luminous, beautiful composition, suited to mood and action; gives effect of third dimension. +2 Exceptionally good, lighting motivated, varied to suit scene. +1 Good, but not unusual, lacks variety, lacks contrast. 0 Ordinary, lack of definition and depth. −1 Meaningless use of light, freakish angles, dull.	+2	10	20
[Item 10] SOUND AND MUSICAL EFFECTS +3 Natural, true to situation; music, if any, outstanding in artistry, well repro- duced (recorded and projected). +2 Satisfying; good effects, definitely contributory to interpretation, some novelty. +1 Adequate, appropriate. 0 Blurred, poor recording of sounds, distracting. −1 Unnatural, ugly, false tones, not carefully synchronized, interferes with story.	+3	10	30

Total weighted score ——→ **190**

[Divide Total Weighted Score) Percentage
[by 3 to get Percentage Score.] Score **63¹/₃**

5.2   *Moving Picture Appreciation Club, High School Yearbook, 1942*

exclusively. Their choices would have been limited if they had, but more important, teenage moviegoers did not see their lives reflected in these portrayals and did not aspire to become the high school characters presented. They admired and fantasized about adult stars and themes, imagining romance with male stars and future roles through female stars.

Movies first dramatized American youth in the 1920s and played an important role in developing a specific youth culture as well as in disseminating information about the role of women in society. Films that addressed female sexuality in the 1920s and 1930s often sensationalized the "ruin" of a beautiful young girl—an innocent virgin tricked down a slippery path to drinking, sexual activity, and often death. The endings pacified censors but did not negate the "excitement" of the fall from grace.

The Road to Ruin (1928) is a good example. High school provides the background in the opening scene as two girls walk together from class. Blond, innocent Sally agrees to spend the night with her friend Eve, whose name, jet-black hair, and visible makeup establish her as a temptress. That evening, Eve reads aloud from a passionate romance novel and persuades Sally to taste alcohol. The following night, Eve convinces Sally to join her on a double date that leads to kissing and more alcohol. Sally has started on the downward path and a few scenes later plays strip poker and is sexually active. The film explicitly blames Sally's mother, who is too lenient, and her father, who is preoccupied with an extramarital affair. After an illegal abortion and discovery in a brothel by her father, who almost becomes her client, Sally dies and her parents repent. Teen culture appears early in the film, in the form of the high school, peer culture, and peer pressure, to provide contrast. Sally quickly graduates to the older men, drinking parties, and sexual activity that lead to her demise.[9]

Images of high school life and teen culture derived from successful characterizations of college life. *Harold Teen,* a 1928 silent film based on a popular comic strip, features Harold, a goofy high school student, who moves from the farm to the city. Harold wears a raincoat covered in sexually suggestive slogans such as, "Teacher's Pet, you bet they do." The students congregate after school at the Sugar Bowl, an ice cream parlor, and laugh at Harold's naiveté. The teens eventually recognize Harold's virtue and he becomes a trendsetter as they all dance "The Harold Teen Drag."[10]

The movie packs in secret fraternity initiations, a high school football game, and competition over the beautiful Lillums. The prominent female characters in this film symbolize the extremes typically offered adult actresses: innocence, portrayed by Lillums Lovewell, "just a downright, upright, all right girl," and lack of innocence, played by Giggles Dewberry, "the perfect vamp: height . . . 5 ft 2 / Waist . . . 25 in / Neck . . . Yes." Although Harold spends a good deal of time kissing Giggles in the film, Lillums forgives him in his moment of crisis and inspires him to score the winning touchdown in the football game. The "gang" celebrates at the Sugar Bowl and the film ends with Harold and Lillums kissing. Teen movies in the 1920s and 1930s, and *Harold Teen* is no exception, typically placed male-female relationships in the forefront, emphasizing girls competing for a boy's attention. Female friendships, central to the media image of bobby soxers, became more central in the 1940s. This slapstick film presents many teen images, from the high school background to the drugstore hangout to the painted slogans on clothes and cars that would become the movie stereotypes of high school life and teen culture in the 1930s and 1940s.[11]

Similar images appear in the opening scenes of two classic juvenile delinquent films, *Are These Our Children?* (1931) and *Wild Boys of the Road* (1933). One begins with a high school debate and the other a high school dance. But despite the painted cars and conventional trappings of teen culture, the institutions of family and school, according to these films, fail to provide viable options for teen characters faced with the Depression and adult temptation. High school serves as a reminder of the stable lives these teens sacrifice. Eddie, in *Are These Our Children?* graduates from alcohol to sex and eventually to murder. Close up shots of newspaper headlines highlight his youthfulness: "High School 'Killers'" and "High School Youth, 18, Named as Killer." Eddie repents as he walks slowly to the electric chair. Sponsored by the National Relief Association, *Wild Boys of the Road* depicts teenagers who leave home to ease the burden on their parents, looking for honest work but surviving by any means necessary. This film ends with a courtroom speech by a firm but kind judge who leads the teenagers back on the path to responsible citizenship.[12]

Even in films without a strong teen presence, the lines between teenager and adult were clearly being drawn. In these juvenile delinquent films of the 1930s, as in the later bobby-sox films, adults play minor roles as absent or ineffective parents, social workers, judges, or as shady characters promoting alcohol and sex. These films often portrayed a loss of innocence, characterized as a fall from "teen culture," assuming an established teenage world from which to fall. In the second half of the 1930s, with the rise to national attention of teenage stars, films began to focus more directly on high school culture. Film scholars often argue that films before the 1940s did not portray a separate teenage culture. While the 1940s do reflect an explosion of adolescent films, pictures in the 1920s and 1930s established the trend.[13]

By the mid-1930s, child stars Shirley Temple and Jane Withers charmed audiences, solving adult problems with innocence and spunk. Spurred by their success, studios moved more young actresses into central roles. In movies from the 1930s, female teenage characters both instigate and resolve adult problems, often dealing with money and love, while longing to be old enough to experience the problems themselves. And they increasingly began to exist in teen-centered worlds. The short film *Every Sunday*

(1936) introduced thirteen-year-old Judy Garland and twelve-year-old Deanna Durbin to film audiences, while Mickey Rooney won national acclaim in *A Family Affair* (1937). *Three Smart Girls* (1936) brought Durbin instant success and inspired a spate of late-1930s films centered on her singing talents. At thirteen, Bonita Granville won an Academy Award nomination as Best Supporting Actress for her role as the teenage troublemaker in *These Three* (1936). By the late 1930s, teens Rooney and Garland joined child stars Temple and Withers among the top-ten box office stars.

In 1938, *Love Finds Andy Hardy* and *That Certain Age* introduced teenage girls trying to act "older" in pursuit of love. Judy Garland, as Betsy Booth, develops a crush on Andy Hardy, played by Mickey Rooney, and poignantly sings "Just an In-Between," a song cited by yearbooks and advertisers in subsequent years. The song describes a girl who sees herself as too old for toys and Mickey Mouse living in a world in which her parents and society deem her too young for romance, Clark Gable, and makeup. Andy Hardy escorts Betsy to a dance at the end of the film and she gratefully accepts the opportunity to wear an evening dress and high heels, even if only for a night.[14]

Deanna Durbin as Alice Fullerton in *That Certain Age* longs for attention from rogue reporter Vince while ignoring the advances of her dependable friend Ken, the boy scout played by former child star Jackie Cooper. Alice refuses to wear a ruffled white dress selected by her mother to a party and instead takes, without permission, a strapless black dress from her mother's closet that conveniently fits. With hair pulled back and makeup artfully applied, precariously balanced in high heeled shoes, she feels glamorous and deserving of Vince's love. Alice's father is amused, but her mother insists that she change clothes immediately. In the end, Alice accepts the limits of youth and accepts Ken as her appropriate beau. This theme, centered on an evening dress and makeup, appeared time and again as teenage girls, in the form of "bobby-soxers," took center stage by the early 1940s. These scenes encouraged teenage girls to imagine themselves as glamorous and feminine, to live in the fantasy of things to come. It also allowed parents to visualize their daughters growing up and allowed the movie industry to experiment with appropriate boundaries for teenage girls' roles.[15]

Child star Jane Withers shifted to teenage roles in *High School* (1940), publicized by Twentieth Century-Fox to coincide with Withers's entrance into high school. Withers's character, also named Jane, has to "grow up" and adjust to the rules of femininity and peer culture. As a child, she had excelled in studies, music, and sports, but the film makes clear that her exuberance and pride are undesirable qualities in a young woman. By the end of the film, after she helps the football star pass a test and apprehends a gang of car thieves, Jane learns humility, accepts a boyfriend, and receives peer approval.[16]

Jane Withers continued to make teenage movies into the early 1940s. *Variety Film Reviews* described her in *Small Town Deb* (1941) as "now considerably grown up, but continuing in the juve idiom." The reviewer concluded, "It won't be long before 20th-Fox will have to take her out of the pigtail class. That the studio already had this in mind may be the reason for the final scene, in which Miss Withers attends a dance considerably glamorized in evening gown, hair-do and makeup." She plays Pat, the younger sister at "that peculiar stage"—around age thirteen. During the country club dance, Jane reunites her sister with the "right" man, rescues a land deal for her father, plays the drums well enough to attract the attention of all the young men present, and finally agrees to dance with Bill, her loyal, adoring friend. In these films, teenagers live in separate worlds, complete with soda shops and high school dances. They interact with the adult world, but it is clear that they do not belong to it.[17]

These themes expanded in the 1940s as the number of teenage characters increased dramatically. The teenage girl, often the central character, served an important role. With her mischievous enthusiasm, she caused problems for her parents and friends and inverted the norms of business, society, and occasionally gender. She also orchestrated solutions by the closing credits that restored order. *A Very Young Lady* (1941), *Her First Beau* (1941), and *Young America* (1942) continued with Withers, while Judy Garland, Deanna Durbin, and eventually Shirley Temple, as well as several newcomers played similar leading roles. *Janie* (1944), starring Joyce Reynolds, epitomized the bobby soxer films in the 1940s. Janie entertains troops stationed in her town while overcoming war shortages, solving her father's business crisis, and having "clean" teenage fun. Each film is marked by the transformation or attempted transformation from child to young woman, the induction into femininity and commercial beauty culture. In some, an evening dress, high heels, makeup, and a permanent wave change the awkward girl into a gracious young woman for a night; in others, an outfit that is too "sophisticated" leads to ridicule and acceptance of one's youthfulness. In both situations, female teenage protagonists exacerbate and then solve adult problems and explore their roles in an adult world while living in a teen world and maturing in the process.[18]

In contrast to these female characters who devoted their energy to helping others, the quintessential teenage boy in 1930s film, Andy Hardy, focused on himself and his immediate concerns, such as how to buy a car or kiss a girl. *A Family Affair* (1937), the first in the series, turned the 1928 Broadway play *Skidding* into a B movie that gave rise to a popular series idealizing middle-class family life. Andy Hardy's naive, comic transition from boyhood to manhood, guided by his judicious father, proved so popular that by the fourth film, the plots and titles centered on this teenage character. Rooney won an Oscar in 1938 for his "significant contribution in bringing to the screen the spirit and personification of youth" and for "setting a high standard of ability and achievement" as a juvenile actor. Rooney appeared on the cover of *Time* magazine in 1940; *Life* and the *New York Times Magazine* also featured him prominently. MGM received a special Academy Award in 1942 in recognition of the Hardy series for "furthering the American way of life."[19]

Teens, however, did not see these characters as role models. Education researcher Paul Witty found in his study of movie preferences in the late 1930s and early 1940s that among high school students, the Hardy series ranked third for white girls and did not reach the top six rankings for white boys or African American boys or girls. Even then, only freshmen "showed considerable interest in series pictures, such as the *Hardy Family.*" Similarly, Marion Edman found that by ninth grade, attention to adult romantic stars replaced interest in juvenile stars. During a radio broadcast of high school student discussions in 1937, Margaret explained the perceived inaccuracy of movies portraying high school life, "The ones I've seen are not good interpretations of high-school students. They are more like . . . what the actors think high-school students should be like."[20]

People of all ages attended movies portraying teenage characters in the 1930s for the humorous plots and happy endings. Children may have looked up to the characters portrayed by Jane Withers, Deanna Durbin, Mickey Rooney, or Jackie Cooper, and to the stars themselves, just as parents might have wished for the family harmony that prevailed by the closing credits. But teens did not take the characters or the actresses seriously as role models of teenage life. Teenage girls admired handsome actors and glamorous actresses rather than aspiring to be comedic high school students. Alleyn Moore, a high school student in the mid-1930s, reminisced years later that in her teens, she "wanted to see Clark Gable making love to somebody. Or Cary Grant" at the movies rather than Andy Hardy's antics.[21]

Studio publicists and merchandisers did not understand and did not try to understand these preferences. By the mid-1930s, studios, media, and marketers promoted the actresses and actors who played teenage characters as model teens, although their lives were far less "normal" than those of their peers.

Marketing Teenage Actresses

A *New York Times* article in December 1936 mentioned the new film careers of two girls in their early teens, Judy Garland and Deanna Durbin, and concluded that their success might "lift the ban from half-grown girls and possibly start a cycle of pictures involving singing ingénues. Girls in their early and mid 'teens have never interested producers." This prediction, buried in the entertainment section, turned out to be remarkably accurate. Actors and actresses in *Harold Teen,* as well as those in the juvenile delinquent and college movies of the 1920s and early 1930s, were rarely teenagers themselves. Mary Pickford portrayed teen and even preteen characters into her thirties. But the success of children, such as Shirley Temple, as main characters in the early- and mid-1930s prompted reconsideration. And the remarkable popularity of Deanna Durbin after the release of *Three Smart Girls* in 1936 ensured serious attention to teenage stars.[22]

After 1936, the number of films with prominent teenage characters, usually musical comedies, increased, as did promotion of their stars. Deanna Durbin and Judy Garland, and a few years later Shirley Temple and Jane Withers, gained national attention portraying teenage girls. Their movies reaped large profits and studios repeated successful formulas. Studio publicists usually emphasized similarities between the actresses and the wholesome characters they played, reinventing their lives—from biographical information to favorite activities—to fit their idealized image of a model teenage girl. And they allowed these reconfigured images to endorse a range of fashion and beauty products, both capitalizing on and furthering their popularity. Marketers depended on the influence of Hollywood stars by the 1920s and 1930s and stars in their teens were no exception.

Mass merchandising the images of child stars, including product endorsements and clothing lines, began by the early 1920s. As female teenage stars such as Durbin and Garland amassed star potential, they too entered the commercial world of marketing. Actress Dawn O'Day legally changed her name to Anne Shirley in 1934 after her starring role in *Anne of Green Gables* (1934). The film's success led Teen Frocks, Inc., to purchase exclusive rights "to promote fashions created for and worn by" Shirley, as seen in figure 5.3. But Teen Frocks marketed Shirley's image to high school girls on the assumption that they would rush to imitate her. An advertisement for Anne Shirley clothes promised fashions "definitely styled for the growing girl, all with just a touch of the 'grand manner' that girls in their 'teens adore." The dresses themselves, though, are pictured on elongated, developed bodies—not those of most teenage girls.[23]

By 1937, Durbin and Garland endorsements appeared on a wide range of products newly designed for high school girls. This demonstrated some awareness among movie merchandisers of a burgeoning teenage culture. Teenage characters and the actresses themselves nonetheless represented an idealized adult version of teenagers more than they reflected the reality of teenage life. The teenage stars who portrayed these idealized

ANNE SHIRLEY

goes formal in CELANESE*

PRINTS AND TAFFETAS

The "Teen Girl," who wears a size 12 to 16 gets a big break in this new collection of Anne Shirley frocks—all formals, all definitely styled for the growing girl, all with just a touch of the "grand manner" that girls in their 'teens adore.

This group is a "natural" for your "Teen Department" promotion . . . an authentic tie-up with a glamorous Hollywood personality. The dresses are created for Anne Shirley and are worn by her. Each dress carries an Anne Shirley tag. Each store merchandising this group of dresses is privileged to use the Anne Shirley name and photograph in the store's newspaper presentation. Photographic displays of Anne Shirley wearing these dresses will be supplied without charge for your "Teen Department."

Write or wire for the franchise for these frocks in your city. Franchises will be granted in order of receipt of applications. Sizes 12 to 16.

PRICE $5.00 and $5.75

*REG U. S. PAT OFF.

Anne Shirley, sensational in her success in "Anne of Green Gables," starring currently in "Steamboat 'Round the Bend," and soon to appear in RKO-Radio's "Long Ago Ladies."

Exclusive in the United States
with

TEEN FROCKS
INCORPORATED
520 EIGHTH AVENUE, NEW YORK CITY

5.3   *Anne Shirley Merchandise,* Women's Wear Daily, *October 1935*

teen characters rarely experienced "normal" teenage life. Throughout their meteoric rise and often equally rapid fall from fame, the trade press and popular media focused on teenage actresses' youthfulness or ability to reflect or rise above the "awkward age." Very few succeeded as adult actors or actresses. And marketers assumed, incorrectly, that high school students wanted to emulate Durbin or Garland rather than Joan Crawford or Greta Garbo.

After the success of Deanna Durbin's second major feature, *One Hundred Men and a Girl* (1937), the press credited her with saving Universal Pictures from bankruptcy. The Academy of Motion Picture Arts and Sciences presented her with a miniature Oscar in 1938 for bringing the "personification of youth" to movie audiences. Journalists emphasized her age: "How a Youthful Prima Donna Triumphed at Thirteen" or "Fifteen . . . And Famous." They also wrote extensively on what studio publicists promoted as Durbin's "firsts": her first "grown-up party dress," first silk stockings, and first kiss.[24]

According to press reports, Durbin received up to sixteen hundred fan letters a week in 1937. At age fifteen, Durbin said that her fans were mostly girls her age. Durbin did not achieve the adoration or status among teenage girls reserved for beautiful, sexy adult actresses, though, and her name rarely appeared in high school yearbooks, letters, or diaries. In a letter to *New York Post* writer Garvin Hudgins in 1958, Durbin conceded that many of her fans had been "frustrated fathers and mothers" who adored her screen image of an idealized daughter full of "sweetness and innocence."[25]

Durbin's image as "America's most famous 'teen girl," however, was used to market products to teenage girls, including dresses, purses, and umbrellas. Manufacturers who licensed Deanna Durbin items claimed to sell fashions "inspired and worn by" Durbin, promising retailers that "girls in their teens . . . will instantly want these gloriously gay garments." They offered free selling aids, usually photographs of Durbin wearing or using the items, and tied products directly to movie releases as seen in figure 5.4. An advertisement for Deanna Durbin handbags in *Women's Wear Daily*, seen in figure 5.5, relied so heavily on the selling power of "the amazing radio and film star" that it did not include a picture or description of the handbag. *Fortune* magazine declared that the sale of Deanna Durbin merchandise totaled $2 million in 1939 and concluded that her career had "tremendous commercial significance." Mothers and preteens, though, were far more likely than high school girls to consume these goods.[26]

Judy Garland's image also promoted a range of products, long before her juvenile Oscar in 1940. Born Frances Ethel Gumm in 1922, she played young girls in the films *Broadway Melody of 1938* (1937) and *Thoroughbreds Don't Cry* (1937), but her role as Betsy Booth in *Love Finds Andy Hardy* first brought her national acclaim. She effectively played the sweet, reliable "girl next door," nurturing her unrequited love for Andy Hardy. Reviewers, admiring her voice and personality, emphasized her youth. After *The Wizard of Oz* (1939), Frank Nugent of the *New York Times* praised her as a "pert and fresh faced miss with the wonder-lit eyes of a believer in fairy tales." In 1938, an article in *Picture Play* celebrated her fifteenth birthday, "She is still just a typical girl of that age."[27]

Articles on Garland emphasized, as did press coverage of Durbin, that she was not in a hurry to grow up: "She prefers gingham dresses, socks and sandals to silken gowns, sheer hosiery and high-heeled shoes." Studios discouraged change, hoping to capitalize on successful images for as long as possible. As teenage actors rose in box office ratings, films made by these young stars brought enormous revenue for studios. *Three Smart*

Closer Tie-Up Between Movie and Movie Fashions Seen in Stern Bros. Promotion

While it is not new in retail circles to capitalize upon the presentation of a new picture by featuring the fashions named for the juvenile star, Stern Bros. achieves a closer than usual tie-up by repeating the Deanna Durbin window display, reproduced here, in the lobby of the Roxy Theatre where "100 Men and a Girl" is now playing. The newspaper ad, a blow-up of which appears in the window, plays up the picture, rather than the clothes—a new stunt that attracted a great deal of attention. The store predicts, under the heading "Movies Are Not in Our Line," that "100 Men and a Girl" will be one of the outstanding hits of the year, and, lower down in the "ad," in very small type, it is noted that the fashions, too, will be hits of the season. Dotted house coat, plaid jacket suit, cotton print frock under a fleece coat and a taffeta bolero party frock with beading are the styles featured in the ad, as well as hats and a handbag.

5.4   Deanna Durbin Merchandise, Women's Wear Daily, *September 1937*

Girls grossed more than $1.5 million dollars for Universal Pictures. Mickey Rooney's films grossed $30 million for MGM in 1939, and films co-starring Judy Garland and Mickey Rooney were top moneymakers. These young stars played teenage characters as long as possible. Judy Garland played pre-pubescent Dorothy in *The Wizard of Oz* at age seventeen and took the part of a high school junior in *Meet Me In St. Louis* (1944) at age twenty-two.[28]

By 1938, Judy Garland fashions also entered the market. Clothes advertised as possessing "Judy Garland *swank*" appeared in the Sears teenage section, as seen in figure 5.6. Promotions for Garland merchandise in 1938 included singing contests with Judy Garland dresses as prizes. The following year, with the release of *The Wizard of Oz,* Macy's prominently featured Garland in a window display advertising back-to-school fashions, seen in figure 5.7. Handbag manufacturers Herz & Kory bought the rights to sell both Garland and Durbin purses to harness competition and advertised the two together, as seen in figure 5.8 when "Deanna Durbin 'The Sing Girl'" handbags appeared alongside "Judy Garland 'The Swing Girl'" handbags. Aggressive marketers took these promotions directly into schools, distributing "special circulars containing photographs of Judy and stills from her pictures" in high school classrooms.[29]

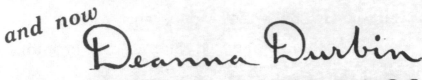

HANDBAGS
Styled for Teen Ages

Herz & Kory are privileged to an-
nounce that the Universal Pictures
Company, Inc., has granted to them
the license to use the name of the
amazing radio and film star, Deanna
Durbin, in the manufacture of handbags for girls in the teen ages.

New Universal
Pictures Star

THIS IS THE AUTHENTIC
DEANNA DURBIN TICKET
ATTACHED TO EACH BAG.

MADE EXCLUSIVELY BY
HERZ & KORY · 330-5TH AVE., N. Y.

5.5   *Deanna Durbin Merchandise,* Women's Wear Daily, *September 1937*

As Garland and Durbin outgrew teen characters, studios turned to famous child actresses, most notably Shirley Temple and Jane Withers, who explored teenage roles by
the early 1940s. Temple's efforts to portray teenage girls received a great deal of attention but even more criticism. Withers made at least five teenage films centered on high
school life before her career faded.[30]

Shirley Temple began her movie career as a toddler and enjoyed enormous success for
years. By age eleven, though, she no longer charmed audiences into theaters. At age thirteen, she wore her first, highly publicized, full-length evening dress in *Kathleen* (1941),
but the movie drew small crowds. Temple's teenage role in *Miss Annie Rooney* (1942) also
received poor reviews. A *New York Times* critic wrote, "We now see a Miss Temple in the
awkward age between paper-doll and the sweater-girl period, an adolescent phenomenon who talks like a dictionary of jive." This film, packed with stilted slang, failed with
audiences of all ages. Despite her marriage at age seventeen, she continued to play
teenage characters. Two years later, at age nineteen, Temple played her quintessential
teenage role in *The Bachelor and the Bobby-Soxer* (1947). Her transition never took hold
and she left Hollywood in 1949, the year she divorced her first husband.[31]

Jane Withers first won acclaim as a dark-haired brat in *Bright Eyes* (1934), a foil for
the sweet, blond Shirley Temple. By the late 1930s, Withers starred in teenage roles. A

For You!

FROM HOLLYWOOD'S ADORABLE GIRL STAR

Judy Garland

FASHIONS

FOR 10 TO 16's

LASTEX WAIST BLOUSE **98c**

ALL WOOL PLAID SKIRT **$1.95**

PLAIN ALL WOOL SKIRT

$1.95

Judy Garland *swank*, girls! And prices are *low!* Blouse in fine-quality Slub yarn Cotton Broadcloth. *Choice of two skirts* in our finest-quality All Wool fabrics, expertly tailored . . . 10-gore Kiltie Plaid or plain Flannel, 15-button-front style with zip pocket. **Sizes: 10, 12, 14, 16.**

Gypsy-Style Blouse
Shipping weight, 6 ounces.
Shirred Lastex band at waist.
Pearl buttons!
27 K 4634—White, Powder
Blue 225, Bittersweet 512.
State color and size.......98c

All Wool Plaid Skirt
Shipping weight, ea., 1 lb. 4 oz.
27 K 4637—Red and Navy
Plaid. Sizes below......**$1.95**
All Wool Flannel Skirt
Sizes below. State size..**$1.95**
27 K 4638—Navy 214
27 K 4639—Brown 614

Skirts, Age-size	10	12	14	16	years
Waist Measure	24	25	26	27	inches
Length	24	26	28	30	inches

5.6   *Judy Garland Merchandise, Sears Catalog, Fall 1938*

Macy's Features Judy Garland Frocks
In "Wizard of Oz" Window Display

How Macy's tied in with the New York showing of the "Wizard of Oz" is illustrated in this window display featuring Judy Garland wool and rayon frocks, suitable for back-to-school wear. The merchandise is displayed against a background of photographs showing scenes from the film. These teen frocks are featured as "designed for and selected by Judy herself."

According to reports these frocks have stimulated business greatly in the store's teen department. The two figures shown on the mannekins are cited as strong reorder numbers, not only in this store, but all across the country in shops carrying Judy Garland fashions. Not shown in the photograph is a two-piece plaid frock similar to the plain one shown at the left of the window.

5.7 Judy Garland Merchandise, Women's Wear Daily, *September 1939*

New York Times review of *Youth Will Be Served* (1940) stated that Withers had "blossomed into a juvenile flower." Withers played a tomboy somewhat transformed into a young lady in her teen roles and of all the young female actresses of this era, she imbued her characters with the most spunk, athletic ability, and independence. Her on-screen "firsts" received attention, and reviewers praised her talent and energy, but by age sixteen she was no longer eligible for high-spirited young teenage roles and was unable to effectively transition to romantic leads.[32]

Hollywood responded unevenly, as did the fashion industry, to an emerging teenage girls' culture. With teenage stars successfully portraying teen characters, studios noticed high school culture without acknowledging teenage audiences. Merchandisers saw potential profit in teen star endorsements, but they failed to ask how teenage girls watched movies or which stars girls admired. Teenage girls found Deanna Durbin and Judy Garland entertaining, but they did not see them as role models. Nor did many of

5.8 *Deanna Durbin and Judy Garland Handbags,* Women's Wear Daily, *September 1938*

the actresses who played those characters see themselves as role models. Studio publicists, however, promoted them as if they were, saying more about the adult desire for teenage girls who were content with gingham dresses and contained sexuality than about girls themselves.

Going to the Movies

At the turn of the twentieth century, itinerant exhibitors brought moving pictures to small towns across the country. By 1907, stationary theaters attracted local audiences. In cities, large, elaborate palaces devoted solely to movies began replacing nickelodeons by 1914. These theaters showed longer "feature" films and offered vaudeville entertainment, orchestras, costumed ushers, and elegant surroundings with the goal of attracting middle-class families and higher ticket prices. Theaters in major cities such as New York and Chicago offered even grander palaces and amenities.[33]

Theaters, whether large or small, provided more than a room for viewing moving pictures and teenage girls described the ambience as integral to their movie experiences. When thirteen-year-old Yvonne Blue visited the Capitol, a grand Chicago movie palace, in 1925, she wrote about it at length in her diary, "The movie wasn't good, but the theater was wonderful. As soon as one enters, he looks up to a sky of Baghdad blue. . . . The carpet under one's feet is as moss." Yvonne continued, describing in elaborate detail, "All along the walls are marble girls holding drinking fountains, with water lilies floating beneath them. Vases of flowers were set in the wall, and gold fish bowls were lighted from underneath by electric lights." The theater experience eclipsed the disappointing movie.[34]

Traveling to a movie palace could also signal an "event." At age fifteen, Yvonne Blue and her friends "went to the Tivoli *in a taxi!* The movie was poor, but they had wonderful, thrilling music and dim lights. That music made us feel wonderful." Yvonne underlined "in a taxi," emphasizing its novelty. Similarly, Beth Twiggar wrote excitedly in her diary at age fifteen, "Oh the thrill of adventure! The Romance of traveling! I've been to Europe. No, that was a mistake, to Tarrytown [New York]! A bunch of us went down via train to the movies. We had a lotta fun. Movie I'd seen before, worst luck. But even so it was worth the trouble." The adventure of travel, exciting music, and exotic decoration provided a thrill even when the movie did not.[35]

Part of the pleasure also derived from recounting movie excursions. Movie magazines, reviews, and advertisements helped create a language for conceptualizing and discussing films. When teenage girls wrote about movies or discussed them with friends, they imitated this format, focusing on lead actors and movie titles as well as plot, genre, and theater in more elaborate descriptions. In 1918, fourteen-year-old Frances Turner received a letter describing a friend's recent movie experience in New York, "Last night I saw Pauline Fredrick in 'A Daughter of the [Old] South.'" Seven years later, fourteen-year-old Yvonne Blue wrote in her diary that she saw "Hoot Gibson in 'Spook Ranch'" and the following week, "Douglas Fairbanks in 'Don Q' Son of Zorro." Arvilla Scholfield wrote in her diary, shown in figure 5.9, in a small town in Northern California in 1926, "went to Mary Pickford in 'Little Annie Roonie'."[36]

A typical movie entry in Arvilla's diary read, "Went to Harold L[l]oyd in 'The Freshman'" or "Went to show with Anna; Norma Shearer in the 'Lady of the Night' was on." Yet subtle differences in these short entries reveal a wealth of information. Some days Arvilla highlighted her companions, "Arthur took me to the show" or

Ther Thurs. Jan. 7, 1926 'Wea

Anna, Irene, and
I went to many
Pickford in "Little Annie
Rooney" last night

Ther   Friday 8   Wea

Glad today is Fri.
no school tomorrow
Oh! Boy! "Hot Dog"
etc

Ther   Saturday 9   Wea

Went to the dance
at shasta had a
pretty good time
wanted to go to Redfield
though

Ther   Sun. Jan. 10, 1926   Wea

The sheik I met at
Shasta came to see
me. We visited Anna
and Irene at work

Ther   Wed. Jan. 13, 1926   Wea

Went to the "Van-
ishing American"
tonight with anna.
kinda sad

5.9 *Diary Entries, Arvilla Scholfield, 1926*

"Ann and I went to Norma Talmadge in Graustark. Pretty good." Other times she highlighted the star or the title of the show. And Arvilla's concise analyses—"it was funny," "Not so bad," or "I should have stayed and studied my lessons"—demonstrate her judgments on films while viewing and reflections on them later while writing in her diary. Schoolwork and family appeared in the diary, but movies shared a privileged space with dances, stimulating the most frequent and descriptive entries.[37]

In 1929, thirteen-year-old Eleanor adopted the same formula. A letter to her friend Adele read, "At 2:00 P.M. we walked to the Victory Theater and saw Dolores Costello and George O'Brien in 'Noah's Ark.' The picture was real good—very exciting, thrilling, etc." Adele included the relevant statistics: where she saw the movie; how she traveled there; the time of day; her companion (a girlfriend); the leading actors; the title; and finally, a brief analysis. In this case, Eleanor's positive response fit so well within a predetermined format of praise for movies that she limited her superlatives and sufficed with "etc." The basic structure remained the same—audiences learned to conceptualize, discuss, and remember movies according to prescribed criteria.[38]

This formula could also include plot analysis. After seeing the Jackie Coogan film *Daddy* (1923), Yvonne Blue wrote, "It was wonderful. It is about a little boy whose mother thinks his father doesn't love her and runs away to see her friends without him. His mother dies and the people are sent to the poor-farm and he runs away." She concluded with the happy ending: "His father becomes a great musician and Jackie's protector was once his teacher. His father at last finds him." Yvonne, at age twelve, sounded remarkably like a film reviewer covering main plot events. Yvonne expressed overall approval for the film and satisfaction that in the end the father "at last" was reunited with his son. Yvonne's diary entries about movies did not always include such detailed summaries, but her use of the language and style of movie reviews demonstrates that she read them frequently, including *Motion Picture Classic,* a gift from her parents.[39]

High school girls also reflected on the frequency of their movie attendance. Yearbooks made special mention of high school students who attended movies often or cultivated a "weakness" for them. One senior's greatest talent was "squeezing four movies into a week-end." Movie theaters provided the physical location for watching movies, but the movie experience far surpassed the setting. Movie companions proved equally important to the experience.[40]

"Will call you to movie it—when I get home," wrote seventeen-year-old Helen in a letter to her friend Frances. By 1920, when Helen wrote this letter, she and her friends were so accustomed to movies and the experience of attending them that she casually made plans, using "movie" as a verb. The point of the correspondence was not to see a specific movie or to arrange plans for a certain date, but to share a pleasurable activity whenever and wherever possible. Frances and her friends attended movies together regularly enough to create their own language, illustrating the important role movies played in their friendship.[41]

Film scholars describe movie audiences in the 1930s and 1940s as multi-generational, with families and people of all ages attending movies together. While movie audiences were more likely to watch the same films and any given audience may have included young and old alike, this did not preclude age segregation inside the theater. Even in the 1920s, teenagers attended movies more frequently with their peers than with their families, creating a teen-centered movie experience within a shared theater.[42]

That potential for teen culture was part of the draw of movie theaters. Movies and the larger movie culture challenged parental supervision, occurring outside of the home and frequently in the realm of peers. High school expanded the number of peer activities but took place within an educational setting. Social and religious clubs also built on adult institutions and traditions. Movie theaters, in contrast, were public spaces presenting mass culture. Unlike dance halls, theaters welcomed teenage consumers, offering them an escape from the gaze of parents, teachers, and adults interested in their moral or cultural development.

Researcher Clarence Perry found in 1922 that between ninth grade and twelfth grade, young people increasingly attended movies with friends rather than alone or with family members. He especially noted the "growing independence of the girls." Saturday morning serials aside, children usually attended movies with their families. The early teen years proved a period of transition from sharing commercial leisure time with family to spending it almost exclusively with peers. The issue of movie companions touches on a significant aspect of teenage movie culture. Peer interactions, from communicating with friends to selecting a movie, from seating location to socializing, and finally post-movie indulgences, were all central to teenage girls' moviegoing experiences. And those experiences helped shape a group identity.[43]

Arvilla Scholfield frequented the movies with her sisters or with dates, sometimes including references to her companions in her diary, "Went to the 'Vanishing American' tonight with Anna [sister]," and other times excluding their presence altogether, "Went to the show Gloria Swanson in Stage Struck." On a special occasion, she wrote, "Ditched school & went to the 'Cat's Pajamas' with mom we liked it lots." Many high school girls were less willing to appear publicly with their families. Thirteen-year-old Katherine Rosner wrote in her diary in 1929, "Tomorrow is Mother's birthday, and she wants us all to go to the show. I hate to go with my family, because if any of the kids see you, they think you were so hard up you didn't have anyone else to go with. But what can a poor girl do?"[44]

Boys attended movies alone more often than girls, in part because of the public nature of theaters. Movie theaters seemed to offer privacy as individuals engaged with a story, but theaters also provided commercial leisure wherein individuals participated as members of a viewing community. And as many couples celebrated, darkened theaters offered rare opportunities for public affection. But the dark also offered opportunities for unwelcome advances, and young girls could be vulnerable targets.

Yvonne Blue recorded an incident in which an unknown man intruded on her personal space. In June 1926, at age fourteen, she saw Adolph Menjou in *The Social Celebrity* and wrote, "It was a good picture, but I'm not going to that theater alone, again." During the show, a man sat next to her in the nearly empty theater and repeatedly asked her questions while moving closer: "I looked down at my lap. His arm was hanging over the seat arm, and his hand was almost touching mine." She continued to move her hand and leg out of reach to thwart his efforts but was "determined that he shouldn't drive me from my seat. I was there first!" When the movie ended, she left the theater quickly, looking over her shoulder as she ran home. Yvonne's combined naiveté and spunk spurred her refusal to move. She felt that she had a right to her seat and, despite being uncomfortable, remained on principle.[45]

Going to the movies in a group offered more security. It also offered the pleasure of peer companionship. In 1917, Margaret wrote to her friend Frances, "Now listen love to my proposition. You come down to my house on Tuesday at quarter of three sharp and we will go to the 'movies.'" Margaret emphasized the novelty of the nickname for moving pictures but felt no need to explain the activity. In 1928, Beth Twiggar described the unique pleasure of going to the movies with a girlfriend, "Gretta and I went to the movies. Never have we had so much fun. Giggled and were silly to the nth degree, but oh what sport! I enjoyed it immensely."[46]

Ten years later, movies had lost some of their novelty. Seeing a film rated above staying home, but teenage girls made such decisions more casually. OGS participants recorded their activities one weekend in 1939 and repeatedly mentioned attending movies with little planning or fanfare. Mary wrote that she "fussed about the house until 12:00 when Sue phoned and wanted to go down to the show. I decided against it but went anyway for lack of other amusements."[47]

A movie date made the prospect more interesting. Participants in sociologist Herbert Blumer's studies in the late 1920s related their high school movie experiences during the early- to mid-1920s. Male students recounted many high school movie dates—popular because of affordability as well as the potential for physical affection. As one recalled, "I thought that if the girl I took saw a real passionate scene it would make it easier for me to neck and kiss her after the show."[48]

Some parents worried about just such an effect, especially on their daughters. In 1935, at age fourteen, OGS participant Lillian told a friend that she usually watched movies with her family: "I go with kids some but my dad doesn't like me to." Her father allowed movie "dates" only under controlled circumstances. In contrast, seventeen-year-old Sarah went to the movies with her boyfriend Friday and Saturday night one weekend in 1939. Friday night was casual, "Bill came for me about 7:00," they joined friends, and the group went "to Jack's afterward. . . . a most enjoyable evening." But the couple reserved Saturday night for themselves. Sarah "dunked into a hot bath—and made myself beautiful for William." After dinner and the movie *Sweethearts* (1939) they "came home on our big yellow limo[u]sine (street car). . . . Bill left me safely at my door at about 12:30." She added that she slept sweetly, dreaming only of the picture "of course."[49]

As demonstrated in Sarah's comments, a movie experience rarely began or ended with the actual movie. Meeting friends or dates and traveling to the movie usually preceded the event, sometimes including a meal. And after the movie, friends socialized. Thirteen-year-old Katherine Rosner described one evening in 1929, "Everybody was there, and quite a few of the kids were sitting near us [in the movie theater]. Afterwards we went to the Commodore for sodas. I like the Commodore. You meet everyone you know there. In fact, there are always a bunch of school kids there. There were, tonight, too, and we had a lot of fun. I really had quite a perfect evening."[50]

At ages thirteen and fourteen, Yvonne Blue increasingly attended movies with friends and recorded post-movie treats, "I ordered a banana split" or "we had a sundae, and bought some candy cigarettes which look very real." These treats enhanced the charm of the movie experience, but they also extended social interaction. OGS students also mentioned snacks frequently: "After the show we went to Edy's [restaurant] to have something to eat" or "After the show we went home to eat" to save money and then went out again. The perfect day in a yearbook "thesis on adolescence" included "an Ingrid Bergman movie, topped off with coffee ice cream and scrambled with giggles."[51]

Movie tickets, streetcar rides, meals, ice cream, and popcorn accompanied the movie experience—all at a price. Even during the height of the nickelodeon, entrance often cost more than a nickel. And with the rise of permanent theaters and movie palaces, prices rose even higher. The Depression economy hurt studio and theater profits, but audience desire for entertainment remained strong. Box-office receipts dropped from a high of more than $700 million in 1930 to a low of $482 million in 1933. But by 1935, movies brought in $566 million annually, with an average ticket price of twenty-five cents, and by 1940 gross income reached $735 million.[52]

Friends sometimes shared costs, buying each other movie tickets and sweets as an expression of friendship. At age fourteen, Katherine Rosner wrote, "I treated Elizabeth both to the show and to ice-cream. It cost me $1.30. That's 30 cents more than my usual allowance!" At age fifteen, Adele's friend Jane "wanted to treat me to a show at the 'St. George' with her birthday money. . . . We saw a darling picture, 'Shipmates.' Jane's a dear." These teenagers kept tabs on available spending money and costs.[53]

Whether treating a date or a friend, companions enhanced the movie experience. Teenagers cultivated friendships through shared movie experiences: making plans, watching movies, sharing meals, and spending time together. Teenage girls attended movies with other girls and, as they grew older, with boys. Although girls who were close to their families, such as Yvonne, continued to share movies with them as well, peer companions provided a very different movie experience.

Teenage Girls Respond to Movies

In diaries and letters, many teenage girls used short but descriptive phrases to explain movies: "it was fine," "Kinda sad" or "I enjoyed [it] very much." But others, such as Yvonne Blue, wrote at length, "we went to the Roosevelt [theater] and saw Harold Lloyd in 'The Freshman.' It was splendid. He thought he was very popular when he was really the college boob. But of course it turned out that he was popular." Yvonne's enthusiasm spread across movie genres and she frequently proclaimed her latest favorite "one of the best movies I have ever seen." Movies acquiring this status ranged from Harold Lloyd in *Safety Last* (1923) to *The Phantom of the Opera* (1925), "the most exciting movie I have ever seen." *The Big Parade* (1925) surpassed all others: "It is the only movie in the world. To call it 'marvelous' or 'good' or 'wonderful' is an insult. It is a realistic picture of the war—the most realistic picture ever filmed."[54]

Despite industry assumptions and fears of educators, teenagers absorbed and interpreted movie messages in complex ways. They did not enjoy all movies, did not approve of everything in movies they did enjoy, and disagreed with each other about favorites. Yvonne Blue, who raved about many movies, was equally willing to criticize. She described *Old Loves and New* (1926) as "nothing much." She placed the movie on a continuum where the worst movies merited an underlined "bad" and an exclamation point.[55]

In addition to recording plot summaries and condensed film analyses, teenagers often responded emotionally to movies and stars. Both boys and girls recalled intense emotional involvement with serial pictures, anxiously awaiting each segment to see the hero resolve impossible dilemmas. Girls felt freer to maintain this enthusiasm as they grew into their teens. The protagonist in a story for teenage girls proclaimed that movies were the only place "where one could weep unquestioned in a modern world. It was in the tenth row of the Crystal, with [girlfriends] all crying softly into handkerchiefs, and wiping their eyes to watch groggily the misfortunes of a heroine." Not all emotional responses involved tears. Beth Twiggar confided in her diary after seeing *We Americans* (1928), a drama about prejudice and intermarriage, that she "came home with a fury of patriotism seething in my chest!"[56]

Researcher Mary Abbott found strong reactions to violence, especially among teenage girls. Although *Mutiny on the Bounty* (1935) achieved widespread popularity among high school students in this 1936 study, several girls disliked the film for its graphic violence. A freshman wrote, "'I don't like to see pictures of this type. It gives me the jitters. Watching people being flogged and murdered and starved is not *my* favorite pastime.'" In addition to violence, young people viewed other "adult" themes through movies—the most restricted usually held the greatest allure. With creativity, determination, and lax restrictions at theaters, teenage girls accessed films forbidden to them by parents or censors. Beth Twiggar told her mother that she had an extra gym session at school to secretly attend a movie; others claimed to be shopping or visiting friends.[57]

Some parents freely allowed their teenage daughters to select films, trusting either in the theaters, the films, or their children. A mother in the OGS told observers that her daughter "select[ed] her own pictures" and added, "'they wouldn't let children in if the pictures were not good for them to see!'" The observer, transcribing an oral interview, presumably added the exclamation mark. Other OGS participants attended movies so frequently that their selections could not have been highly discriminatory. Not all parents were so permissive, but as Beth demonstrated, deceit could create opportunity.[58]

Before the Production Code actively controlled film content, films about college, ranging from comedy to musical to drama, emphasized social life, romance, and athletics, often containing "adult" themes. A highly popular genre of the 1920s, teenagers flocked to see college films and to admire the glamorous lifestyle of "youth." Fourteen-year-old Katherine Rosner saw the college film *Hot Stuff* (1929) and wrote, "the cutest picture I've ever seen . . . . a snappy, modern, adorable picture." She then summarized the plot, "a girl who goes to college and pretends to drink and smoke and neck because she thinks fellows prefer whoopee" until a valiant college man "calls her bluff, and tells her she has a wrong idea." Yvonne Blue incorporated college film images in her language at age seventeen when describing her friend as "popular & co-edish like a girl in the movies." Some students credited movies with the inspiration to pursue higher education; others realized that college life consisted more of lectures and assignments than glamorous parties.[59]

Love, Sex, and Movies

College movies contained idealized images of love, physical intimacy, and relationships, themes that generally interested girls entering their teenage years. At age twelve, OGS participant Mary intensely disliked the romantic comedy *Springtime for Henry* (1934): "'There was nothing to it but love all the time.'" Three years later, teenage girls in the study resoundingly approved of such films. Sharon publicly expressed her approval of movie love scenes and Rebecca "raved unreservedly about Nelson Eddy in 'Maytime'— especially the love-making scenes." In a study by sociologist Earl Sullenger in 1930, several girls explained that John Gilbert was their favorite actor because "'he is so handsome'" or has "'sex appeal.'" A female college junior reminisced, "As I grew older I began to like the 'love' pictures" and spent hours "dreaming that I sprained my ankle . . . and some great movie actor carried me to his car, told me I was fit for his picture, etc." The "etc." implied that her fantasy followed a predictable path as she alluded to an inevitable happy ending complete with wedding bells and stardom.[60]

Some teenage girls were more influenced by these images than others. Beth Twiggar longed for idealized movie romance and found her life lacking in comparison. She wrote in 1928, at age fourteen, "Having seen Greta Garbo in the 'Divine Woman' I have decided to throw [away] George's letter . . . but the question is, if I accomplish that, where am I going to find a larger or better love affair?" The following year she saw another romantic film and "enjoyed it immensely, although it filled one with girlish longings for what looks oddly hopeless in my eyes."[61]

Many teenage girls imitated actresses or love scenes in daydreams and real life. In a story for teenage girls, the shy, awkward protagonist practiced saying "I love you" as she had seen in movies: "It embarrassed her to say the [words]. How did you learn to say it naturally? Like Dorothy Lamour, or Betty Grable, or Ingrid Bergman. Especially Bergman." She experimented with the oft-repeated words: "the Bergman way. More 'lov' than 'love,' she decided; sort of between them. 'I love you, Robert.'" Imagining herself as Bergman allowed her to participate in an idealized, romantic heterosexual relationship, a dream that became reality by the end of the story when Robert invited her, not surprisingly, to the movies.[62]

Teenage girls and boys reported comparing dates to favorite movie stars or studying on-screen love "techniques." Although this confirmed observers' worst fears, the results could be fairly innocuous. A high school senior joked that her ideal prom date "must have the physical perfection of Tyrone Power." A college junior reminisced about a high school experience reenacting a movie scene with a girlfriend, "My first heavy necking party was brought on mainly through a picture which showed a harem with several beautiful girls, lightly clad, dancing while a man and woman were lying in each other's arms on a couch-like affair." Another high school girl found less charm in reenactment. She complained that one of her dates only wanted to "neck" and "I have a sneaking suspicion that he got his method from the screen. . . . It makes him appear silly."[63]

Herbert Blumer studied the relationship between movies and sexual desire and the influence on the sexual behavior of young people. In this research, girls generally appeared in Blumer's section on "the milder forms of sexual agitation resulting from the witnessing of passionate or suggestive pictures." One college sophomore admitted that some "sensational love scenes" left her "with a rather goose-fleshy feeling." Another girl saw *Flesh and the Devil* (1926) twice at age sixteen and noted, "I would have gone the third time but I didn't have the money. The love scenes were so amorous and during them I throbbed all over. I will have to admit that I wanted someone so bad to make love to me that way."[64]

Girls in the 1920s struggled with sexuality. They were taught at home to refrain from sexual activity until marriage, but they enjoyed sexual images in movies, print media, and on the radio and admired the freedom of the idealized flapper. Teenage girls, often aware of their awakening desires, expressed these conflicting values through denial, contradiction, and occasionally insightful reflection. Until age seventeen, a college student wrote, "I firmly believed that I would be a ruined woman if ever I let a man kiss me, and all the desires that the movies aroused were counterbalanced by my father's lectures." Another student described sitting with a boy after a romantic movie, writing that she "had known it all along, from the moment [she] had seen that perfect embrace in the movies" that she wanted to kiss someone, "So, I struggled no longer, and I learned the charm which before I had only dreamed of."[65]

Blumer grew so concerned that he abruptly ended his research and never published his monograph, "Movies and Sex." Despite his fears, watching movies did not always lead to sexual intercourse, even when it aroused sexual curiosity. Movies generally perpetuated the norms and practices of heterosexuality and femininity. Teenage girls fantasized about sex and their own sexuality and acted on those fantasies to a limited degree, but they also accepted the dream of perfect romance and longed for marriage. Most high school girls in the 1920s explored sexual desire through fantasy, kissing, or petting. Teenage dating was fraught with insecurity and experimentation. Innocent flirting and sexual tension occurred far more frequently than sexual intercourse. One girl wrote that she and her friends attended movies because they "loved the pictures" but also because "there were always high school boys there . . . a row or two behind us, and aware of us." She described the excitement of "the thrilling march down the [theater] aisle, during which we were exquisitely aware of the eyes that followed [us]. . . ."[66]

Affordable, accessible, and requiring limited conversation, movies offered a popular dating option. But a movie date was still a date, with as much potential for awkwardness as for magic. Beth Twiggar was almost sixteen when she wrote, in 1929, about a movie date that was "rather uncomfortable." The date improved after the movie when she and the boy were "seen" together by her friends at a popular restaurant. Fifteen-year-old Adele Siegel quickly made a transition in 1931—much to her delight—from movies with her family or friends to three movie dates in three weeks. All movie dates were not equal, though. When she saw *Monkey Business* (1931) with John, she "didn't enjoy the picture or [the] company." Her outlook improved, though, when Eugene took her to see Eddie Cantor in *Palmy Days* (1931): "I hadn't enjoyed myself or laughed as much for ages, and it's partly Eugene's company—he's such fun to be with."[67]

High school girls learned about heterosexual romance, dating, passion, and sexuality from the movies they frequently attended. These messages were not new to movies, but grew more powerful when dramatized by glamorous stars on the big screen in a darkened theater. Girls often accepted these images of idealized relationships, incorporating them into fantasies and expectations. Despite the fears of researchers, watching movies did not cause most teenage girls to engage in sexual activity. It did, however, further their initiation into the norms of femininity. Movie fan culture extended this process but also opened possibilities for challenging tradition.

"How is Doug?": Teenage Girls and Movie Fan Culture

In 1919, Helen wrote to her fifteen-year-old friend Frances, "How is Doug? Have you seen 'His Majesty, the American' his new picture?" Helen's casual question about movie star Douglas Fairbanks provides some insight into her relationship with movie fan culture. She asked "How is Doug?" as though inquiring about a mutual friend—without introduction or context. She used a nickname, knowing that Frances would understand that only one "Doug" existed. And in reference to his latest movie, Helen wrote as though she, Frances, and Douglas Fairbanks shared an intimate bond. With these questions, Helen participated in a growing movie fan culture. Helen also asked Frances to "Save the movie classics," insisting, "Please do and you can see all my mags, too." Helen's excitement centered on a newly restyled movie magazine, *Motion Picture Classic,* introduced in 1915 by the editors of *Motion Picture Magazine.* Renamed *Classic,* the magazine offered larger pages, numerous glamour photographs, and expanded articles on beauty, fashion, and the personal lives of stars. By 1919, Helen represented the emerging image of movie fans, teenage girls.[68]

Movie fan culture developed in the early twentieth century with little understanding of the gender and socioeconomic background of movie fans. Film exhibitors and producers, hoping to appeal to all potential consumers, initially envisioned movie fans as representative of society as a whole—male and female, all ages, all class backgrounds. Movie fan magazines helped shape the concept of the movie fan as consumer, predominantly female and increasingly young, replacing technical information on movie production with advice columns and recipes. By the early 1920s, more than a dozen movie fan magazines competed for the attention of readers. *Photoplay* editor James R. Quirk first attempted to change the image of movie fans from "a mass of gum-chewing, giggling schoolgirls" to "knowledgeable, middle-class film consumers." After a marked lack of success, he embraced youth and presented his magazine to advertisers as a favorite of young people.[69]

With the rise of the star system and the development of an elaborate publicity infrastructure, many teenage girls became active fans, deriving pleasure, building friendships, and exploring fantasy through shared fan culture. And movie magazines provided a main staple. Frances and Helen shared their passion for movie fan magazines. They traded issues, pored over pictures and articles together, and shared juicy details. High school yearbooks and newspapers similarly recorded widespread interest in movie magazines between 1920 and 1945. Fan culture was not only a teenage phenomenon, but teenage girls were among the most active fans. Some teenagers, male and female, never read movie magazines, but studies suggest that by the 1920s and 1930s, teenage girls read movie fan magazines regularly and far more often than boys did. In studies of high school movie habits, researchers consistently found more star preferences among girls than among boys.[70]

In addition to knowing who read movie magazines, it is important to understand how they read them. As Helen's letter demonstrated, reading could be a group activity that strengthened friendships through shared possessions and ideas. Movie magazines supplied the raw material for movie fan culture—plot summaries, details of stars' private lives, often fabricated, and most importantly, pictures. Supplemented by photographs from studio publicity offices, magazine pictures of stars and movie advertisements became the currency of dreams. In addition to reading movie magazines, girls actively wrote fan letters requesting autographs or photographs.

Teenage girls used these materials to personalize rooms, decorate belongings, construct scrapbooks, or trade images. Irene Scholfield, a high school student in Northern California in the late 1920s, lovingly drew pictures of movie stars based on movie magazine photographs, as seen in figures 5.10–5.13, turning mass produced images into personal art. And she was not alone. Seniors in 1933 nostalgically remembered their younger high school days of "desk-covers hidden by drawings and photographs of movie stars." Similarly, seniors in 1936 remembered "bring[ing] Hollywood to [school] by decorating the locker doors with pictures of our favorite movie stars. Between periods we traded them around and admired each other's collection with a regrettably noisy enthusiasm." Creating their own movie fan culture at home and school offered teenage girls a pleasurable way to interact with stars, dreams, and with each other.[71]

These pictures served as decoration, but also as a medium for communication. At age thirteen, Yvonne Blue loved the movie *Peter Pan* (1924). She and her best friend collected pictures, pasted them into diaries and scrapbooks, and perused them together. Yvonne wrote next to a recently acquired picture, "I just adore Betty Bronson in Peter Pan . . . I wish I had the cute pictures of Peter that Bobby has." Jealousy prevailed even more for other girls, "Gasps and screams shook the hall as someone beheld her favorite's picture in another girl's locker." Although these girls knew realistically that they did not have private relationships with their adored stars or a monopoly on the commodified images, part of the fantasy included imagining a meaningful, unique relationship between fan and star.[72]

A yearbook caption from 1942, "Runs, does not walk, to see the newest Nelson Eddy picture," characterized one senior's passion, but it also acknowledged degrees of "fandom." Many girls enjoyed movies regularly but retained strong interests unrelated to them. Movie fans, on the other hand, had to run to the theater on opening day to see a favorite star's latest release, read every word of studio publicity, and cover all personal belongings with photographs and drawings. Girls teased each other about such devotion, as seen in figure 5.14. This yearbook drawing from 1925 explicitly stated that only a

Hommel

Clara Bow

Clara is the perpetual flapper, the symbol of S. A.
Things begin brightening up when she breezes around.
Someone asked the saucy Bow what she intended to do
about Leap Year and *that* wink may be the answer.
Who can tell?   Richee

5.10   *Photograph, Clara Bow, c. 1928*

5.11   *Clara Bow, Drawing by Irene Scholfield, 1928*

Photo by Ruth Harriet Louise

Greta Garbo and John Gilbert make Russia the scene of their latest film romance, which means that the temperature of the picture will be in inverse ratio to the ice and snow of the background. The story, called "Love," is an adaptation of Tolstoy's novel, "Anna Karenina," and depicts the tragic adventure in love of a cabinet minister's wife, whose fatal allure destroys all who succumb to it, and, eventually, *Anna* herself.

5.12   *Photograph, Greta Garbo and John Gilbert, c. 1928*

5.13   Greta Garbo and John Gilbert, Drawing by Irene Scholfield, 1928

film magazine could bring "an unprecedented hush in the vicinity of Chattering Chita." As with portrayals of Sinatra fans, however, media often presented teenage movie fans more negatively, as silly and uncontrolled, as seen in figure 5.15.[73]

Movie fan magazines, in combination with studios and fans, helped create an active movie fan culture—a culture that teenage girls often turned into an engaging hobby and that studios and manufacturers turned into enormous financial gain. Girls started with the building blocks of movie fan culture, often provided by studios and magazines, and transformed them into personalized memories through scrapbooks, diaries, and fan letters. This enjoyment, also embodied by the senior's "noisy enthusiasm," was the key. Fans took ownership of the dreams and movie star images and created a pleasurable subculture, often using it as a foundation for developing friendships, fantasizing about romance, and exploring sexuality. Girls explored teen identity and fantasies about adult life while creating a peer culture around shared interest in movies and stars. Fan culture profited from teenage girls' enthusiasm for stars but was slow to recognize its significance.[74]

Female fan culture can demonstrate acceptance of traditional gender roles. It can also signify resistance against gender norms and prescribed identities. Movie fans infatuated with romantic male stars participated in the active, desiring side of sexual attraction, as did teenage Sinatra fans. Girls explored and expressed sexual desire privately, safely imagining an unattainable star as their ideal mate or experimenting with a different male persona every night. Movies and fan magazines offered high school girls a chance to flirt with sexuality safely.[75]

In an early effort to understand fans, Leo Rosten interviewed studio fan mail department heads and studied fan mail received by two movie stars, one male and one female, in January 1939. He found that girls under age twenty-one wrote most frequently, primarily directing their correspondence to romantic male stars. High school girls composed an important and distinct component of this "under twenty-one" group. In addition to general praise and requests for photographs, autographs, or memorabilia, however, Rosten found that letter writers solicited advice and shared private emotions, "Many fans indicated a marked desire to unburden their ambitions and unhappiness." He was impressed by "the earnestness and naiveté of the effort to make the star seem more 'real' to the fan writers" by revealing personal information and urging reciprocation.[76]

Margaret Thorp's 1939 examination of movie audiences, *America at the Movies*, also offers rich, contemporary descriptions of American movie audiences, studio gimmicks, and fan culture. Thorp detailed the commercialization of fan culture, warning readers that fan magazines were "stimulants of the most exhilarating kind. Everything is superlative, surprising, exciting." She analyzed the marketing of dreams in the form of luxury, beauty, and romance as well as the sale of fan materials, from magazines to guided tours. Although Hollywood showed little interest in teenage girls as fans, Thorp recognized that many girls avidly followed stars' lives and fan magazines. She also referred to teenage characters and, more perceptive than the studios or movie merchandisers, acknowledged that high school girls responded more enthusiastically to the glamorous adult actresses they admired and longed to emulate. Only the preteen girl "fashion[ed] herself on such heroines as Judy Garland, Deanna Durbin, and the Lanes."[77]

Adoration of movie stars developed out of a tradition of celebrity for stage stars, but stage actors and actresses rarely gained national fame. The motion picture industry, due to national circulation and the power of the medium, was well positioned to create new

The recent arrival of "Film Favorites" will cause an unprecedented hush in the vicinity of Chattering CHITa.

5.14   Drawing, High School Yearbook, 1925

5.15   *Movie Fan Culture,* Ladies' Home Journal, *March 1946*

American heroes. Rudolph Valentino, a young Italian tango dancer, stood poised to take the evolving hero status to new heights, bringing passion and sexuality to the screen. Audiences, including teenage girls, responded exuberantly. Theaters capitalized immediately on his unexpected death in August 1926 at age thirty-one. Yvonne Blue saw a revival showing of *The Sheik* the day newspapers announced his death. Her response reflected the emerging notion of visual authenticity: "It was rather queer seeing him move across the screen and knowing that all the time he was lying in state, and covered with flowers." For many, though, Valentino retained his magnetism even in death. Years later, high school students used his name freely, confident that the reference would be understood. A teenage girl described her ideal prom date in 1940, "His personality must be tantamount to that of Rudolph Valentino," and a yearbook in 1943 dubbed a popular boy the school's Rudolph Valentino.[78]

Valentino was not the only actor adored by teenage girls in the 1920s. Douglas Fairbanks, "the smiling, clean-cut, genteel American hero," also received much attention. Yvonne Blue, after seeing *Don Q, Son of Zorro* (1925), wrote in her diary at age fourteen, "It was wonderful! Everything that Doug is in is wonderful." Sixty years later, women who were teenagers in the 1930s and 1940s vividly recalled their high school movie idols. Louise Armstrong remembered adoring Errol Flynn and his adventure movies, although she and her friends preferred "love stories whenever we could get to them." Nancy Boyce recalled that Gary Cooper and Tyrone Power were "the leading men who could really attract you."[79]

OGS participants freely expressed their views on movie stars to observers and to each other. Shirley wrote at age fourteen, "I never miss George Arliss" in a film. Amy wrote that her favorite actor was Will Rogers until his death after which she "changed to William Powell, because of his marvelous acting in mysterious motion pictures." A few years later, Helen told an interviewer that she remained faithful to Robert Taylor, even though "All the others have gone back on him. . . . He's been in some bad pictures. That's all." Well into the 1940s, yearbooks cataloged teenage girls "addicted to" Lawrence Olivier and Orson Welles or "eager to meet Spencer Tracy" and listed heroes such as Cary Grant and Errol Flynn.[80]

Teenage girls also admired actresses for a variety of traits—beauty, daring, skill, and on- or off-screen romances. Young women in Blumer's study remembered idolizing female serial stars for their bravery. As small girls, they admired Pearl White's courage or found an outlet in Alberta Vaughn's "sense of adventure." Other childhood favorites included actresses who crossed gender lines to play male roles and access adventure and freedom, such as Betty Bronson in *Peter Pan* and Mary Pickford in *Little Lord Fauntleroy* (1921).[81]

As girls grew into teenagers, their idols shifted from daring heroines to romantic beauties. Girls wrote that they loved Norma Talmadge because she "seemed the perfection of the beautiful" or admired "the languid lasciviousness of Greta Garbo." Thirteen-year-old Katherine Rosner excitedly shared with her diary in 1929, "I received a picture today from Alice White. I'm crazy about her—I think she's adorable, and the picture is simply darling. It's on a black background, so it's very distinct. If ever, as is my hope, I become a movie star, I'll have my fan pictures made on a black background." Rosner admired Alice White's publicity photo and used it as a vehicle for imagining her future and dreams of stardom. Colleen Moore and Clara Bow topped the list of favorites in a study conducted in 1930. Jean Harlow, credited with initiating the "platinum blond" craze and, according to *New York Times* writer Frank Nugent, for possessing "the impudence to make that nasty three-letter-word S-E-X comic," was very popular among OGS participants until her death in 1937 at age twenty-six. Actresses Joan Crawford, Lana Turner, and Hedy Lamarr received attention from girls who hoped to emulate them. High school characters, such as Judy Garland and Deanna Durbin, were admired for their singing talents but did not receive the same devotion—they did not inspire imitation or allow exploration of sexual and romantic fantasy.[82]

Yearbooks usually mentioned girls whose fan activities extended beyond casual interest. One girl collected autographs from any movie star, while another collected only photographs of Tyrone Power. The girls mentioned in these entries most likely relished recognition of their devotion. OGS participants who actively collected movie paraphernalia proudly shared information about their collections. Rebecca, at age fourteen, wrote that her hobby was "collecting movie star pictures. . . . I have over ten hundred pictures." Most fans never saw their idols in person, but seeing any star was exhilarating. Kat wrote excitedly to her friend Frances, "among those present were Mary Eaton of Ziegfield Management and the star in 'Kid Boots' with Eddie Cantor, and also the movie actress, Betty Bronson, so you see what celebrities were in our midst." The pleasure of seeing stars was potent enough to experience vicariously.[83]

Some teenage girls expressed more cynicism about the Hollywood star system, such as this high school senior in a poem entitled "Twentieth Century":

The beautiful goddesses of the screen,
Tony, and Pony, and Marly and Harla,
And, perhaps, as a by-product of the press-agent's

Over-worked brain,
'Tabasco' or 'Sherry' or 'Candy'.
Different names, cute names,
But somehow, their bearers all look alike.
Put on the conveyor belt
And molded and pounded and poured and moulded again
Until the finished product is as sleek
And shining and polished and hard
As a new car.

The false, bright gaiety of the interviewer
And the publicity photo.

She sits, reclining gracefully,
Her body fitted to the curve of the *chaise lounge*
Her head tilted just enough to be pert.
And her beautifully manicured hands
Holding the heavy volume so that its title shows.
And underneath, a caption—
"She reads Tolstoy, to improve her mind."[84]

Many fans could suspend doubt, wanting to believe that the beautiful star read Tolstoy, but others looked beyond the glitter to see the publicity machine. This author resented the manufactured movie star personas, the bodies, names, and interests crafted to sell movie tickets, fan magazines, and a host of consumer goods. Although selling products may have been the intent, an unforeseen outcome was helping teenage girls create a culture of their own, made partially out of the products of movie culture.

Movies and Real Life

In 1940, *Scholastic* magazine published the poem "Never-Ending" by a New York City high school student. The author chided the temporary escape experienced by moviegoers, "regardless of gary cooper, the gasbill will be a little higher this month" and "regardless of her getting him in the end, you'll get a cold early next week." The poem concluded, "Mickey Mouse can do nothing about it / The dirty dishes are still waiting in the sink / Pathe News has no solution for a cheaper washing machine." According to this poem, movies do not shape reality outside theaters and despite the powerful attraction of momentary escapism, audiences leave with nothing tangible: no solutions, paid bills, or clean dishes.[85]

Although this prescient cultural criticism highlights the marketing of dreams and illusions of grandeur, it ignores the powerful messages that moviegoers do take with them as they leave the theater—images of beauty, romantic love, fashion, and the optimistic faith that problems can be resolved in two hours. Teenage girls compared their faces, hair, and figures to those of actresses, bought clothing and accessories endorsed by stars, imitated actions, repeated lines, and sometimes aspired to become actresses. They teased each other about being "movie struck," and used movie stars as cultural references with mutual understanding. Although movies did not wash dishes, they did seep out of theaters and into reality in a multitude of ways.

Movies filtered into the conversations, writings, and self-images of OGS participants. In a dressing room conversation, two thirteen-year-old girls complained about the minimal clothing provided for examinations, "Kid these are terrible, but they wear things just like these in the movies. Just as bad. Right out in the open too." The following year, Gretchen similarly remarked, "Just think the girls in 'Gold Diggers' wear things just exactly like this." When drawing pictures and self-portraits, girls in the study often drew movie stars. Edith commented that her self-portrait looked "more like Janet Gaynor than me." When asked by the interviewer if she wanted to look like Gaynor, she laughed, "Yeah. But I don't." Edith's humor and realism allowed her to accept that she did not resemble Gaynor, especially the highly perfected version on screen or in magazines.[86]

Yearbooks from the 1920s, 1930s, and 1940s frequently mentioned movie stars as points of reference, willing a "Garboish" figure in a 1932 yearbook. Other yearbooks praised girls with a "Scarlett O'Hara waist," for providing "plenty of competition" for Ginger Rogers, or for being "a second Hedy Lamarr." Comparisons with movie stars could also be light-hearted. Beth Twiggar wrote in her diary at age fourteen, "I saw 'Gentle Men Prefer Blonds' today, and I came out firmly resolved to become a gold digger." She then looked into a mirror and wrote, "circumstance plus fate and the weather caused my ambitions to melt. All the gold digging I can ever do will be in overalls with an ax!" Despite Beth's lighthearted humor, comparison brought insecurity and anxiety for many girls. No high school student could achieve the polished, constructed images presented on screen and in movie magazines, and the effort left some girls discouraged.[87]

When teenage girls adopted "personality" as easily as dress and hairstyles, they incorporated the childhood realm of playacting into their increasingly "grown-up" worlds. A college sophomore remembered practicing dance steps from movies as well as "little flourishes; for example we all accepted the hand shake exhibited by Harold Lloyd in 'The Freshman.'" Nancy Boyce remembered her excitement at seeing *The Wizard of Oz,* recalling sixty years later that she and a friend "learned to do that dance, 'We're off to see the Wizard.'" OGS participants discussed learning dance steps or songs, as well as star qualities, from movies. Shirley wished to emulate Kay Francis: "She speaks so beautifully and naturally. The big words just drop out of her mouth." Her friend George joked, "All she says is 'I love you, but I'm going to marry another man.' It's just about love."[88]

Where did this imitation and idealization lead? For some, it led to fantasies of stardom and occasionally to serious acting ambition. For others, glamorized and usually highly gendered careers, such as nursing, caught their attention. Still others aspired to work in the industry itself, as illustrators, writers, or costume designers. Most teenage girls outgrew these adolescent dreams, but their intensity at the time could be strong. One yearbook recorded a senior's "vain longing to act in the movies or on the stage," but another confidently listed a senior's future as "actress." Frances Turner wrote to a friend, "My dear, if Christmas holidays hadn't come when they did I think I would have gone into the movies or eloped or I would have done something rash." For this high school girl in 1922, becoming a movie star or eloping were equally far-fetched fantasies jokingly used for dramatic emphasis. But the reference also demonstrates the existence of such a dream, however remote, for teenage girls frustrated with school, work, or family.[89]

Teenage girls' writings, diaries, and yearbooks demonstrate that movies shaped their lives in many ways. Movies provided a meeting place, date activity, and entertainment. And whether imitating styles, practicing handshakes, or dreaming about careers, teenage girls learned about fantasy and sometimes about reality. Where they drew the lines between fantasy and reality, though, varied, and sometimes caused concern among peers and adults.

One high school junior complained that Hollywood caused the problems of her contemporaries: "No wonder girls of older days before the movies were so modest and bashful. They never saw Clara Bow and William Haines. They didn't know anything else but being modest and sweet." Although she underestimated the imaginations and level of sexual activity among previous generations, she remained convinced that "the movies have a great deal to do with present day so-called 'wildness.' If we didn't see such examples in the movies where would we get the idea of being 'hot'? We wouldn't." Teenagers obviously knew about sex before movies. As seen in Blumer's study, movies may have shifted the boundaries of acceptable behavior, but they did not cause unprecedented "wild" actions. Movies served primarily to reinforce societal norms and ideals.[90]

Yet movie fans also developed media skills—learning how to enjoy movies as well as how to understand and scrutinize them. Although studies usually noted boys' interest in film production, teenage girls also noticed technical aspects. Yvonne Blue wrote in her diary at age fourteen, after seeing *The Ancient Mariner* (1925), "it was wonderful! The part where the poem was filmed was delicately tinted, and it was so soft and beautiful." Yvonne recognized the use of special effects to enhance the mood and appreciated its aesthetic value. After *Phantom of the Opera* (1925), she again discussed filmic qualities: "A great many of the scenes were colored. One beautiful scene was the masquerade ball where the Phantom appeared clothed in a scarlet silk robe with a plumed hat to match." After a French film, Adele Siegel wrote, "I liked only the beautiful photography." Despite her distaste for the plot, characters, and film itself, she was able to appreciate its cinematic achievements.[91]

High school girls also analyzed plot and character development and felt comfortable disagreeing with filmmakers. Students in Perry's study criticized entire genres: "'Those stories in which the hero comes out without a scratch and gets the girl he wants are bunk," or "'I dislike many of the so-called comedies which are humorous only to the feeble-minded." Yvonne Blue differentiated between modes of humor when she saw *Hands Up* (1926): "It was a humorous picture. . . . It was most horribly funny, but not slap sticky like Harold Lloyd, or Charlie Chaplin, tho I like them both."[92]

Finally, some teenage girls analyzed their relationships with the entire movie experience, including responses. Yvonne Blue wrote in her diary in 1926, "I've seen lots of movies—good ones that I haven't written about because the entries dealing with those . . . are so dull." She had previously recorded all movie experiences, listing titles and favorite stars as well as evaluations of plot, cinematography, writing, and direction. She wrote at length about the theaters she patronized and the activities surrounding each visit, from a taxi ride to a date, from ice cream with a friend to unwelcome advances by strange men. After this entry in 1926, at age fifteen, she suddenly found such details tedious and stopped recording her moviegoing, though she continued to attend movies.[93]

Beth Twiggar also stopped writing about movies as her nights and weekends filled with dances, dates, and bridge parties. The authors of Blumer's movie autobiographies frequently commented that as teenage girls grew older, the role of movies in their lives waned. School, a wider circle of friends, greater mobility, and increased social activity consumed their time. Movies did not retain their unique status, but girls continued to see them, form opinions, and remember how it felt to be "movie struck."

ᖇᖇᖇ

By the 1920s, movies had become a way of life for most Americans. Educators, politicians, religious leaders, and some social scientists felt they had lost control of cultural standards and, more importantly, that those who had gained control did not operate in the best interests of young people. Condemnation and calls for censorship appeared with the first kinescopes and continue today, usually exploding at certain crossroads of cultural tension. Those who did not support censorship or thought it ineffective focused instead on education, although their efforts to divert high school students away from "inferior" films were rarely successful.[94]

In the 1920s and especially the 1930s, moviemakers began to include teenagers more systematically as main characters in films and to cultivate actors to play those roles. They did so in the interest of attracting audiences, not of shaping or reflecting teenage culture, but they demonstrated some awareness of this emerging group even when they reconfigured it to promote idealized images. Despite new recognition of the marketability of high school culture, there was little attention paid to high school students as a distinct audience for movies. And the notice they did receive from those promoting movie images and endorsements usually misinterpreted their interest in movies and movie fan culture.

Studios presented high school culture as innocent, light-hearted, and fun. To some extent, moviemakers, and most noticeably creators of movie merchandise, assumed that high school audiences admired and perhaps imitated the bumbling antics of Andy Hardy giddy with excitement over a kiss on the cheek. Yet studies and girls' writings demonstrate that teenage girls learned much more from movies. Through their fascination with adult actors and actresses, as well as with movie fashion and romance, high school students accessed a far different world through fantasy and screen portrayals. Movies challenged parental authority and in contrast to portrayals of high school youth, promoted more adult behaviors through the marketing of adult stars and movies.

Despite the fact that fourteen-year-old OGS participant Edna spoke about movie stars as frequently as other girls in the group did, her mother claimed that her daughter's "interests were on a loftier plane." Edna's mother exhibited distaste for teenage girls' movie culture, perhaps presuming that movie fans were frivolous, uncultured, or less intelligent than she wished her daughter to be. Yet the evidence shows that girls from all backgrounds enjoyed movies and participated in creating their own movie culture. Although some participated more enthusiastically than others, high school girls regardless of education and socioeconomic background shared movie interests and that shared culture served to strengthen their emerging group identity.[95]

Teenagers comprised an important segment of the moviegoing public, attending a range of movies, influencing movie popularity, cultivating fan culture, and purchasing products endorsed by movie stars. Yet studios, publicists, and merchandisers continued to imagine them as little girls who wanted to emulate teen characters rather than romantic leads. Girls ignored this misperception by selecting which movies to attend and which stars to idolize. At some point during their teenage years, most girls replaced passion for movies with real-life infatuations closer to home. Researchers, educators, and community leaders studied, criticized, and sometimes censored girls movie habits. Studio publicists, movie magazines, and merchandisers sought their box office dollars. But girls also felt entertained and empowered. Although Edna's mother flatly denied her daughter's movie interests, Edna felt no shame. She enjoyed the many pleasures of attending movies, as well as the sense of community she experienced while sharing her movie interests with friends. Edna did not consider herself devoid of "loftier" interests.

Teenage girls learned about fashion, beauty, and romance from movies. They adapted movies to their lives and, as with fashion, commercial beauty products, and music, consumed the messages and material goods of movies and movie culture in distinct ways. Despite the industry's tendency to overlook teenage girls as an important group at the box office, girls constructed their own fan culture through scrapbooks, letters, diary entries, decorations, and stories. They shared the accoutrements of movie fan culture with their friends, from photographs and magazines to gossip and fantasy, and formed strong bonds around them. They teased each other about movie interests in school hallways, invented movie star games, imagined themselves as stars and with stars, and shared emotional responses to movies. But as in their relationship with fashion, beauty culture, and music, girls also absorbed, although not unquestioningly, the norms of consumption, femininity, and heterosexual romance.

Conclusion

When is a girl worth $11,690,499?

*... when 1738 advertisers spend just that much money in four years—to sell
her their product and their name in the magazine she reads*

*... when the magazine devoted to her interests surveys her needs—sets up a re-
search department, a consumer panel, a library of fifteen market studies to determine her powerful present, her promising future*

*... when the magazine she buys on the newsstands or subscribes to can show a
150% circulation gain—400,000 copies sold in September '44; 1,000,000 in
September '48*

Seventeen—the magazine that keeps pace with each new generation of teens.

—*Seventeen* Magazine Promotional Brochure, 1948[1]

By 1948, when *Seventeen*'s promotional director circulated this brochure, seen in figure 6.1, to thousands of manufacturers, marketers, and retailers, she confidently presented the magazine's success in reaching teenage girls, conducting research about teenage girls, selling teenage girls to advertisers, and selling products to teenage girls. The teenage girl was "worth" almost $12 million because businesses were willing to invest that much into selling her their products. She was worth this to advertisers because she purchased the magazine and the products advertised in it, spending an estimated $2 billion annually on food, clothing, cosmetics, and entertainment.

Seventeen magazine was instrumental in expanding the consumer market for teenage girls and in reaching readers. The first magazine to target high school girls exclusively, it was well received. Many credited timing with *Seventeen*'s enormous success. During World War II, high school students experienced greater freedom as the country focused on war. They had more opportunity to work and, given the limited availability of durable goods, could spend more money on amenities. A poll in the mid-1940s found that the vast majority of teens felt satisfied with the size of their discretionary spending budgets. By the end of the war, manufacturers promoted a range of products designed

6.1   Seventeen Magazine *Promotional Campaign*

specifically for high school girls, including clothing lines, shoes, jewelry, barrettes, and even greeting cards.[2]

The magazine also appealed to readers because it attempted to make them better teenagers. Helen Valentine, *Seventeen's* first editor-in-chief, envisioned a magazine that would treat teenage girls seriously, that combined "boys and books, clothes and current events, people and politics, cooking and careers" and addressed the future doctor as well as the future homemaker. *Seventeen* was primarily a fashion and beauty magazine that, given its advertising content, cultivated insecurity and the constant need for personal improvement. But true to the editor's promise, *Seventeen* also recommended books on inflation and atomic energy, offered articles on politics and world affairs, and encouraged readers to become active, questioning citizens. The result was a kind of civic consumerism, combining one's duty as a consumer with civic responsibility. *Seventeen's* success, however, was not inevitable. Timing was one factor, but success also drew upon the lessons of the previous twenty-five years. The magazine approached manufacturers and department stores attuned to teenage sizes, styles, and fads, utilizing tested marketing strategies and responding to the enormous interest teenage girls demonstrated in reading about themselves as well as about fashion and beauty culture and their favorite music and movies.[3]

The development of the concept "teenager" was inextricably linked to girls and to the marketplace. As girls entered high school from 1920 to 1945, they exhibited strong interest in commercially defined ideals of fashion and beauty. They eagerly consumed mass-produced fashions, beauty advice and products, music, and movies, responding to industries that attempted to cater to their desires and establishing their own relationships with industries that did not. They used mass-produced commodities to imitate flappers and college students, but they also used them to create fads and define themselves as teenage girls. Girls integrated various products, ideals, and messages into their lives in uniquely "teen" ways and, in doing so, strengthened their emerging group identity and challenged age and gender boundaries as well as mass media prescriptions for their lives.

Defining teenage girls' culture also involves telling a story of manufacturers, retailers, advertisers, and creators of popular culture. Some marketers became aware of high school girls' potential as consumers as early as the 1920s but were unsure of how to approach them and attract their business. Many other industries sold products to teenage girls for decades before noticing their demographic and consumer importance. The clothing industry began to notice high school girls by the 1920s, however unevenly and awkwardly. Movie studios, in contrast, unknowingly depended on the frequent attendance of teenagers at theaters. They experimented with teenage characters in the 1920s, 1930s, and 1940s in films for a general audience, but with little attention to high school life. Long before market researchers specialized in translating teen desires and websites catered to their interests, though, messages from the creators of commercialized fashion, beauty, music, and movies permeated girls' thoughts and world-views, promoting narrow gender roles, insecurity, and self-consciousness about success.

Many factors shaped the creation of a gendered teenage culture, based in large part on the interactions between high school girls and the producers of consumer culture and commercial popular culture. Beyond consumption, it is also a story of identity formation, gender, stages of life, the importance of institutions, and induction into mainstream norms of femininity, commercial beauty, consumer culture, romance, and marriage. Nationally and individually, identity formation and market formation occurred together. From fashion and beauty to music and movies, girls were active in the development of teenage girls' culture, but they were also greatly influenced by the commercial, media, and academic interest in their lives and consumer choices.

Important institutional, social, and cultural changes shaped the formation of teenage girls as a separate group. The rise of high school set the stage, bringing young people together into an age-segregated setting. Psychologists, educators, and social scientists began to recognize the teen years as a distinct stage of life, and the media recognized a provocative subject. The explosion of teenage culture and media attention in the years after World War II, especially in the 1950s, with the strong emphasis on boys has led many to conceptualize teenagers as postwar and primarily male. But the preceding years, 1920 to 1945, were filled with activity by and attention to teenage girls, the first "teenagers" and, in the eyes of marketers, still the most important young consumers.

High school girls responded to adult messages and to teen-directed advertising in many ways. As high school culture emerged, girls found themselves striving to be individuals and members of a group while simultaneously aspiring to be young women. In addition, girls navigated myriad messages about femininity, responsibility for attractiveness, and the primary importance of looks in achieving success in all aspects of life. The degree to which girls absorbed these messages is clear from their diaries, letters, yearbooks, and stories. Girls from the 1920s, 1930s, and 1940s exhibited strong interest in commercial beauty culture and expressed a firm belief in the relationship between commercial goods and looks as well as the connection between looks and popularity. Some girls questioned these mantras more than others, but most repeated them frequently.

Parents, advice columnists, educators, and social scientists applauded and supported these messages. They promoted girls' initiation into the culture of consumption and glamour, emphasizing grooming and self-consciousness about looks. Conflict between adults and girls arose over timing, degree, and standards. Conflict over timing generally centered on when girls could or should begin experimenting with women's—and increasingly "teen"—clothing styles, haircuts, cosmetics, music, dances, and movies. Occasionally this trend reversed itself and girls were hurried into adult grooming practices before they were ready.

Degree and standards were more problematic in relation to norms of femininity and sexuality. Parents expressed interest in having high school girls use cosmetics sparingly with the goal of enhancing a demure femininity and not displaying overt sexuality or "loud" teenage fads. Many girls accepted the emphasis on grooming and appearance, but wanted to experiment, express themselves, and display group loyalties. They wanted to explore the "adult" meanings and fantasies of sexy dances, fast music, romantic movies, cosmetics, and hair dye, often to the dismay of parents. They also wanted to participate in fads and bond with friends through autographed skirts, hats made from phonograph records, or pajama top shirts. Aware of resistance from many parents, the "Tricks for Teens" editor advised mothers in 1941 to "be tolerant" and reminded them that any attention to looks was a "good" sign, the first step in building lifetime habits of grooming, attention to appearance, and devotion to the role of commercial products in perfecting or constructing beauty.[4]

Not all commercial products worked in the same way, however. Fads and bobby sox served to separate girls and heighten group conformity and identity. Evening gowns, lipstick, and some hairstyles allowed girls to dress as young women, to move even further from the ruffles and pigtails of childhood. Music and movies introduced teenage girls to adult themes but also became integral to teenage life and further defined group boundaries. These various media and modes of expression worked in different ways, but all were used by high school girls to explore their roles as teenage girls, as consumers of goods and culture, and as emerging young women.

Manufacturers, marketers, and retailers of clothing were among the first to notice teenage girls as potential consumers in the 1920s and 1930s. Early efforts included direct appeals to girls, such as advertising in high school yearbooks, but these ads often marketed clothes and styles designed for "juniors," primarily women in their twenties. In the 1930s, interest in high school girls heightened, and manufacturers began to create sizes for girls' growing bodies. Attention to special styles took longer and occurred amidst uneven and often poorly designed efforts to create clothing for teenage girls' lifestyles. Marketers were often unsure how to pitch these new styles and sizes and whether to address mothers or daughters directly. Messages, slang, styles, and even sizes shifted throughout the 1930s, but by the end of the decade teenage girls' clothes had become a permanent segment of the industry. By the early 1940s, the size ranges, styles, and marketing strategies began to solidify.

During these industry attempts to define and reach a niche market, high school girls became important shapers of their own fashions. The overall trend was marked by increasingly casual styles, replacing dresses and stockings with skirts, sweaters, and socks. After-school options expanded to include pants, jeans, and even shorts. Although high school girls imagined themselves as flappers and movie stars, they also identified themselves visually as teenagers through fads. Fads highlighted a tension between individuality and conformity that is especially acute during the high school years. Clothing, increasingly expendable in the twentieth century, became a medium for self-expression and self-creation. Girls experimented with casual styles and with adult fashions, trying on roles and testing identities. In an increasingly differentiated market with styles designed for specific times and places, girls fantasized about formal dresses and silky underwear and wore them for special events without abandoning everyday teen styles.

High school girls became active consumers, interested in the range of teenage clothing styles. But they also shopped creatively, aware of the fashions they desired. Girls shopped in the newly formed teen departments, but if the dresses were not sophisticated enough or the sweaters sturdy enough, they borrowed from juniors, women's, or men's departments. Wearing bow ties or their fathers' pajamas, girls explored the boundaries of gender, appearance, and fashion, sometimes using clothes to highlight their figures or femininity, other times to obfuscate them. Through the acts of shopping, manipulating clothes, and experimenting with fads, girls debated parents, educators, and each other. They also rebelled, strengthened friendships and group identity, expressed individuality, and explored adult looks.

In contrast to fashion industry efforts to understand and reach high school girls, decidedly uncertain and inconsistent, the commercial beauty and health industries were slower to recognize girls as consumers. But teenage girls would not wait. They avidly read women's magazines, purchased cosmetics, creams, and beauty aids as they became available, and adopted popular hairstyles. Girls often used beauty products in creative ways, integrating them into friendship rituals, explorations of sexuality and romantic fantasies, and modes of self-expression. Although girls did not naively accept all beauty messages, they frequently mimicked the language of advice literature and advertising, reiterating the need to subdue nature in order to appear "natural." A few companies, such as those manufacturing feminine hygiene products or acne medicine, began to target teenage girls in the 1930s, but not until the 1940s and 1950s did beauty manufacturers offer inexpensive products, smaller sizes, and color names that incorporated slang or song lyrics, such as "Hound Dog Orange" and "Heartbreak Hotel Pink." Long before that time, though, teenage girls used women's beauty culture to be teenagers and to emulate adult women.[5]

High school girls were also in the forefront of their interactions with the music industry in the 1920s, 1930s, and into the 1940s. Despite the occasional mention of young people, the music industry as a whole did not recognize the passion high school students nurtured for music, dancing, and records until the fan and media response first to Benny Goodman and then to Frank Sinatra. Girls, on the other hand, cared deeply about music, whether accessed via radio, records, jukeboxes, or in person. The most dedicated amassed large record collections and skipped school to attend concerts. Others integrated song lyrics into their lives and memories, socialized through dance and music, and analyzed the structure of popular culture through the production of commercial music. High school girls often accepted the norms of heterosexual romance and femininity presented in popular music, but they also found freedom to express independence and release sexual energy through singing and dancing.

The movie industry was similarly slow to assess its audience, despite efforts by social scientists, educators, reformers, and parents to understand the impact of movies on young people. Studies emphasized the frequency of movie attendance among high school students as well as their preferences, and assessed student choices. These studies led to both censorship and education, but neither altered viewing habits. Studio portrayals of high school characters also had little impact on the viewing habits of teenage girls. Movie producers noticed the rising popularity of teenage stars and responded with more, but did so without analyzing who admired these idealized characters. Marketers assumed that high school students comprised the fan base for Deanna Durbin and Judy Garland and advertised endorsed products ranging from school dresses to hair ribbons. Those in the business of promoting movie fan culture, though, filled frequent requests by teenage girls for information and photographs of their favorite romantic leads, handsome male stars and glamorous actresses.

Movies and movie stars, primarily adult actors and actresses, played an important role in the lives of teenage girls, even if the industry as a whole did not notice. Movies provided images of fashion, beauty, and romance, as well as language, music, and dance that teenage girls imitated. The whole movie experience provided an accessible activity for girls, from attending a movie to socializing. Girls used these experiences and the collective culture of movies to define their group, sharing fan magazines and discussing movie-inspired locker decorations at school. Despite contemporary researchers' fears about the insidious influence of movies, most girls found the same messages in movies that they acquired through other forms of consumer and popular culture with which they came into contact, from fashion advertisements to advice literature to music. Some teenage girls questioned the structure and sincerity of the production of movies and other forms of commercial popular culture, but overall they accepted the hegemonic ideals of physical perfection, femininity, and romance. Girls incorporated movies and movie culture into their lives and used them to define their peer group, but they were limited by the prescribed gender roles.

As with the emergence of teenage girls in the 1920s, 1930s, and 1940s, the story of market formation is complex. Manufacturers, marketers, and retailers cultivated girls' consumer desires and insecurities to sell products. Those in the fashion industry actively sought the consumer dollars of high school girls, targeting schools, holding teen fashion shows and contests, and striving to increase self-consciousness about fashion, figures, and grooming. Other industries shaped girls' consumer desires unknowingly, convincing high school girls that they needed commercial beauty products to achieve a "schoolgirl complexion." Teenage girls navigated consumer messages, creating fads, dancing to jazz and swing, and idolizing film stars. Yet they also absorbed societal messages about femininity, heterosexuality, consumerism, and commercial beauty. They challenged parents, schools, adult advisors, and even peers over when and how to interact with these messages, but they did not object to their central tenets. High school girls used consumer culture and popular culture to define their group identity while the producers of those products helped shape that identity, knowingly or unknowingly, and profit from it.

Epilogue

At the beginning of the twentieth century, teenagers did not exist. The cultural conditions for their emergence were in formation, and the years between childhood and adulthood were increasingly viewed as a distinct life stage. One hundred years later, at the beginning of the twenty-first century, it was virtually impossible to avoid teenagers. There were more teenagers than ever before, they spent large amounts of money, and their cultural presence was incontestable. They existed not only as members of a distinct institution and stage of life, but as highly sought-after consumers, carefully watched trendsetters for fashion, entertainment, and new technologies.

Despite the prevalence of teenagers in American culture and life, several authors have predicted their disappearance. Walter Kirn, in a *Time* magazine report on the new millennium, anticipated the end of the teenage years as a distinct phase of life. Kirn argued that high school students increasingly felt the pressures of adult life, such as financial success, the need for health and fitness, and the full legal ramifications of their actions. He also wrote that teenagers increasingly used adult solutions, such as spending money, using drugs and alcohol, taking prescription medication, and consulting professional advice, to handle these pressures. Thomas Hine concluded his book on teenagers with the chapter, "Life After Teenagers." Such predictions are usually based on the argument that teens are growing up faster than ever before and that they are exposed to new responsibilities and enticements that their parents did not experience. This trend, however, leads to a stronger teenage identity. As teenagers gain more household responsibility and fiscal control, their consumer strength increases yet remains specifically "teen."[1]

As with the discovery of the teenage market, proclamations of youth "growing older, younger" have appeared throughout the twentieth century. A young woman in 1922 wrote an appeal to her parents' generation on behalf of flappers, "The times have made us older and more experienced than you were at our age. It must be so with each succeeding generation if it is to keep pace with the rapidly advancing and mighty tide of civilization."[2]

Another meaning of the maxim "They're growing older, younger" that becomes more true each year is the fact that marketers are targeting girls at younger ages than ever before as consumers of clothing, beauty products, music, and movies. Lisa Bannon wrote in 1998 in the *Wall Street Journal*, "Today's kids are growing up sooner than previous generations." She described the growth of children's retail stores that target six- to twelve-year-olds, as well as the rise in fitness clubs, personal trainers, investment funds, and car commercials designed for this age group. Girls, long before they reach their teenage years, want to wear teen fashions and makeup, and stores trying to attract their business are spreading rapidly.[3]

Bannon credited the success of Limited Too, a clothing store for six- to fourteen-year-old girls, with its ability to convince kids "that the store is for them, not their parents or older teen siblings." The stores "are designed as a place to hang out, with comfortable flower-shaped chairs, the latest music and psychedelic flowers and designs flashed on the walls." In addition, the store carries "so-called aspirational clothing, which looks like teen clothing but is cut for a younger girl. Thus, the minis aren't so high and hip-huggers aren't so low, and parents—who still pay for the majority of the clothes—aren't alienated."[4]

The number of companies that specialize in researching and advertising to teenagers and preteens has increased dramatically since the 1940s. Businesses earn large profits by "coolhunting," searching for the hottest trends among teenagers, and selling that information to manufacturers, marketers, and retailers for hefty fees. Teenage Research Unlimited (TRU) declares itself "the nation's foremost market researcher specializing in the teen market" and boasts more than 225 clients, including Abercrombie & Fitch, Kraft Foods, MGM, Verizon, and State Farm Insurance. TRU's client list included ten cosmetic companies in 2003, as competition for teen beauty dollars intensified. Estée Lauder acquired Sassaby in 1997 with the goal of "expanding its line of cosmetics aimed at preteen and teen-age girls." By 2002, many new cosmetic lines sought teen and preteen consumers, including Mary-Kate and Ashley makeup, Mary Kay's teen line "Velocity," and Urban Decay's industrial-colored products. Avon created a "Teen Business" division in 2001 and unveiled its new teen line in 2003.[5]

The teen media market was equally strong in the early twenty-first century. The Magazine Publishers of America announced in 2000 that 233 magazines offered content "aimed at 12- to 17-year old girls." In 2002, circulation of *Seventeen* magazine reached 2.43 million, including fifteen overseas editions, and revenues exceeded $100 million. Newcomers in the twenty-first century included *Teen People, CosmoGIRL, ELLEgirl, Teen Vogue, Latinagirl, Honey* for African American girls, *Jump* for active girls, a host of prom magazines, and *TeenStyle* specifically for hair and beauty. A *New York Times* article in 2003 described the commercial success of AOL Time Warner's WB, "A Network that Serves Youth, and Sells It as Well." A thirty-second advertising slot for the show *Smallville* sold for $110,000, more than a thirty-second slot during the CBS staple *60 Minutes.* In addition, the proliferation of non-commercial girls' magazines and Internet sites has ensured that a multitude of voices speak to and for teenage girls. These zines and virtual magazines have created a new kind of competition but have not hurt commercial sales.[6]

The teenage girls' market is larger, stronger, and more profitable than ever before. As seen in the bottom right corner of figure 7.1, this attention merited a separate section called "Teen Fashions & Accessories" with eighteen store listings in a shopping mall directory in Northern Virginia. All of these stores offer products for teenage girls and many sell items only for girls, still defining the teenage consumer as primarily female. Not only are high school students targeted as viable consumers, but their younger siblings in junior high school and even elementary school are shopping in stores or on websites designed just for them by marketers who study their habits and hold focus groups to determine their preferences on everything from fashion and movies to snacks and cell phones. In 1999, Paul Herman co-created iCanBuy.com, a website that allowed teenagers to maintain a "digital allowance" (funded by a parent's credit card), surf teen-friendly stores, and purchase goods. When he encountered criticism from parents that

ATHLETIC WEAR

Active Edge	A
Champs Sports	I
Eddie Bauer	D
Finish Line	H
Foot Locker	N
Hudson Trail Outfitters, Ltd.	K
Just Sports	D
Lady Foot Locker	C
Washington Redskins Official Store	A

BEAUTY SALONS

The Barber of Seville	B
Blooming Beauty Supply & Salon	N
Bubbles Hair Salon	D
Cartoon Cuts	G
Christie-Adam Salon & Spa	C
Glamour Nails	H
Heidi's Salon	K
JCPenney Beauty Salon	
Nail Pro	P
Outersphere	O
Regis Hairstylists	K

BOOKS, CARDS & STATIONERY

Carlton Cards	E
CVS	I
Family Christian Stores	D
Hallmark, Banner's	P
Papyrus	H
Waldenbooks	D

CANDLES

Bombay Company, The	B
Carlton Cards	E
Creative Candles	H
Hallmark, Banner's	P
Wicks 'n' Sticks	D

CHILDREN'S FASHIONS & ACCESSORIES

abercrombie	D
The Children's Place	H
Gap Kids	G
Gymboree	C
Limited Too	I
Strasburg Children	G
Talbots Kids	K

CHILDREN'S SHOES

Foot Locker	N
Gymboree	C

HOME FURNISHINGS & KITCHEN

Art & Frame	H
The Bombay Company	B
Domain Home Fashions	F
Dry Ice	I
Harry and David	J
Mastercraft Interiors	C
Michael Round - China Silver • Crystal • Gifts	G
Oriental Decor	M
Pottery Barn	G
Pottery Barn Kids	C
Sleep Number Store By Select Comfort	C
Williams-Sonoma Grande Cuisine	O

JEWELRY

Bailey Banks & Biddle	G
Christian Bernard	O
Claire's Boutique	B
Helzberg Diamonds	P
The Icing	F
J.B. Robinson Jewelers	P
Kay Jewelers	D
Littman Jewelers	N
Shaw's Jewelers	K
Watch Station	G
Zale's Jewelers	I

LUGGAGE & LEATHER

Coach	F
Eddie Bauer	D
Fossil	I
Leather Store	D
Travel 2000	N

MEN'S FASHIONS & ACCESSORIES

Abercrombie & Fitch	D
Active Edge	A
After Hours Formalwear (tuxedo rental)	J
American Eagle Outfitters	N
Banana Republic	H
Coach	F
Eddie Bauer	D
Fossil	I
Free Styles	H
The Gap	O
Guess?	J
Hollister Co.	P
Hot Topic	B
Hudson Trail Outfitters, Ltd.	K

SERVICES

After Hours Formalwear (tuxedo rental)	J
Chevy Chase Bank ATM	A
CVS	I
DMV	J
Fairfax Custom Tailors	J
Greensleeves Florists	O
H&R Block	Sears
Hakky Shoe Repair	N
Heartland Cash Network ATM	E, N
InfoExpress Kiosk	E
JJ Watch and Jewelry Repair	J
Jiffy Lube	Sears
Masters Tuxedo	Sears
Mortgage Center of America	O

SPECIALTY GIFTS

Art & Frame	H
Brookstone	K
Chesapeake Knife & Tool	D
Creative Candles	H
Dollar Days	O
Discovery Channel Store	O
Dry Ice	I
Harry and David	J
Michael Round - China Silver • Crystal • Gifts	G
People's Pottery	G
Things Remembered	I
Wicks 'n' Sticks	D

TEEN FASHIONS & ACCESSORIES

Abercrombie & Fitch	D
Active Edge	A
American Eagle Outfitters	N
Claire's Boutique	B
Express	J
Forever 21	H
Fossil	I
The Gap	O
Guess?	J
Hollister Co.	P
Hot Topic	B
Pacific Sunwear of California	P
The Icing	F
The Limited*	N
United Colors of Benetton	C
Water Water Everywhere	K
Wet Seal	D
Mr. Rags	H

TOBACCO

John B. Hayes Tobacconist K

7.1 *Shopping Mall Directory, Fair Oaks Mall, Fairfax, Virginia, 2003*

he was "'turning kids into little consumers,'" he responded, "kids are consumers today anyway." The ideas behind this exchange lie at the heart of the complicated relationship between consumers and creators of commercial popular culture and mass-produced goods. Some claim that marketers and advertisers create desire and turn people into consumers; others maintain that consumers already exist and sellers simply fulfill their wishes. It is a complicated and, to a large degree, symbiotic relationship.[7]

In the 1920s, 1930s, and 1940s, few marketers worked to turn young people into consumers. The emerging advertising industry strove to turn people in general into consumers, promoting new products and ephemeral fashions, but it did not target high school students specifically. Teenage girls established relationships with many industries that remained unaware of their purchasing power and self-identification. During these years, girls absorbed messages of consumerism, yet had some freedom to explore a range of media and messages, selecting among them and trying on new identities. By the turn of the twenty-first century, teenagers were closely watched, studied, and analyzed by fashion, beauty, music, and movie industries. Their preferences were catalogued and their dollars sought after. Attention from the consumer market helped shape an emerging teenage identity, but it also responded to a group identity formed by high school girls. In the twenty-first century, marketers cater to and imitate teenage styles and fashions so closely that teenage culture is less clearly defined by teenagers. And the effort to entice younger and younger girls into a world of consumer goods and self-consciousness intensifies each year.

Notes

Introduction

1. Maureen Daly, "Sixteen," in *Saplings* (New York: Scholastic, 1938), 1–6. Daly's story won a *Scholastic* award in 1938, was reprinted in several women's magazines, such as *Redbook* and *The Woman's Day,* and was produced as a radio play in 1940. Daly published her first novel, *The Seventeenth Summer,* while in college in the early 1940s and after graduating wrote teen columns in the *Chicago Tribune* and *Ladies' Home Journal* as well as advice books for teenagers and novels about young love.

2. Teenage Research Unlimited specializes in market research on teenagers aged twelve to nineteen (TRU, http://www.teenresearch.com/home.cfm, April 3, 2003). Figures from press release, "Store chains get hot catering to teens" (TRU, http://www.teenresearch.com/NewsView.cfm?page_id=150, April 3, 2003).

3. Kathleen Stanley, "When Teens Go to Their Rooms; Gen-Y's Cocooning Now," *Washington Post* (February 6, 1999): C4; Fred Kaplan, "Tapping the Teen Market," *Boston Globe* (December 29, 1998): A1.

4. "A New, $10–Billion Power: The U.S. Teen-Age Consumer," *Life* (August 8, 1959): 78, 83–85; "Teenage Consumers," *Consumer Reports* (March 1957) in Eugene J. Kelley and William Lazer, eds., *Managerial Marketing: Perspectives and Viewpoints* (Homewood, IL: Richard Irwin, 1958), 97–101; Louis Kraar, "Teenage Customers: Merchants Seek Teens' Dollars, Influence Now, Brand Loyalty Later," *Wall Street Journal* (December 6, 1956): 1, 11.

5. Dwight MacDonald, "A Caste, A Culture, and A Market–I," *New Yorker* (November 22, 1958): 57; James Gilbert, *A Cycle of Outrage: America's Reaction to the Juvenile Delinquent in the 1950s* (New York: Oxford Univ. Press, 1986), 205–10; Eugene Gilbert, *Advertising and Marketing to Young People* (Pleasantville, NY: Printers' Ink Books, 1957), 43, 103.

6. *Seventeen* (March 1947): 2; Estelle Ellis, interview by author, tape recording, New York, NY, November 15, 1994; Estelle Ellis Collection, National Museum of American History, Archives Center; Kelly Schrum, "'Teena Means Business': Teenage Girls' Culture and *Seventeen* Magazine, 1944–1950" in Sherrie A. Inness, ed., *Delinquents and Debutantes: Twentieth-Century American Girls' Cultures* (New York: New York Univ. Press, 1998), 134–63.

7. Stanley C. Hollander and Richard Germain, *Was There a Pepsi Generation Before Pepsi Discovered It?: Youth-Based Segmentation in Marketing* (Lincolnwood, IL: NTC Business Books, 1992), 13–14; Margaret V. Cobb, "How College Girls Buy," *Printers' Ink* (August 25, 1921): 111; Ray Giles, "Making Youth the Bull's-Eye of the Advertising Target," *Printers' Ink* (September 14, 1922): 57–60; Kathryn H. Fuller, *At the Picture Show: Small-Town Audiences and the Creation of Movie Fan Culture* (Washington, D.C.: Smithsonian Institution Press, 1996), chs. 8, 9.

8. "Twenty Years of Scholastic: A Brief History of the American High School Weekly," *Scholastic* (October 21, 1940): 21–24, 30; "Campaigning on Future Big Buyers While They Are Students," *Printers' Ink* 93 (December 30, 1915): 10.

9. "Are You A Buyer for Your Family?" *Scholastic* (May 27, 1932): 26; Robert F. Allen, "Talking to the 6,000,000 Rulers," *Printers' Ink* (October 26, 1933): 12–13; "30 Million Young, Eager Prospects for Advertisers," *Printers' Ink* (February 16, 1933): 16; Amos Bradbury, "Advertising to Seven Million Young Skeptics," *Printers' Ink* (February 2, 1933): 17–20; Dewey H. Palmer and Frederick J. Schlink, "Education and the Consumer," *Annals of the American Academy of Political and Social Science* 173 (May 1934): 188–96.

10. For a discussion of the concept of "culture" and its use in historical research, see William H. Sewell, Jr., "The Concept(s) of Culture," and Victoria E. Bonnell and Lynn Hunt, "Introduction," in Victoria E. Bonnell and Lynn Hunt, eds., *Beyond the Cultural Turn: New Directions in the Study of Society and Culture* (Berkeley: Univ. of California Press, 1999), 1–61.

11. Joseph Kett invigorated the study of youth in America in 1977 with *Rites of Passage.* He used the word "teenager" freely, discussing boys almost exclusively, and located the importance of consumer and popular culture in the period after World War II. Writing in the 1980s, James Gilbert looked at the role of consumer and popular culture in creating a new youth culture after World War II, the period, he argued, when "adolescents gained recognition as a distinct new consumer group." Grace Palladino opened her book, *Teenagers,* with high school culture in the 1920s, but argued that the concept of teenagers first became popular around World War II. The rich history before the war has remained largely unexplored. Joseph Kett, *Rites of Passage: Adolescence in America, 1790 to the Present* (New York: Basic Books, 1977), 3–7, 215, 238; Gilbert, *A Cycle of Outrage,* 204–11; Grace Palladino, *Teenagers: An American History* (New York: Basic Books, 1996), xv, xx, 93.

12. In 2001, teens, primarily teenage girls, spent an estimated $17 billion on personal care items, including beauty, hair, and skin products, expressing strong preferences for goods designed for teens with special colors, sizes, and prices. Marylin Johnson, "Hey, Girls, Companies Are Creating Cosmetics Just for You (and Your Wallet)," *Atlanta Journal-Constitution* (May 2, 2002): 13GE.

13. *The Reflector,* Armstrong Technical High School (1923), n.p.

14. Frances Turner Papers, Bryn Mawr School (Baltimore, MD); Beth Twiggar Goff diary, Schlesinger Library, Radcliffe Institute, Harvard University, Beth Twiggar Goff Papers, 90–M130.

15. Yvonne Blue Skinner diary, Schlesinger Library, Radcliffe Institute, Harvard University, Yvonne Blue Skinner Papers, 85–M195; Arvilla Scholfield diary, Walters Family Papers; Katherine Rosner (pseudonym) diary, Schlesinger Library, Radcliffe Institute, Harvard University, Katherine Rosner Papers, 92–M10; Adele Siegel Rosenfeld diary, Schlesinger Library, Radcliffe Institute, Harvard University, Adele Siegel Rosenfeld Papers, 90–M109. Diaries are a unique primary source, personal records that provide insight into daily lives and friendships and record how societal messages are internalized and personalized. By their nature, diaries are incomplete texts, selectively describing feelings and interpretations. But diaries also serve as an outlet, a place to reflect, vent, and interpret one's surroundings. For more on diaries as sources, see Margo Culley, ed., *A Day at a Time: The Diary Literature of American Women from 1764 to the Present* (New York: The Feminist Press, 1985), 11–23; and Joan Jacobs Brumberg, *The Body Project: An Intimate History of American Girls* (New York: Random House, 1997).

16. Betty Goldstein Friedan, high school autobiography and high school diary, 1937–1938, Schlesinger Library, Radcliffe Institute, Harvard University, Betty Goldstein Friedan Papers, 71–62; June Goyne Corotto, Typescript reminiscences, 1984, Schlesinger Library, Radcliffe Institute, Harvard University, June Goyne Corotto Papers, A/C822.

17. June Calender diary, Schlesinger Library, Radcliffe Institute, Harvard University, June Calender Papers, 89-M55; Ruth Teischman (pseudonym) diary, Schlesinger Library, Radcliffe Institute, Harvard University, A–T265.

18. Nancy Winslow (high school graduate 1932), interview by author, tape recording, Baltimore, MD, January 18, 1997; Mary Streeter Farber (high school graduate 1936), interview by author, tape recording, Baltimore, MD, February 24, 1997; Alleyn Moore (high school graduate 1937), interview by author, tape recording, Baltimore, MD, March 28, 1997; Louise Armstrong (high school graduate 1938), interview by author, tape recording, Baltimore, MD, April 4, 1997; Nancy Boyce (high school graduate 1941), interview by author, tape recording, Baltimore, MD, February 28, 1997; Alma Bond (high school graduate 1944), interview by author, tape recording, Baltimore, MD, April 17, 1997; Betsy Smith Hughes (high school graduate 1947), interview by author, tape recording, Baltimore, MD, January 23, 1997; Betsy MacDonald, Jo Booze, and Dorothy Wolff (high school graduates 1950), interview by author, tape recording, Baltimore, MD, April 21, 1997.

19. Mary Cover Jones, et al, eds., *The Course of Human Development: Selected Papers from the Longitudinal Studies, Institute of Human Development, The University of California, Berkeley* (Waltham, MA: Xerox College Publishing, 1971), 4–15; Carol L. Huffine and Elaine Aerts, "An Introduction to the Intergenerational Studies," (Berkeley, CA: Institute of Human Development, 1998): 1–6.

20. Huffine and Aerts, "Introduction," 2–3.

21. A complete list of the names and corresponding numbers is available at the IHD. Jones, et al., *The Course of Human Development*, 4–15; Huffine and Aerts, "An Introduction," 1–6.

Chapter 1—Emergence of Teenage Girls

1. Harvey J. Graff, ed., *Growing Up in America: Historical Experiences* (Detroit: Wayne State Univ. Press, 1987); Joseph Kett, *Rites of Passage: Adolescence in America, 1790 to the Present* (New York: Basic Books, 1977), 4–7, 245; Howard P. Chudacoff, *How Old Are You?: Age Consciousness in American Culture* (Princeton: Princeton Univ. Press, 1989), 82–91, 172–78; John Modell, *Into One's Own: From Youth to Adulthood in the United States, 1920–1975* (Berkeley: Univ. of California Press, 1989), 13–14.

2. G. Stanley Hall, *Adolescence: Its Psychology and Its Relations to Physiology, Anthropology, Sociology, Sex, Crime, Religion, and Education* (New York: D. Appleton and Co., 1904); Dorothy Ross, *G. Stanley Hall: The Psychologist as Prophet* (Chicago: Univ. of Chicago Press, 1972), 309–67; Kett, *Rites of Passage*, 215–45.

3. Kett, *Rites of Passage*, 221–34; Chudacoff, *How Old Are You*, 66.

4. Kett, *Rites of Passage*, 215, 238, 243.

5. *Digest of Education Statistics*, NCES (http://nces.ed.gov/pubs2002/digest2001/tables/dt036.asp); Stephen J. Provasnik, "The Historical Development of Public Schooling in the United States" (unpublished manuscript, 2000).

6. Thomas D. Snyder, *120 Years of American Education: A Statistical Portrait* (National Center for Education Statistics, 1993), 36–37, 55; *Digest of Education Statistics*, 2001, National Center for Education Statistics (http://nces.ed.gov/pubs2002/digest2001/index.asp, February 15, 2003); U.S. Department of Commerce, *Historical Statistics of the United States: Colonial Times to 1970* (Washington, D.C., U.S. Bureau of the Census, 1975), 379.

7. Edward A. Krug, *The Shaping of the American High School, 1920–1941*, vol. 2, (Madison: Univ. of Wisconsin Press, 1972), 120–30.

8. Paula Fass, *The Damned and the Beautiful: American Youth in the 1920s* (New York: Oxford Univ. Press, 1977), 123–29; David Nasaw, *Schooled to Order: A Social History of*

Public Schooling in the United States (New York: Oxford Univ. Press, 1979), 104–30, 161; Paula Fass, *Outside In: Minorities and the Transformation of American Education* (New York: Oxford Univ. Press, 1989), 73–111; Harl R. Douglass, *Secondary Education for Youth in Modern America: A Report to the American Youth Commission of the American Council on Education* (Washington, D.C.: American Council on Education, 1937), 15; Barbara Brenzel, Cathy Roberts-Gersh, and Judith Wittner, "Becoming Social: School Girls and Their Culture Between the Two World Wars," *Journal of Early Adolescence* 5 (1985): 480–82. Historian Reed Ueda writes that high schools at the turn of the twentieth century "institutionalized" a peer society, but this did not coalesce into a distinct teenage culture until high school enrollment rose in the 1920s, 1930s, and 1940s. Reed Ueda, *Avenues to Adulthood: The Origins of the High School and Social Mobility in an American Suburb* (Cambridge: Cambridge Univ. Press, 1987), 119, 150.

9. Kett, *Rites of Passage,* 236–37; Gottlieb and Reeves, *Adolescent Behavior,* 63; Krug, *Shaping of the American High School,* 131–32.

10. I. Keith Tyler and High School Students of the University School, Ohio State University, *High School Students Talk It Over* (Bureau of Educational Research, 1937), 25–30.

11. Robert S. Lynd, "The People as Consumers," in *Recent Social Trends in the United States: Report of the President's Research Committee on Social Trends,* v. 2 (New York: Arno Press, 1979 [1933]), 857; Roland Marchand, *Advertising the American Dream: Making Way for Modernity, 1920–1940* (Berkeley: Univ. of California Press, 1985), xxii, 7, 347.

12. Ray Giles, "Making Youth the Bull's-Eye of the Advertising Target," *Printers' Ink* 120 (September 14, 1922): 57.

13. Oakland Growth Study, Advertisement Test, 1937; Yvonne Blue Skinner diary, May 10, 1924; Adele Siegel Rosenfeld diary, June 13, 1931. These references most likely referred to a game that involved creating puns from common advertising slogans. The individual or team to create the cleverest puns or to distinguish between original slogans and changed ones won. Harry Edwin Eiss, *Dictionary of Language Games, Puzzles, and Museums* (New York: Greenwood Press, 1986), 23.

14. Kathy Peiss, *Cheap Amusements: Working Women and Leisure in Turn-Of-The-Century New York* (Philadelphia: Temple Univ. Press, 1986); Elizabeth Ewen, *Immigrant Women in the Land of Dollars: Life and Culture on the Lower East Side, 1890–1925* (New York: Monthly Review Press, 1985); Mary E. Odem, *Delinquent Daughters: Protecting and Policing Adolescent Female Sexuality in the United States, 1885–1920* (Chapel Hill: Univ. of North Carolina Press, 1995); Fass, *Damned and the Beautiful,* 88–89.

15. Fass, *The Damned and the Beautiful,* 5–25, 380.

16. Fass, *The Damned and the Beautiful,* 5–25, 125–29; Ellen Welles Page, "A Flapper's Appeal to Parents," *Outlook* 132 (December 6, 1922): 607; Maude A. Royden, "The Destructive Younger Generation" *LHJ* (March 1924): 31; Frank Crane, "The Flapper," *Collier's* (October 11, 1924): 23; Bruce Bliven, "Flapper Jane," *New Republic* 44 (September 9, 1925): 65–67.

17. Marguerite Aspinwall, "The Sub-Deb," *LHJ* (July 1928): 79; Aspinwall, "The Sub-Deb," *LHJ* (May 1930): 86; Elizabeth Woodward, "The Sub-Deb," *LHJ* (August 1931): 90; Woodward, "The Sub-Deb," *LHJ* (September 1931): 130.

18. Chudacoff, *How Old Are You,* 3, 118–19; Letter to Adele Siegel. Schlesinger Library, Radcliffe Institute, Harvard University, Adele Siegel Rosenfeld Papers, 90–M109, August 29, 1929.

19. Beth Twiggar Goff diary, December 21, 1928, February 15, 1929.

20. Katherine Rosner (pseudonym) diary, Schlesinger Library, Radcliffe Institute, Harvard University, Katherine Rosner Papers, 92–M10 (hereafter Katherine Rosner diary), February 23, 1929.

21. Katherine Rosner diary, April 4, 1929, May 11, 1929.

22. Modell, *Into One's Own*, 85–105; Fass, *Damned and the Beautiful*, 262–73, 324–25; Beth Bailey, *From Front Porch to Back Seat* (Baltimore: The Johns Hopkins Univ. Press, 1988).

23. Katherine Rosner diary, February 25, 1929; Beth Twiggar Goff diary, Schlesinger Library, Radcliffe Institute, Harvard University, Beth Twiggar Goff Papers, 90–M130 (hereafter Beth Twiggar Goff diary), 1928.

24. Elaine Tyler May, *Homeward Bound: American Families in the Cold War Era* (New York: Basic Books, 1988), 37–57.

25. Richard M. Ugland, *The Adolescent Experience During World War II: Indianapolis as a Case Study* (Ph.D. Dissertation, Univ. of Indiana, 1977), 1, 348; J. A. Simpson and E. S. S. Weiner, *Oxford English Dictionary*, 2d ed. (Oxford: Clarendon Press, 1989), 712–14; Robert K. Barnhart, *Barnhart Concise Dictionary of Etymology* (New York: Harper Collins, 1995), 799. The *Dictionary of American Slang* places "teenager" in 1930 for colloquial use and as standard since 1945. Harold Wentworth and Stuart Berg Flexner, *Dictionary of American Slang*, 2d ed., sup ed. (New York: Thomas Y. Crowell, 1975), 538–39; *Readers' Guide to Periodical Literature* (Minneapolis: H. W. Wilson, 1945), 1667. Advice literature for parents and educators used the terms "teen" and "teen-age" by 1920. M. V. O'Shea, *The Trend of the Teens* (Chicago: Frederick J. Drake and Co., 1920); Leora M. Blanchard, *Teen-Age Tangles: A Teacher's Experiences with Live Young People* (Philadelphia: The Union Press, 1923).

26. See, for example, *Women's Wear Daily* (hereafter *WWD*), August 19, 1930, 3:5; *WWD*, October 18, 1933, 1:6; Sears, Roebuck & Co. catalog (fall 1934), 98.

27. *America's Youth, The March of Time* (Time Life, Inc., 1940); "Life Goes to a Slumber Party," *Life* (January 4, 1943): 72–75; "High-School Fads," *Life* (May 15, 1944): 65–71; "Teen-Age Girls: They Live in a Wonderful World of their Own," *Life* (December 11, 1944): 91–95; *Teenage Girls, The March of Time* (Time Life, Inc., 1945).

28. PTA magazine quoted in Thomas Doherty, *Teenagers and Teenpics: The Juvenilization of American Movies in the 1950s* (Boston: Unwin Hyman, 1988), 42; Dwight MacDonald, "A Caste, A Culture and A Market–II," *New Yorker* (November 29, 1958): 58; Kenneth Leech, *Youthquake: The Growth of a Counter-Culture through Two Decades* (London: Sheldon Press, 1973), 1–2.

29. John Fiske, *Understanding Popular Culture* (New York: Routledge, 1989), 20–21.

Chapter 2—Fashion and Teenage Girls

1. *Forester*, Forest Park High School (Spring 1926), 25.

2. See Elizabeth Ewing, *History of Twentieth-Century Fashion* (New York: Costume and Fashion Press: 1992 [1985]), 119; Lynn Schnurnberger, *Let There Be Clothes: 40,000 Years of Fashion* (New York: Workman, 1991), 357; Sandra Ley, *Fashion for Everyone: The Story of Ready-to-Wear* (New York: Charles Scribner's Sons, 1975), 104–6; and Grace Palladino, *Teenagers: An American History* (New York: Basic Books, 1996), 51–55; 108–18.

3. Sylvia Silverman, *Clothing and Appearance: Their Psychological Implications for Teen-Age Girls* (New York: Bureau of Publications, Teachers College, Columbia Univ., 1945), 12–13; Mary Mildred Knoebber, *The Self-Revelation of the Adolescent Girl: An Analysis of the Attitudes, Ideals, and Problems of the Adolescent Girl from the Viewpoint of the Girl Herself* (New York: Bruce Publishing Co., 1937), 129; Lucretia P. Hunter, *The Girl Today: The Woman Tomorrow* (Boston: Allyn and Bacon, 1936), 7, 25–60.

4. F. F. O'Donnell, "The Adolescent and His Clothes," *The Parents' Magazine* (hereafter *Parents*) 6 (April 1931): 20–21.

5. Oakland Growth Study, Institute of Human Development, Berkeley, California (hereafter OGS), Maria, March 31, 1939; OGS, Peggy, October 2, 1935; OGS, Sue, August 25, 1936; OGS, Sharon, October 2, 1935. Jeanne Eagles played Sadie Thompson, "a woman with an unsavory background" in the stage version of *Rain*. She died of a heroin

overdose in 1929. Joan Crawford played the role in the movie in 1932. *The American Film Institute Catalog of Motion Pictures Produced in the United States* v. F3 (Berkeley: Univ. of California Press, 1971), 1731.

6. Beth Twiggar Goff diary, Schlesinger Library, Radcliffe Institute, Harvard University, Beth Twiggar Goff Papers, 90–M130, 1930 (hereafter Beth Twiggar Goff diary); Adele Siegel Rosenfeld diary, Schlesinger Library, Radcliffe Institute, Harvard University, Adele Siegel Rosenfeld Papers, 90–M109 (hereafter Adele Siegel Rosenfeld diary), January 29, 1931, December 14, 1931; David L. Cohn, *The Good Old Days: A History of American Morals and Manners as seen through the Sears Roebuck Catalogs, 1905 to the Present* (New York: Simon and Schuster, 1940), 285.

7. *Liber Anni,* Dunbar High School (1936), n.p.; *Shepherdess,* Seaton High School (1942), 48–95; *Forester* (June 1945), 21–30.

8. Leora M. Blanchard, *Teen-Age Tangles: A Teacher's Experiences with Live Young People* (Philadelphia: The Union Press, 1923), 160–65; Robert S. Lynd and Helen Merrell Lynd, *Middletown: A Study in Modern American Culture* (New York: Harvest/Harcourt Brace Jovanovich, 1956 [1929]), 159–67, 184–86, 522. See also August B. Hollingshead, *Elmtown's Youth and Elmtown Revisited* (New York: John Wiley and Sons, Inc., 1975 [1949]) on the impact of clothing on high school girls, their friendships, and social world.

9. Knoebber, *The Self-Revelation of the Adolescent Girl,* 122, 128–30. Studies over the next few decades found similar responses. See Mary Shaw Ryan, *Clothing: A Study in Human Behavior* (New York: Holt, Rinehart and Winston, Inc., 1966).

10. Alice Barr Grayson, *Do You Know Your Daughter?* (New York: D. Appleton-Century Co, 1944), 25, 48, 174–76.

11. *Ladies' Home Journal* (hereafter *LHJ*) (April 1941): 125, 128.

12. Silverman, *Clothing and Appearance,* 49–61.

13. Beth Twiggar Goff diary, October 23, 1928.

14. Martha Neall Hogue, "The Scarf," *Saplings* (Pittsburgh: Scholastic Publishing Co., 1931), 89.

15. OGS compilations.

16. *The Reflector,* Armstrong Technical High School (1923); *Quid Nunc,* Roland Park Country School (1943), 8–35.

17. Estelle Ellis Collection, National Museum of American History, Archives Center; Kelly Schrum, "'Teena Means Business': Teenage Girls' Culture and *Seventeen* Magazine, 1944–1950" in Sherrie Inness, ed., *Delinquent Daughters: Twentieth-Century American Girls' Culture* (New York: New York Univ. Press, July 1998), 143; OGS, Margaret, 1945.

18. Fredonia J. Ringo, *Girls' and Juniors' Ready-to-Wear* (Chicago: A. W. Shaw Co., 1924), 33–44.

19. "Dressing the 'Difficult Age' of Thirteen to Seventeen" (May 8, 1926), Oversize Scrapbook 1, Hutzler Brothers Company Papers, Maryland Historical Society (hereafter Hutzler Papers).

20. *Quid Nunc* (1930), 83; *Sidelights,* Towson High School (1930), 140.

21. *Westward Ho,* Western High School (January 1923), 58; *Better Service Bulletin* 83 (June 4, 1930), Hochschild Kohn Company Collection, Maryland Historical Society.

22. *Forester* (Spring 1926), 30; *Forester* (Fall 1926), 83; *Bryn Mawrtyr,* Bryn Mawr High School (1926), 103; *Westward Ho* (Jan 1925), 55; *Bryn Mawtyr* (1925), n.p.

23. *Westward Ho* (January 1925), 54.

24. "Mary Lynn Frocks," *Women's Wear Daily* (hereafter *WWD*) (July 29, 1930): 3:33; "Mary Lynn Frocks," *WWD* (August 19, 1930): 3:35, italics and capitals in original.

25. *LHJ* (September 1932): 24.

26. "Merchandising News from Out-of-Town," *WWD* (September 12, 1934): 19; "Saturday-Sunday Frocks," *WWD* (September 4, 1934): 23.

27. "Dark Color Trend in Teen Party Frocks," *WWD* (September 23, 1936): 23; "Party Dresses Big Feature for 'Teens," *WWD* (October 7, 1936): 10; "High School Girls Want to Dress Like College Girls," *WWD* (August 25, 1937): 23; "'Sophistication' Is It a Teen Dept. Boomerang?" *WWD* (September 21, 1938): 20.

28. *Forester* (1930), 114.

29. *Forester* (1933), 56; OGS, Margaret, May 25, 1938.

30. Sears, Roebuck & Company Catalog (hereafter Sears) (Spring 1933), 14; Sears (Spring 1934), 52.

31. "High School Style Advisory Board in Chicago Stores," *WWD* (September 21, 1938): 22; "'Teen Style Show," *WWD* (September 2, 1936): 12; "At R. H. Macy & Co. Alterations Allow for Teen Dept," *WWD* (August 25, 1937): 22; "Stix, Baer & Fuller opens Hi-School Shop," *WWD* (August 18, 1937): 12; "Saks–5th to Stress 'Little Originals,'" *WWD* (September 9, 1936): 22; "Hecht 'Teen Age' Shop Meets Good Response," *WWD* (September 30, 1936): 21; "Opens 'Hy-Teen' Shop," *WWD* (September 14, 1938): 22; "Twix-Teen Shop," *WWD* (September 11, 1940): 9; "Emphasis on Teen Fashions," *WWD* (September 29, 1937): 22.

32. Sears (Spring 1939), 120; Sears (Spring 1940), 217–18.

33. *General Rule Book,* 1940, 1943, 1944, Hutzler Papers; Inter-office Memos, 1940–1973, Bulletins 146 and 358, Hutzler Papers.

34. *Parents* (January 1942): 72–73.

35. *Maiden Form Mirror* (April 1945): 5, Maidenform Collection, Archives Center, National Museum of American History (hereafter *Maiden Form Mirror*).

36. *Seventeen* (March 1946): 194; Sears (Spring 1934): 90.

37. *LHJ* (February 1936): 60.

38. Frances Coleman, "How High School Girls Buy Clothing," *Journal of Home Economics* (February 1939): 99.

39. Hogue, "The Scarf," 88.

40. OGS, Edna, 1937; Natsuki Aruga, "Continuity During Change in World War II Berkeley, California, As Seen Through the Eyes of Children" (Ph.D. diss, Stanford Univ., 1996), 237–72.

41. Paula Fass, *The Damned and the Beautiful: American Youth in the 1920s* (New York: Oxford Univ. Press, 1977), 227–34.

42. *Westward Ho* (January 1926), 54; "Beer Jackets Worn," *WWD* (July 7, 1937): 25; Advertisement, "Singing in the Rain," *WWD* (September 28, 1938): 30.

43. "Teen-Age Girls: They Live in a Wonderful World of their Own," *Life* (December 11, 1944): 91–95; *The March of Time, Teenage Girls, 1945,* v. 11, no. 11; *Senior Scholastic* (October 22, 1945), 42, italics in original.

44. "Tricks for Teens" (hereafter "Tricks"), *Parents* (February 1941): 84; "Tricks," *Parents* (March 1941): 92; "Tricks," *Parents* (April 1941): 108, italics in original.

45. "Tricks," *Parents* (October 1941): 104; "Tricks," *Parents* (February 1942): 82; "Tricks," *Parents* (May 1942): 94.

46. "Tricks," *Parents* (July 1941): 78, italics in original; Elizabeth Woodward, "The Sub-Deb," *LHJ* (February 1936): 60.

47. *Brownie,* Park School (1938), 17.

48. "Tricks," *Parents* (September 1941): 86; "Tricks," *Parents* (February 1942): 83; *Eastern Echo,* Eastern High School (1946), 125.

49. Berkeley Guidance Study, Institute of Human Development, Berkeley, California, Irene, February 21, 1945.

50. Memo from Arthur Rosenberg Company to Maidenform (December 1930), Maidenform Collection, Archives Center, National Museum of American History; Alice Dowd, "Going After New Customers," *Maiden Form Mirror* (August 1931): 5; Sears (Spring 1934), 90; Sears (Fall 1934), 98; Sears (Spring 1935), 119, italics in original; Schrum,

"'Teena Means Business,'" 151. See also Jane Farrell-Beck and Colleen Gau, *Uplift: The Bra in America* (Philadelphia: Univ. of Pennsylvania Press, 2002), 63, 71–72.

51. Advertisement, *Maiden Form Mirror* (March 1937): 8; "Selling the Young Girl—As the Trade-Editors See It," *Maiden Form Mirror* (April 1939): 6; *Maiden Form Mirror* (July 1945): 7; "New 'Adagio' Series," *Maiden Form Mirror* (February 1939): 1; "Sound Advice to Juniors," *Maiden Form Mirror* (October 1939): 6.

52. "Cooperation of Junior Departments Builds Up Extra Foundation Sales," *Maiden Form Mirror* (October 1935): 5.

53. *Maiden Form Mirror* (July 1944): 6.

54. OGS, Judy, August 30, 1933; OGS, Rita, October 17, 1934; OGS, Evelyn, November 20, 1935; OGS, Rose, November 13, 1935.

55. *Maiden Form Mirror* (February 1944): 2, italics in original; Marjorie Lederee, "We're telling you!" *LHJ* (December 1944): 21.

56. Joan Jacobs Brumberg, *The Body Project: An Intimate History of American Girls* (New York: Random House, 1997), especially introduction and chapter 4.

57. OGS, Spring Vacation Trip, 1938.

58. Editorial Advertisement, *Parents* (June 1942): 90; "Tricks," *Parents* (May 1942): 94; "Tricks," *Parents* (October 1942): 104; "Tricks," *Parents* (August 1942): 80; Brumberg, *The Body Project,* 99–100, 125–30.

59. Woodward, "Sub-Deb," *LHJ* (September 1932): 26; "Girl Hikers Haled for 'Scanty' Attire," *New York Times* (hereafter *NYT*) (June 17, 1935): 19; "Hikers in Shorts Defy Yonkers Ban," *NYT* (June 24, 1935): 3; "Warring Against Shorts," *NYT* (July 26, 1936): IX:9.

60. Yvonne Blue Skinner diary, Schlesinger Library, Radcliffe Institute, Harvard University, Yvonne Blue Skinner Papers, 85–M195 (hereafter Yvonne Blue Skinner diary), February 5, 1927; June Calender diary, Schlesinger Library, Radcliffe Institute, Harvard University, June Calender Papers, 89–M55, February 3, 1954, February 18, 1954.

61. Woodward, "Sub-Deb," *LHJ* (March 1939): 6.

62. "Tricks," *Parents* (July 1941): 79.

63. Helen Wills, "Emancipated Legs Mean Better Sports," *LHJ* (April 1927): 33; "Miss Wills Sets New Style, Plays Tennis Without Socks," *NYT* (April 29, 1929): 18; *Quid Nunc* (1930), 34; *Forester* (1934), n.p.

64. *Quid Nunc* (1933), 33; *Westward Ho* (1939), 101; OGS, Sandra, October 11, 1936; OGS, Deborah, November 4, 1936.

65. Woodward, "Sub-Deb," *LHJ* (August 1935), 58; Woodward, "Sub-Deb," *LHJ* (February 1936): 60; Woodward, "Sub-Deb," *LHJ* (August 1938): 6.

66. Sears (Spring 1938), 164; Sears (Fall 1938), 37, 312.

67. *Eastern Echo* (1940), 52; *Clipper* (1943) 29; *Quid Nunc* (1943), 22; *Brownie* (1944), 40.

68. *Time* (July 5, 1943): 76; *NYT Magazine* (March 5, 1944): 23; *Newsweek* (March 6, 1944): 88; "The Voice and the Kids," *Reader's Digest* (January 1945): 12–14; *Britannica Book of the Year* (Chicago: Encyclopedia Britannica, 1945), 771; *Newsweek* (January 1, 1945): 12, 74; *American Speech* 20 (October 1945): 223.

69. Katherine Rosner (pseudonym) diary, Schlesinger Library, Radcliffe Institute, Harvard University, Katherine Rosner Papers, 92–M10, February 16, 1929.

70. Woodward, "Sub-Deb," *LHJ* (January 1934): 24; Betty Thompson, "Other Deans Waiting," *Saplings* (New York, Scholastic Publishing Co, 1934), 99.

71. Mary Newell Schultz, "Margaret's Debut," *Forester* (1926), 8.

72. Advertisement, *WWD* (September 13, 1939): 11.

73. Yvonne Blue Skinner diary, November 10, 1925.

74. Jean Knight Graham, "Monday to Monday," *Saplings* (New York: Scholastic Publishing Co., 1939), 30; Adele Siegel Rosenfeld diary, December 4, 1931.

75. OGS summary materials; OGS, Maria, March 20, 1936; OGS, Linda, March 25, 1938.

Chapter 3—Commercialized Beauty and Health

1. *Forester,* Forest Park High School (Spring 1926), 25. Similar jokes appeared in multiple yearbooks in this era.

2. Kathy Peiss, *Hope in a Jar: The Making of America's Beauty Culture* (New York: Henry Holt, 1998), 3–4, 53–55; Joan Jacobs Brumberg, *The Body Project: An Intimate History of American Girls* (New York: Random House, 1997), xx-xxi.

3. Peiss, *Hope in a Jar,* 134, 169–73, 190; Brumberg, *Body Project,* 70–76.

4. Peiss, *Hope in a Jar,* 122–33; Roland Marchand, *Advertising the American Dream: Making Way for Modernity, 1920–1940* (Berkeley: Univ. of California Press, 1985), 10–16, 103–4.

5. Elizabeth Woodward, "The Sub-Deb," *Ladies' Home Journal* (hereafter *LHJ*) (May 1931): 138; Woodward, "The Sub-Deb," *LHJ* (October 1932): 27

6. Woodward, "The Sub-Deb," *LHJ* (August 1935): 58; Woodward, "The Sub-Deb," *LHJ* (August 1940): 6; Woodward, "The Sub-Deb," *LHJ* (November 1940): 6.

7. Joan Jacobs Brumberg, *Fasting Girls: The History of Anorexia Nervosa* (New York: Penguin Books, 1988), 246–55; Brumberg, *Body Project,* 97–107.

8. Yvonne Blue Skinner diary, Schlesinger Library, Radcliffe Institute, Harvard University, Yvonne Blue Skinner Papers, 85–M195 (hereafter Yvonne Blue Skinner diary), July 1926, April 17, 1927.

9. Beth Twiggar Goff diary, Schlesinger Library, Radcliffe Institute, Harvard University, Beth Twiggar Goff Papers, 90–M130 (hereafter Beth Twiggar Goff diary), February 25, 1928, May 3, 1928, July 11, 1928, March 1930.

10. *Dictum Est,* Red Bluff Union High School (1928), n.p.; *Quid Nunc,* Roland Park Country School (1928), 33; *Bryn Mawrtyr,* Bryn Mawr School (1931), 16; *Right Angle,* Maryland Park High School (1932), 22; *Quid Nunc* (1943), 35; *What-Not,* Girls' Latin School (1946), n.p.

11. Louise Paine Benjamin, "What Daughters Know About Beauty," *LHJ* (October 1937), 31; Alice Barr Grayson, *Do You Know Your Daughter?* (New York: D. Appleton-Century Co., 1944), 46.

12. Brumberg, *Body Project,* 98; Peiss, *Hope in a Jar,* 106; Marchand, *Advertising,* 18–20, 355.

13. Marchand, *Advertising,* 18–20; Advertisement, "Odorono," *LHJ* (July 1928): 82.

14. Marchand, *Advertising,* 114, 218–20; Oakland Growth Study, Institute of Human Development, Berkeley, California (hereafter OGS), Barbara, fall 1932; OGS, Elizabeth, November 14, 1934.

15. Beth Twiggar Goff diary, 1928.

16. Beth Twiggar Goff diary, October 21, 1928; Benjamin, "What Daughters Know," 121.

17. Beth Twiggar Goff diary, August 7, 1931.

18. OGS, Jean, November 14, 1933; OGS, Helen, September 26, 1934.

19. Peiss, *Hope in a Jar,* 150–51; *Quid Nunc* (1936), n.p.; *Brownie,* The Park School (1938), 17.

20. Marchand, *Advertising,* 187; *Forester* (1933), 56; *Forester* (1939), 84; *Clipper,* Patterson Park High School (1944), 27. The election of 1876 was notorious for extensive allegations of fraud, leading to the establishment of an electoral commission and the eventual although embittered approval of Rutherford B. Hayes as the nineteenth president of the United States.

21. Girls in the early nineteenth century typically began to menstruate at age fifteen or sixteen. The average age has remained relatively constant for the past fifty years, although the age of the youngest girls to begin menstruating has dropped. Brumberg, *Body Project,* 3–25, 30; U.S. Department of Health, Education, and Welfare, "Age at Menarche, United States" (Rockville, MD: National Center for Health Statistics, 1973).

22. Brumberg, *Body Project,* 29–55; Advertisement, "Kotex," *LHJ* (1921) in Ad*Access (http://scriptorium.lib.duke.edu:80/adaccess/index.html), Ad number BH0231, November

15, 2002; Advertisement, "Kotex," *LHJ* (1922) in Ad*Access (http://scriptorium.lib. duke.edu:80/adaccess/index.html), Ad number BH0232, November 15, 2002.

23. OGS, Anna, fall 1932.

24. OGS, Mary, January 11, 1933; OGS, Doris, April 1, 1936.

25. Brumberg, *Body Project*, 45–49; Advertisement, "Kotex," *Delineator* (September 1935), inside back cover.

26. Advertisement, "Kotex," *The Parents' Magazine* (hereafter *Parents*) (February 1942): inside front cover.

27. June Goyne Corotto, Typescript reminiscences, 1984, Schlesinger Library, Radcliffe Institute, Harvard University, June Goyne Corotto Papers, A/C822, 27; Ruth Teischman (pseudonym) diary, Schlesinger Library, Radcliffe Institute, Harvard University, A-T265, September 17, 1959.

28. *Sidelights,* Towson High School (1931), 133. For an example of the "Schoolgirl Complexion" campaign, see Ad*Access (http://scriptorium.lib.duke.edu:80/adaccess/index. html), Ad number BH1245, July 17, 2003.

29. *Quid Nunc* (1931), 89; *Pine Tree,* Bethesda-Chevy Chase High School (1933), 62; *Brownie* (1944), 40.

30. Brumberg, *Body Project*, 59–94.

31. Beth Twiggar Goff diary, 1928; Letter from Leon Lessler to NBC President, Mr. Aylesworth, October 11, 1935, Library of Congress, Performing Arts Reading Room.

32. Louise Paine Benjamin, "Young Skin Needs Watching," *LHJ* (July 1941): 94, 104; Advertisement, "Poslam," *Scholastic Magazine* (November 2, 1942): 39.

33. Peiss, *Hope in a Jar,* 99–100, 121–22.

34. Beth Twiggar Goff diary, 1928.

35. Beth Twiggar Goff diary, 1928.

36. *Rarebit,* Oldfields School (1932), n.p.; *Bryn Mawrtyr* (1935), 95; *Westward Ho,* Western High School (1945), 29; *Eastern Echo,* Eastern High School (1947), 108; *Liber Anni,* Dunbar High School (1931), n.p.

37. Peiss, *Hope in a Jar,* 97, 103, 151–55.

38. Peiss, *Hope in a Jar,* 194–95; OGS, Evelyn, March 16, 1937.

39. Peiss, *Hope in a Jar,* 252; Brumberg, *Body Project,* 66–70; *Westward Ho* (March 1925), 9, 45.

40. Woodward, "The Sub-Deb," *LHJ* (May 1931): 138; Woodward, "The Sub-Deb," *LHJ* (May 1932): 104; Woodward, "The Sub-Deb," *LHJ* (October 1932): 27; Yvonne Blue Skinner diary, January 10, 1925, October 25, 1925.

41. Beth Twiggar Goff diary, 1928, March 17, 1928.

42. Mary Elizabeth Evernden, "Sonnet to the Lady of the Sign-Board," *Saplings* (New York: Scholastic Publishing Co., 1933), 70; OGS, Rita, March 30, 1938.

43. *The Reflector,* Armstrong Technical High School (1924), n.p.; *Forester* (1937), 105.

44. Beth Twiggar Goff diary, 1928, 1929.

45. Beth Twiggar Goff diary, 1929.

46. OGS, Judith, October 12, 1934; OGS, Lillian, May 29, 1935; OGS, Jean, April 5, 1934.

47. OGS, Margaret, June 2, 1936; Kathy Peiss, *Cheap Amusements: Working Women and Leisure in Turn-of-the-Century New York* (Philadelphia: Temple Univ. Press, 1986); Elizabeth Ewen, *Immigrant Women in the Land of Dollars: Life and Culture on the Lower East Side, 1890–1925* (New York: Monthly Review Press, 1985), 197–201.

48. OGS, Elizabeth, 1934; OGS, Olivia, September 12, 1934; OGS, Meredith, 1934.

49. OGS, Mary, October 10, 1934; OGS, Wilma, September 12, 1934; OGS, Dorothy, October 7, 1936; OGS, Beverly, November 18, 1936, emphasis in original.

50. OGS, Anna, March 9, 1938; OGS, Nancy, December 2, 1936; OGS, Joyce, November 20, 1935; OGS, Deborah, October 10, 1934; OGS, Anna, March 31, 1937; OGS, Rita, October 23, 1935; OGS, Olivia, February 19, 1936; OGS, Eloise, April 3, 1935.

51. Promotional material from *Seventeen* magazine, Estelle Ellis Personal Collection.

52. Peiss, *Hope in a Jar*, 129–30; Frances Turner Papers, Bryn Mawr School, n.d.; *Forester* (fall 1926), n.p.

53. Yvonne Blue Skinner diary, March 26, 1927; Beth Twiggar Goff diary, June 30, 1928, July 21, 1928.

54. Beth Twiggar Goff diary, 1930; *Silverlogue*, Takoma-Silver Spring High School (1931), 40; *Quid Nunc* (1933), 26; *Forester* (June 1937) 105; *Forester* (1938), 106.

55. OGS, Virginia, August 23, 1933; OGS, Lillian, December 4, 1935; OGS, Elizabeth, May 20, 1936.

56. *Bryn Mawrtyr* (1932), n.p.; *Sidelights* (1939), 45; *Forester* (1932), 23; *Eastern Echo* (1940), 35–59.

57. *Quid Nunc* (1935), 10, 13; *Shepherdess*, Seaton High School (1942), 79; *Quill*, newsletter, Bryn Mawr School (March 11, 1942): 1.

58. Peiss, *Hope in a Jar*, 103, 245–46; Marguerite Aspinwall, "The Sub-Deb," *LHJ* (June 1930), 77; OGS, Sue, September 6, 1933.

59. OGS, Sharon, October 2, 1935; *Quid Nunc* (1936), n.p.; *Bryn Mawrtyr* (1937), 21; *Sidelights* (1939), 32, 35.

60. Peiss, *Hope in a Jar*, 19–20, 98; Yvonne Blue Skinner diary, July 26, 1923.

61. Advertisement, "Seventeen Perfume," *LHJ* (October 1930), 141; *Bryn Mawrtyr* (1932), 16.

62. *Forester* (1939), 84.

63. "Tricks for Teens" (hereafter "Tricks"), *Parents* (February 1941): 84; "Tricks," *Parents* (April 1941): 113; Advertisement, "Tween-Age Jewelry," *Parents* (June 1941): 94; Advertisement, "Beau Belle Jewelry," *Parents* (March 1942): 88.

64. "Tricks," *Parents* (February 1941): 84; "Tricks," *Parents* (March 1941): 92; "Tricks," *Parents* (April 1941): 113; "Tricks," *Parents* (August 1941): 80.

65. "Tricks," *Parents* (August 1941): 80; "Tricks," *Parents* (February 1942): 83; "Tricks," *Parents* (March 1944): 107.

66. Mary Trasko, *Daring Do's: A History of Extraordinary Hair* (Paris: Flammarion, 1994), 109–10; Betty Smith, *A Tree Grows In Brooklyn* (New York: Harper Collins, 1992 [1943]), 217, 327.

67. Trasko, *Daring Do's*, 110, 113; Letter to Frances Turner, Bryn Mawr School (hereafter Letter to Frances Turner), November 5, 1918.

68. Yvonne Blue Skinner diary, September 3, 1924, September 14, 1924, June 21, 1925, May 4, 1927.

69. Letter to Frances Turner, January 9, 1926; Aspinwall, "The Sub-Deb," *LHJ* (May 1930), 86.

70. *Quid Nunc* (1928), 7; *Forester* (1929), 100.

71. Peiss, *Hope in a Jar*, 61–62.

72. Trasko, *Daring Do's*, 107; *Bryn Mawrtyr* (1922), 18; *Bryn Mawrtyr* (1926), 26, italics in original; *Quill* (February 15, 1926), 2.

73. Advertisement, "Gerardine," *LHJ* (October 1931): 176; *Dictum Est* (1928), n.p.; OGS, Betty, August 29, 1938; OGS, Edna, April 13, 1934; OGS, Doris, April 14, 1937.

74. Yvonne Blue Skinner diary, August 13, 1926; *Bryn Mawrtyr* (1941), 40: Peiss, *Hope in a Jar*, 206–15; *Liber Anni* (1931), n.p.

75. Trasko, *Daring Do's*, 117–18; *Pine Tree* (1933), 62; *Rarebit* (1932), n.p.

76. OGS, Virginia, September 4, 1935; OGS, Grace, November 14, 1934; OGS, Anna, October 14, 1936; OGS, Anna, September 29, 1937; OGS, Betty, January 20, 1938; *Bryn Mawrtyr* (1942), 23; *Bryn Mawrtyr* (1945), 9, 10; *Westward Ho* (1945), 36; *Brownie* (1948), 23.

77. OGS, Louise, January 7, 1939; OGS, Joyce, March 9, 1938; OGS, Sally, n.d.

78. *Brownie* (1946), 38; "Tricks," *Parents* (August 1942): 80; *Bryn Mawrtyr* (1947), 12.

79. Yvonne Blue Skinner diary, January 9, 1926; *Bryn Mawrtyr* (1941), 40; OGS, Maria, October 31, 1936; OGS, Cynthia, 1937.
80. *Quill* (March 11, 1942): 2.
81. Grace Watson, "Results," *Saplings* (New York: Scholastic Publishing Co., 1932), 59.

Chapter 4—Music, Radio, and Dance

1. Ray Giles, "Making Youth the Bull's-Eye of the Advertising Target," *Printers' Ink* (September 14, 1922): 60.
2. For a discussion of reading popular culture and examining multiple meanings in popular culture, see John Fiske, *Understanding Popular Culture* (New York: Routledge, 1991).
3. Theodor W. Adorno, with George Simpson, "On Popular Music," in *Studies in Philosophy and Social Science* 9 (New York: Institute of Social Research, 1941), 25–42.
4. Ross Firestone, *Swing, Swing, Swing: The Life and Times of Benny Goodman* (New York: W. W. Norton and Co., 1993), 149; Philip K. Eberly, *Music in the Air: America's Changing Tastes in Popular Music, 1920–1980* (New York: Hastings House, 1982), 86.
5. Lewis Erenberg, "Things to Come: Swing Bands, Bebop, and the Rise of a Postwar Jazz Scene," in Lary May, ed., *Recasting America: Culture and Politics in the Age of Cold War* (Chicago: Univ. of Chicago Press, 1989), 224–26; Peter Gammond, *The Oxford Companion to Popular Music* (Oxford: Oxford Univ. Press, 1991), 290–94, 560–61; Benny Goodman, "What Swing Really Does to People," *Liberty* (May 14, 1938): 6.
6. James Lincoln Collier, *Benny Goodman and the Swing Era* (New York: Oxford Univ. Press, 1989), 190–92; Erenberg, "Things to Come," 234; Firestone, *Swing,* 197–201.
7. Henry A. Steig, "Profiles: Alligators' Idol," *New Yorker* (April 17, 1937): 27–33; "1,500 Storm Theatre to Receive Goodman," *New York Times* (hereafter *NYT*) (January 17, 1938): 17; "Vendetta, Or A Clarinetists' Revenge: Benny Goodman Swings Into a Campaign to Drive Films from the Theatres," *NYT* (January 30, 1938): X:5; "Swing Bands Put 23,400 in Frenzy," *NYT* (May 30, 1938): 13.
8. Editorial, "Hot Music at Carnegie," *NYT* (January 18, 1938): 22; "Swing Viewed as 'Musical Hitlerism,'" *NYT* (November 2, 1938): 25; Adorno, "On Popular Music," 42–48; "Warns of Effects of 'Swing' on Youth," *NYT* (October 26, 1938): 20.
9. Firestone, *Swing,* 239–40; "From Toscanini to Memphis Minnie," *Printers' Ink Monthly* (November 1938): 5, 58.
10. "News of the Night Clubs: The Decline of Swing," *NYT* (August 7, 1938): IX:8.
11. Letter to Frances Turner, Bryn Mawr School, August 28, 1925; Katherine Rosner (pseudonym) diary, Schlesinger Library, Radcliffe Institute, Harvard University, Katherine Rosner Papers, 92–M84 (hereafter Katherine Rosner diary), February 21, 1929.
12. Katherine Rosner diary, March 9, 1929, March 10, 1929; *Bryn Mawrtyr,* Bryn Mawr School (1939), 8; *Bryn Mawrtyr* (1940), 22; "Tricks for Teens" (hereafter "Tricks"), *The Parents' Magazine* (hereafter *Parents*) (April 1941): 110; "Tricks," *Parents* (December 1941): 102.
13. *Westward Ho,* Western High School (1926), 51; *Shepherdess,* Seaton High School (1942), 60; *Britannica Book of the Year* (Chicago: Encyclopedia Britannica, Inc., 1945), 771; *Quid Nunc,* Roland Park Country School (1939), 40–41.
14. Gammond, *Oxford Companion,* 308; Eberly, *Music in the Air,* 86; June Goyne Corotto, Typescript reminiscences, 1984, Schlesinger Library, Radcliffe Institute, Harvard University, June Goyne Corotto Papers, A/C822 (hereafter June Goyne Corotto papers), 27; *Yearling,* Cambridge High School (1944), 27.
15. *Eastern Echo,* Eastern High School (1940), 24; *Brownie* (1947), 26.
16. U.S. Bureau of the Census, *Historical Statistics of the United States, Colonial Times to 1970,* Bicentennial ed. (Washington, D.C.: U.S. Government Printing Office, 1976), 796; U.S.

Census Bureau, *Statistical Abstract of the United States: 1999,* 119th ed. (Washington, D.C.: U.S. Government Printing Office, 1999), 885.

17. *Dictum Est,* Red Bluff Union High School (1928), n.p.; Beth Twiggar Goff diary, Schlesinger Library, Radcliffe Institute, Harvard University, Beth Twiggar Goff Papers, 90–M130 (hereafter Beth Twiggar Goff diary), 1929.

18. *The Ship,* Federalsburg High School (June 1934), 41; *Rarebit,* Oldfields School (1932), n.p.; Letter to Adele Siegel, Schlesinger Library, Radcliffe Institute, Harvard University, Adele Siegel Rosenfeld Papers, 90–M109, February 2, 1930.

19. Paul Witty, Sol Garfield, and William Brink, "Interests of High-School Students in Motion Pictures and the Radio," *Journal of Educational Psychology* 32 (March 1941): 176–84, italics in original; Alice P. Sterner, *Radio, Motion Picture, and Reading Interests: A Study of High School Pupils* (New York: Teachers College, Columbia Univ., 1947), 31–36.

20. I. Keith Tyler and High School Students of the University School, Ohio State University, *High School Students Talk It Over* (Bureau of Educational Research, 1937), 37.

21. Oakland Growth Study, Institute of Human Development, Berkeley, California (hereafter OGS), compilations, 1936–1938; OGS, Margery, October 13, 1937, emphasis in original.

22. *Your Hit Parade* was also known as *Hit Parade* and *Lucky Strike Hit Parade.* Eberly, *Music in the Air,* 126–30; Russell Sanjek, *American Popular Music and Its Business: The First Four Hundred Years, v. 3, From 1900 to 1984* (New York: Oxford Univ. Press, 1988), 87, 165–66, 433; *Your Hit Parade* (October 1936); "Reminiscences," June Goyne Corotto Papers, 27; Betsy Smith Hughes (high school graduate 1947), interview by author, tape recording, Baltimore, MD, January 23, 1997.

23. Tyler, *High School Students,* 39, 40; OGS, Advertisement Test, 1937; *Your Hit Parade* (October 1936); *Your Hit Parade* (October 1936); "Your Hit Parade," Museum of Broadcast Communications, Archives (http://www.museum.tv/archives/etv/Y/htmlY/yourhitpara/yourhitpara.htm), November 8, 2003.

24. *Bryn Mawrtyr* (1945), 19; *Westward Ho* (1940), n.p.

25. Tyler, *High School Students,* 35.

26. Jean Breeskin, "Impressions," *Bryn Mawrtyr* (1936), 53–54.

27. Laurette Virginia Pizer, "The Radio Is Democratic," *Saplings* (New York: Scholastic Publishing Co., 1940), 68–69.

28. Arvilla Scholfield diary, 1926, Walters Family Papers, January 22, 1926, March 20, 1926, February 27, 1926.

29. Katherine Rosner diary, March 9, 1929; *Bryn Mawrtyr* (1931), 25; *Bryn Mawrtyr* (1932), 9; *Quid Nunc* (1935), 10; *Liber Anni,* Dunbar High School (1925), n.p.; Yvonne Blue Skinner diary, Schlesinger Library, Radcliffe Institute, Harvard University, Yvonne Blue Skinner Papers, 85–M195 (hereafter Yvonne Blue Skinner diary), July 31, 1923.

30. Beth Twiggar Goff diary, 1929, July 28, 1930; *Forester,* Forest Park High School (1933), 114; *Westward Ho* (1936), 107.

31. *Bryn Mawrtyr* (1937), 11; *Forester* (1937), 50; *Bryn Mawrtyr* (1939), 16; *Towers,* Notre Dame of Maryland Preparatory School (1943), 14; *Quid Nunc* (1943), 43; Cecilia McGee, "Modern Graduate," *Westward Ho* (1940), n.p.; Helen Daufmann, "From Ragtime to Swing: A Short History of 'Popular Music,'" *Scholastic* 32 (April 30, 1938): 29–32.

32. Yvonne Blue Skinner diary, July 31, 1923; *Quid Nunc* (1928), 28; *Bryn Mawrtyr* (1931), 25; *Quid Nunc* (1935), 10.

33. OGS, compilations, 1935–1939; *Bryn Mawrtyr* (1940), 20; *Westward Ho* (1945), 20.

34. Beth Twiggar Goff diary, September 5, 1928.

35. *Rarebit* (1932), n.p.; *Sidelights,* Towson High School (1939), 6.

36. *Sidelights* (1939), 37, 45.

37. "Tricks," *Parents* (November 1941): 102; "Tricks," *Parents* (March 1944): 107; "Tricks," *Parents* (December 1943): 125; "Tricks," *Parents* (January 1944): 77.

38. *Bryn Mawrtyr* (1939), n.p.

39. Kathy Peiss, *Cheap Amusements: Working Women and Leisure in Turn-of-the-Century New York* (Philadelphia: Temple Univ. Press, 1986), especially chapter 4; Eberly, *Music in the Air,* 86; John Modell, *Into One's Own: From Youth to Adulthood in the United States, 1920–1975* (Berkeley: Univ. of California Press, 1989). On the creation of teen canteens, see Richard M. Ugland, *The Adolescent Experience During World War II: Indianapolis as a Case Study* (Ph.D. Dissertation, Univ. of Indiana, 1977), 313–15; Grace Palladino, *Teenagers: An American History* (New York: Basic Books, 1996), 86–89; California Department of Youth Authority, *Teen Centers* (Waterman, CA: California Youth Authority, 1944).

40. *Shasta Daisy,* Shasta Union High School (1928), 96.

41. Arvilla Scholfield diary, January 9, 1926, January 16, 1926, March 13, 1926, April 24, 1926, July 31, 1926, December 11, 1926.

42. *Liber Anni* (1932), n.p.; OGS, Virginia, September 4, 1935; OGS, Ruth, April 1, 1936; OGS, Sharon, February 24, 1937.

43. *Sidelights* (1939), 36; OGS, Nancy, March 20, 1936.

44. *Bryn Mawrtyr* (1937), 11; *Bryn Mawrtyr* (1938), 23; *Quid Nunc* (1939), 58; *Eastern Echo* (1940), 58; *Bryn Mawrtyr* (1940), 22.

45. OGS, compilations, 1935–1939.

46. OGS, Betty, February 19, 1937; OGS, Milk Fund Dance, November 21, 1938; OGS, Linda, March 25, 1938.

47. *Quid Nunc* (1928), 27; *Forester* (1929), 30; *Shepherdess* (1942), 55; *Clipper,* Patterson Park High School (1943), 35; *Liber Anni* (1939), n.p.

48. OGS, Caroline, October 24, 1935; OGS, Melinda, March 5, 1936.

49. OGS, Ruth, April 1, 1936; OGS, Frances, October 6, 1938.

50. Peiss, *Cheap Amusements,* 89; Angela McRobbie, "Dance and Social Fantasy," in Angela McRobbie and Mica Nava, *Gender and Generation* (London: MacMillan, 1984), 130–42.

51. Arvilla Scholfield diary, January 17, 1926; January 26, 1926.

52. OGS, Virginia, September 16, 1936; OGS, Sarah, August 31, 1937; *Quid Nunc* (1943), 9; OGS, Anna, January 7, 1939.

53. Advertisement, Arthur Murray dance lessons, *Senior Scholastic* (February 16, 1929):15.

54. Elizabeth Woodward, "The Sub-Deb," *Ladies' Home Journal* (hereafter *LHJ*) (May 1933): 89; Woodward, "The Sub-Deb," *LHJ* (October 1934): 76.

55. Woodward, "The Sub-Deb," *LHJ* (February 1938): 6; Woodward, "The Sub-Deb," *LHJ* (August 1938): 6; Woodward, "The Sub-Deb," *LHJ* (December 1939): 6.

56. *Women's Wear Daily* (hereafter *WWD*) (September 29, 1937): 19; *WWD* (September 14, 1938): 22.

57. J. A. Simpson and E. S. C. Weiner, *Oxford English Dictionary,* 2d ed., v. 8 (Oxford: Clarendon Press, 1989), 244–45; J. E. Lighter, ed., *Random House Historical Dictionary of American Slang,* v. 2 (New York: Random House, 1997), 285; Harold Wentworth and Stuart B. Flexner, *Dictionary of American Slang,* 2d sup. ed. (New York: Thomas Y. Crowell, 1975 [1962]), 293.

58. "Speaking of Pictures . . . Jitterbugs and Ickeys," *Life* (February 21, 1938): 4–5, 7; Steig, "Profiles," 27–33; "Swing Bands Put 23,4000 in Frenzy."

59. *Quid Nunc* (1939), 21; *Clipper* (February 1943), 17; *Clipper* (June 1943), 29–38; *Agnesian,* Mt. Saint Agnus High School (1941), 21.

60. Gammond, *Oxford Companion,* 27, 138, 582–83.

61. Gammond, *Oxford Companion,* 138–39; Neil McCaffrey, "I Remember Frankee," in Steven Petkov and Leonard Mustazza, eds., *The Frank Sinatra Reader* (New York: Oxford Univ. Press, 1995), 17–21, 50–52.

62. Shaw, "Sinatrauma," 20; E. J. Kahn, Jr., "Phenomenon: I—The Voice with the Gold Accessories," *The New Yorker* (October 26, 1946): 36–37.

63. E. J. Kahn, Jr., "Phenomenon: II—The Fave, The Fans, and the Fiends," *The New Yorker* (November 2, 1946): 35–48; Bruce Bliven, "The Voice and the Kids," *Readers' Digest* (January 1945): 12–14; "Swoonatra Girl," *Hi There High School* (New York: Scholastic Corp., 1944), 72; *Eastern Echo* (1946), 125.

64. Bliven, "The Voice," 14; Petkov and Mustazza, *The Frank Sinatra Reader,* 18; E. J. Kahn, Jr., "Phenomenon: II," 35; "The Sinatra Effect," in Gene Lees, *Singers and the Song* (New York: Oxford Univ. Press, 1987), 101–15.

65. Martha Weinman Lear, "The Bobby Sox Have Wilted, but the Memory Remains Fresh," in Petkov and Mustazza, *The Frank Sinatra Reader,* 47–48, italics in original.

66. Lisa Lewis, *Gender, Politics, and MTV: Voicing the Difference* (Philadelphia: Temple Univ. Press, 1990), 149, 152; Barbara Ehrenreich, Elizabeth Hess, and Gloria Jacobs, *Re-making Love: The Feminization of Sex* (Garden City, NY: Anchor Press/Doubleday, 1986), 10–38.

67. Lewis, *Gender, Politics, and MTV,* 163–69; Kahn, "Phenomenon: I," 38; Bliven, "The Voice," 13; *Eastern Echo* (1946), 125.

68. Lear, "The Bobby Sox," 47–48; Kahn, "Phenomenon: II," 35–48; Lewis, *Gender, Politics, and MTV,* 153–54; Bliven, "The Voice," 14; Ehrenreich et al, *Re-making Love,* 10–38.

69. Goodman, "What Swing Really Does to People," 6–7; Benny Goodman and Ted Shane, "Now Take the Jitterbug," *Collier's* (February 25, 1939): 11–13, 60.

70. *Rarebit* (1932), n.p.; OGS, Kay, June 9, 1936, September 23, 1936, March 3, 1937, March 2, 1938.

71. *Bryn Mawrtyr* (1938), 13, 20; *Brownie* (1938), 16; *Eastern Echo* (1940), 51; *Forester* (February 1939), 84.

72. *Towers* (1943), 14; *What-Not,* Girls' Latin School (1943), n.p.; *Eastern Echo* (1945), 125.

73. *Bryn Mawrtyr* (1932), 9; OGS, Eloise, April 6, 1937; *Bryn Mawrtyr* (1938), 23; *Eastern Echo* (1940), 38.

74. "Swing It!" *NYT* (May 23, 1937): IV:2; Firestone, *Swing,* 239–40.

75. *Brownie* (1942), 16; *Bryn Mawrtyr* (1946), 34; *Forester* (June 1937), 53.

Chapter 5—Teenage Girls and Movies

1. This quote comes from a series of motion picture autobiographies collected by sociologist Herbert Blumer in the late 1920s as part of the Payne Fund studies. These previously unpublished autobiographies are reprinted in Garth S. Jowett, Ian C. Jarvie, and Kathryn H. Fuller, *Children and the Movies: Media Influence and the Payne Fund Controversy* (New York: Cambridge Univ. Press, 1996), 246.

2. Garth Jowett, *Film: The Democratic Art* (Boston: Little, Brown and Co., 1976), 77.

3. Robert Sklar, *Movie-Made America: A Cultural History of American Movies* (New York: Vintage Books, 1994 [1974]), 124–39; Leora M. Blanchard, *Teen-Age Tangles: A Teacher's Experiences with Live Young People* (Philadelphia: The Union Press, 1923), 32–33; Robert S. Lynd and Helen Merrell Lynd, *Middletown: A Study in Modern American Culture* (San Diego: Harcourt Brace Javonavich, 1956 [1929]), 264–68; Robert S. Lynd and Helen Merrell Lynd, *Middletown in Transition: A Study in Cultural Conflicts* (New York: Harcourt, Brace and World, 1965 [1937]), 176, 261–63.

4. Clarence Arthur Perry, "Frequency of Attendance of High-School Students at the Movies," *The School Review* 31 (October 1923): 573–87; Oakland Growth Study, Institute of Human Development, Berkeley, California, (hereafter OGS), compilations, 1935–1939.

5. "What Students Think of Movies," *Photo-Era Magazine* (January 1929): 49; "What Students Think of Movies," *Photo-Era Magazine* (February 1929): 102–3; Alice P.

Sterner, *Radio, Motion Picture, and Reading Interests: A Study of High School Pupils* (New York: Teachers College, Columbia Univ., 1947), 69, 31–32; Marion Edman, "Attendance of School Pupils and Adults at Moving Pictures," *The School Review* 48 (December 1940): 755–56, 760–62. Researchers continued debating these questions and reporting conflicting conclusions. Paul Witty, Sol Garfield, and William Brink argued in 1941 that "youth is deplorably lacking in resources or inclination to participate in many wholesome pursuits." In contrast, A. L. McGuinnes found just as conclusively in 1943 that high school students made good movie selections and had "the ability to discriminate." Paul Witty, Sol Garfield, and William Brink, "Interests of High-School Students in Motion Pictures and the Radio," *Journal of Educational Psychology* 32 (March 1941): 176; A. L. McGuinnes, "Can Youth Select Good Movies?" *High Points in the Work of the High Schools of New York City* 25 (May 1943): 64.

  6. Edgar Dale, *How to Appreciate Motion Pictures: A Manual of Motion-Picture Criticism Prepared for High-School Students* (New York: Macmillan Company, 1933).

  7. Sarah MacLean Mullen, *How to Judge Motion Pictures: A Pamphlet for High School Students* (New York: Scholastic Corporation, 1934); Sarah MacLean Mullen, *How to Organize a Photoplay Club* (New York: Scholastic Corporation, 1934); Lea Jacobs, "Reformers and Spectators: The Film Education Movement in the Thirties," *Camera Obscura* 22 (January 1990): 30; *Purple Wave,* Cardozo High School (1942), n.p.; Mary Allen Abbott, "A Sampling of High-School Likes and Dislikes in Motion Pictures," *Secondary Education* 6 (March 1937): 821, italics in original.

  8. Paul Cressey, "The Motion Picture Experience as Modified by Social Background and Personality," *American Sociological Review* 3 (August 1938): 516–25; James Gilbert, *A Cycle of Outrage: America's Reaction to the Juvenile Delinquent in the 1950s* (New York: Oxford Univ. Press, 1986); Jowett, *Film: A Democratic Art,* 269–71.

  9. *Road to Ruin* (Cliff Broughton Productions, 1928).

10. *Harold Teen* (First National, 1928).

11. *Harold Teen;* Georganne J. Scheiner, *Signifying Female Adolescence: Film Representations and Fans, 1920–1950* (Westport, CT: Praeger, 2000), 68.

12. *Are These Our Children?* (RKO, 1931); *Wild Boys* (Warner Brothers Studio, 1932); David Considine, *The Cinema of Adolescence* (Jefferson, NC: McFarland, 1985), 158.

13. Historian David Considine writes in *The Cinema of Adolescence* that "there was no such creature as an adolescent" in the 1930s, much less the 1920s, while in the 1940s there was "almost an obsession with adolescence, treated as a separate stage of life replete with its own views, values, tribal customs." Considine, *The Cinema of Adolescence,* 42.

14. *Love Finds Andy Hardy* (MGM, 1938).

15. *That Certain Age* (Universal Pictures, 1938).

16. *High School* (Twentieth Century–Fox, 1940).

17. *Variety* (October 29, 1941); *Small Town Deb* (Twentieth Century–Fox, 1941).

18. *Janie* (Warner Brothers, 1944).

19. Considine, *The Cinema of Adolescence,* 13–31; Richard Shale, *The Academy Awards Index: The Complete Categorical and Chronological Record* (Westport, CT: Greenwood Press, 1993), 286.

20. Witty, Garfield, and Brink, "Interests of High-School Students," 181–82, italics in original; Edman, "Attendance of School Pupils," 761–63; I. Keith Tyler and High School Students of the University School, Ohio State University, *High School Students Talk It Over* (Bureau of Educational Research, 1937), 17.

21. Alleyn Moore (high school graduate 1937), interview by author, tape recording, Baltimore, MD, March 28, 1997; Betsy Smith Hughes, interview by author, tape recording, Baltimore, MD, January 23, 1997.

22. *New York Times* (hereafter *NYT*) (December 13, 1936): XI:7.

23. "Initial Anne Shirley 'Teen' Series Considers the Fall Wardrobe," *Women's Wear Daily* (hereafter *WWD*) (October 2, 1935): 16; Advertisement, Anne Shirley formals, *WWD* (October 9, 1935): 15.

24. *Time* (January 31, 1938): 13; "Deanna Durbin," *Current Biography* 1941 (New York: H. W. Wilson Co. 1941), 247; Shale, *Academy Awards Index,* 286; *NYT* (September 17, 1939): VII:11; *NYT* (December 6, 1940): 29; "Fifteen . . . And Famous," *Scholastic* 31 (January 15, 1938): 12.

25. "Deanna Durbin, Spinster" *NYT* (September 12, 1937): XI:3; "One Smart Girl," *NYT* (September 17, 1939): VII:11; *NYT* (March 23, 1941): IX:4; Georganne Scheiner, "The Deanna Durbin Devotees: Fan Clubs and Spectatorship," in Joe Austin and Michael Nevin Willard, eds., *Generations of Youth: Youth Cultures and History in Twentieth-Century America* (New York: New York Univ. Press, 1998), 83, 90.

26. *WWD* (August 4, 1937): 26; *WWD* (September 15, 1937), 11; Sears, Roebuck & Company Catalog (hereafter Sears) (Spring 1939), 62; "Closer Tie-Up Between Movie and Movie Fashions Seen in Stern Bros. Promotion," *WWD* (September 22, 1937): 19; "More 'Personalized' Fashion Ideas in Deanna Durbin Film," *WWD* (September 22, 1937), 19; "Watch Your Movie Release Dates for Fashion Tie-Ups," *WWD* (September 28, 1938): 30; Advertisement, "Singing in the Rain With a Deanna Durbin Stormy Weather Ensemble," *WWD* (September 28, 1938): 30; *Fortune* (October 1939): 66–67, 158; *Business Week* (June 8, 1946): 74.

27. *Love Finds Andy Hardy; NYT* (August 18, 1939): 16; Joe Morella and Edward Z. Epstein, *The Complete Films and Career of Judy Garland* (New York: Carol Publishing Group, 1990 [1969]), 14–25; Shale, *Academy Awards Index,* 287; Ted Magee, *Picture Play* (June 1938): 52.

28. Magee, *Picture Play* (June 1938): 52–53; "Success Story," *Time* (March 18, 1940): 84; "Fifteen . . . And Famous," 12; Morella and Epstein, *The Complete Films,* 16–41.

29. "Opens 'Hi-Teen' Shop," *WWD* (September 14, 1938): 22; "Watch Your Movie Release Dates for Fashion Tie Ups," *WWD* (September 28, 1938): 30; "Macy's Features Judy Garland Frocks in 'Wizard of Oz' Window Display," *WWD* (September 6, 1939): 20; Sears (Fall 1938), 177, italics in original; "Judy Garland Dress Success in England," *WWD* (September 28, 1938): 30; Thorp, *America at the Movies,* 51–52.

30. Cobbett Steinberg, *Reel Facts: The Movie Book of Records* (New York: Vintage Books, 1981 [1978]), 169–72.

31. *NYT* (June 1942): 11

32. James R. Parish, *Great Child Stars* (New York: Ace Books, 1976), 191–95; Norman Zierold, *The Child Stars* (London: MacDonald, 1965), 102–3; *Variety* (October 29, 1941); T. M. P., *NYT Film Reviews* (New York: New York Times, 1943).

33. Kathryn H. Fuller, *At the Picture Show: Small-Town Audiences and the Creation of Movie Fan Culture* (Washington: Smithsonian Institution Press, 1996), 1–74, 98–114; Sklar, *Movie-Made America,* 3–64; Jowett, *Film: The Democratic Art,* 30–59; David Nasaw, *Going Out: The Rise and Fall of Public Amusements* (New York: Basic Books, 1993), chapters 12, 14.

34. Yvonne Blue Skinner diary, Schlesinger Library, Radcliffe Institute, Harvard University, Yvonne Blue Skinner Papers, 85–M195 (hereafter Yvonne Blue Skinner diary), April 11, 1925.

35. Yvonne Blue Skinner diary, October 23, 1926, emphasis in original; Beth Twiggar Goff diary, Schlesinger Library, Radcliffe Institute, Harvard University, Beth Twiggar Goff Papers, 90–M130 (hereafter Beth Twiggar Goff diary), September 1928.

36. Letter to Frances Turner, Bryn Mawr School (hereafter Letters to Frances Turner), October 22, 1918, November 29, 1918 (*A Daughter of the Old South* was released in 1918); Yvonne Blue Skinner diary, September 10, 1925, (*Spook Ranch* was released in 1925); September 16, 1925 (*Don Q Son of Zorro* was released in 1925); Arvilla

Scholfield diary, Walters Family Papers, January 7, 1926 (*Little Annie Roonie* was released in 1925).

37. Arvilla Scholfield diary, January 20, 1926 (*The Freshman* was released in 1925), 1926 (*Lady of the Night* and *Graustark* were both released in 1925).

38. Letter to Adele Siegel, Schlesinger Library, Radcliffe Institute, Harvard University, Adele Siegel Rosenfeld Papers, 90–M109, November 14, 1929 (*Noah's Ark* was released in 1928).

39. Yvonne Blue Skinner diary, May 3, 1923, December 25, 1926. A review of *Daddy* in *Variety* read, "Jackie's Dad in the story was a well-known violinist. Mother was jealous of his attention to pupils and walked out on him. She goes back to the home town and is taken in by poor farmers, who were friends. She dies and Jackie [Coogan] remains with the old couple until they are forced out of their home and into a poor farm. Jackie runs away and comes to the big city, where he meets a street violinist who takes him in . . . finally the boy's dad and he come together for a happy ending." *Variety Film Reviews* (April 19, 1923) (New York: Garland Publishing, Inc., 1983).

40. *Forester,* Forest Park High School (1933), 15; *The Towers,* Notre Dame of Maryland Preparatory School (1943), 9; *Eastern Echo,* Eastern High School (1946), 36, 58.

41. Letter to Frances Turner, September 9, 1920. Despite industry efforts to encourage the popularity of "film" and "cinema," the appellation "movie" became popular by 1915 as a noun. Its popularity as a verb never spread. Harold Wentworth and Stuart Berg Flexner, eds., *Dictionary of American Slang,* 2d sup. ed. (New York: Thomas Y. Crowell, 1975), 346.

42. Thomas Doherty, *Teenagers and Teenpics: The Juvenilization of American Movies in the 1950s* (Boston: Unwin Hyman, 1988), 3.

43. Perry, "Frequency of Attendance," 584–85.

44. Arvilla Scholfield diary, January 12, 1926 (*Vanishing American* was released in 1925); February 3, 1926 (*Stage Struck* was released in 1925); December 21, 1926 (*Cat's Pajamas* was released in 1926); Katherine Rosner (pseudonym) diary, Schlesinger Library, Radcliffe Institute, Harvard University Katherine Rosner Papers, 92–M10 (hereafter Katherine Rosner diary), February 21, 1929.

45. Yvonne Blue Skinner diary, June 25, 1926.

46. Letters to Frances Turner, November 21, 1917, November 29, 1918; Beth Twiggar Goff diary, December 24, 1928.

47. OGS, Mary, January 6–7, 1939.

48. Motion picture autobiography in Jowett, Jarvie, and Fuller, *Children and the Movies,* 253, 281–301.

49. OGS, Lillian, December 4, 1935; OGS, Sarah, January 6–7, 1939.

50. Katherine Rosner diary, March 6, 1929.

51. Yvonne Blue Skinner diary, August 10, 1924, March 28, 1925, September 10, 1925; OGS, Gwen, January 7, 1939; OGS, Paul, January 8, 1939; *Brownie,* Park School (1947), 24.

52. Fuller, *At the Picture Show,* 74; Steinberg, *Reel Facts,* 44–47.

53. Katherine Rosner diary, March 6, 1929; Adele Siegel Rosenfeld diary, Schlesinger Library, Radcliffe Institute, Harvard University, Adele Siegel Rosenfeld Papers, 90–M109 (hereafter Adele Siegel Rosenfeld diary), June 22, 1931 (*Shipmates* was released in 1931).

54. Letter to Frances Turner, October 16, 1917; Arvilla Scholfield diary, January 12, 1926; OGS, Deborah, August 29, 1935; Yvonne Blue diary, September 19, 1925, June 1, 1923, September 14, 1924, January 10, 1925, February 3, 1926, July 31, 1927. *The Freshman* was released in 1925.

55. Yvonne Blue diary, July 1, 1926.

56. Brooke Hanlon, "All the Boys," in Frances Ullmann DeArmand, ed., *When Mother Was a Girl: Stories She Read Then* (New York: Funk and Wagnalls Co., 1964), 70 (originally published in *Ladies' Home Journal* 1942); Beth Twiggar Goff diary, August 6, 1928.

57. Abbott, "A Sampling of High-School Likes and Dislikes," 75, italics in original; Beth Twiggar Goff diary, March 1929.

58. OGS, Sandra, Spring 1934.

59. Katherine Rosner diary, May 14, 1929; Yvonne Blue Skinner diary, October 26, 1928.

60. OGS, Mary, September 22, 1934; OGS, Sharon, Summary, November 11, 1957; OGS, Rebecca, May 5, 1937 (*Maytime* was released in 1937); Earl T. Sullenger, "Modern Youth and the Movies," *School and Society* 32 (October 4, 1930): 460; Motion picture autobiography in Jowett, Jarvie, and Fuller, *Children and the Movies*, 243.

61. Beth Twiggar Goff diary, March 1928 (*Divine Woman* was released in 1928); April 1929.

62. Lucille Vaughan Payne, "Sunday Afternoon," in Bryna Ivens, ed., *Nineteen from Seventeen* (Philadelphia: J. B. Lippincott Co., 1952), 154.

63. *Westward Ho*, Western High School (1940), n.p.; Motion picture autobiographies in Jowett, Jarvie, and Fuller, *Children and the Movies*, 276, 254, 288–89, 276.

64. Motion picture autobiographies in Jowett, Jarvie, and Fuller, *Children and the Movies*, 80, 281–285.

65. Motion picture autobiographies in Jowett, Jarvie, and Fuller, *Children and the Movies*, 269, 258–59.

66. Paula S. Fass, *The Damned and the Beautiful: American Youth in the 1920s* (Oxford: Oxford Univ. Press, 1977), 260–90; Beth L. Bailey, *From Front Porch to Back Seat: Courtship in Twentieth-Century America* (Baltimore: Johns Hopkins Univ. Press, 1988), especially 77–96; John Modell, *Into One's Own: From Youth to Adulthood in the United States* (Berkeley: Univ. of California Press, 1989); Motion picture autobiography in Jowett, Jarvie, and Fuller, *Children and the Movies*, 278, 257.

67. Beth Twiggar Goff diary, 1929; Adele Siegel Rosenfeld diary, October 25, 1931, November 2, 1931, November 7, 1931.

68. Letter to Frances Turner, September 5, 1919 (*His Majesty, the American* was released in 1919), September 22, 1919; Fuller, *At the Picture Show*, 116.

69. Fuller, *At the Picture Show*, 133–46.

70. Sullenger, "Modern Youth and the Movies," 459–460; Abbott, "A Sampling of High-School Likes and Dislikes," 75; Edman, "Attendance of School Pupils," 761–63.

71. *Quid Nunc*, Roland Park Country School (1933), 54; *Bryn Mawrtyr*, Bryn Mawr School (1936), 30.

72. Yvonne Blue Skinner diary, February 15, 1925; *Bryn Mawrtyr* (1937), 39.

73. *Shepherdess*, Seaton High School (1942), 69; *Westward Ho* (March 1925), 45.

74. Fuller, *At the Picture Show*, 115, 150–67; Janice Radway, *Reading the Romance: Women, Patriarchy, and Popular Literature* (Chapel Hill: Univ. of N. Carolina Press, 1984), 46–118.

75. Scheiner, *Signifying Female Adolescence*; Lisa Lewis, *Gender, Politics, and MTV: Voicing the Difference* (Philadelphia: Temple Univ. Press, 1990), 151–52; Barbara Ehrenreich, Elizabeth Hess, and Gloria Jacobs, *Re-Making Love: The Feminization of Sex* (Garden City, NY: Anchor Press, 1986), 19.

76. Leo Rosten, *Hollywood: The Movie Colony, The Movie Makers* (New York: Harcourt, Brace, and Co., 1970 [1941]), 409–11.

77. Margaret Farrand Thorp, *America at the Movies* (New Haven: Yale Univ. Press, 1939), 69–98, 114.

78. Miriam Hansen, "Pleasure, Ambivalence, Identification: Valentino and Female Spectatorship," *Cinema Journal* 25 (Summer 1986): 6–32; "Crowds Wait in Vain," *NYT* (September 4, 1926): 3; "Last Valentino Film Draws London Throng," *NYT* (September 21, 1926): 9; Yvonne Blue Skinner diary, August 24, 1926; Clementine Barship, "On Dating a Boy for the Prom," *Westward Ho* (1940), n.p.; *Clipper*, Patterson Park High School (1943), 23.

79. Sklar, *Movie Made America,* 99; Yvonne Blue Skinner diary, September 16, 1925; Louise Armstrong (high school graduate 1938), interview by author, tape recording, Baltimore, MD, April 4, 1997; Nancy Boyce (high school graduate 1941), interview by author, tape recording, Baltimore, MD, February 28, 1997.

80. OGS, Shirley, August 29, 1935; OGS, Amy, August 29, 1935; OGS, Helen, February 23, 1938; *Bryn Mawrtyr* (1940); n.p.; *Eastern Echo* (1940), 72.

81. Motion picture autobiography in Jowett, Jarvie, and Fuller, *Children and the Movies,* 243–269.

82. Letter to Frances Turner, September 5, 1919; Motion picture autobiography in Jowett, Jarvie, and Fuller, *Children and the Movies,* 257–58; Katherine Rosner diary, January 9, 1929; Sullenger, "Modern Youth," 459–61.

83. *Quid Nunc* (1930), 25; *Eastern Echo* (1941), 95, 120; OGS, Rebecca, August 29, 1935; Letters to Frances Turner, March 31, 1927 (*Kid Boots* was released in 1926).

84. Patricia Tate, "Twentieth Century," *Bryn Mawrtyr* (1948), 56–57, italics in original.

85. H. Feigenbaum, "Never-Ending," *Senior Scholastic* 37 (October 21, 1940): 20.

86. OGS, Rita, October 17, 1934; OGS, Sue, March 27, 1935. Gretchen most likely referred to *Gold Diggers of 1935* (Warner Brothers, 1935); OGS, Edith, June 1, 1938.

87. *Right Angle,* Maryland Park High School (1932), n.p.; *Westward Ho* (1945), 28; *Westward Ho* (1935), 59; *Eastern Echo* (1940), 55; Beth Twiggar Goff diary, 1928 (*Gentle Men Prefer Blonds* was released in 1928).

88. Motion picture autobiography in Jowett, Jarvie, and Fuller, *Children and the Movies,* 272–73; Boyce interview; OGS, Shirley, August 30, 1937.

89. Letter from Frances Turner, 1922.

90. Motion picture autobiography in Jowett, Jarvie, and Fuller, *Children and the Movies,* 276.

91. Yvonne Blue Skinner diary, January 9, 1926, February 3, 1926; Adele Siegel Rosenfeld diary, January 4, 1931.

92. Perry, "What Students Think of Movies," 103; Yvonne Blue Skinner diary, January 1926.

93. Yvonne Blue Skinner diary, August 24, 1926.

94. Gilbert, *A Cycle of Outrage,* esp. 162–77.

95. OGS, Edna, December 9, 1936.

Conclusion

1. Estelle Ellis Collection, Archives Center, National Museum of American History.

2. Richard M. Ugland, *The Adolescent Experience During World War II: Indianapolis as a Case Study* (Ph.D. Dissertation, Indiana Univ., 1977), 195–96; Dwight MacDonald, "A Caste, A Culture, and A Market–I," *New Yorker* (November 22, 1958): 62; "Neat Greet," *Business Week* (May 18, 1946): 92.

3. *Seventeen* magazine (September 1944): 33; Kelly Schrum, "'Teena Means Business': Teenage Girls' Culture and *Seventeen* Magazine, 1944–1950" in Sherrie Inness, ed., *Delinquent Daughters: Twentieth-Century American Girls' Culture* (New York: New York Univ. Press, July 1998), 134–163.

4. "Tricks for Teens," *The Parents' Magazine* (February 1941): 84.

5. "Teenage Consumers," *Consumer Reports* (March 1957): 139–42, reprinted in Eugene J. Kelley and William Lazer, *Managerial Marketing: Perspectives and Viewpoints* (Homewood, IL: Richard D. Irwin, Inc., 1958), 97–102.

Epilogue

1. Walter Kirn, "Will Teenagers Disappear?" *Time* (February 21, 2000): 60–61; Thomas Hine, *The Rise and Fall of the American Teenager* (New York: Avon Books, 1999), 298.

2. Ellen Welles Page, "A Flapper's Appeal to Parents," *Outlook* 132 (December 6, 1922): 607. See also Lisa Bannon, "Little Big Spenders: As Children Become More Sophisticated, Marketers Think Older," *Wall Street Journal* (October 13, 1998): A1.

3. Bannon, "Little Big Spenders," A6.

4. Ibid.

5. Jamie Beckett, "New Marketing Study Targets Teenagers," *San Francisco Chronicle* (April 17, 1989): C3; Stuart Elliot, "Hey, Dude, That's One Serious Pitch," *New York Times* (hereafter *NYT*) (May 10, 1991): D1; Malcolm Gladwell, "The Coolhunt," *The New Yorker* (March 17, 1997): 78–88; PBS-Frontline documentary, "The Merchants of Cool" (Coolhunt, http://www.pbs.org/wgbh/pages/frontline/shows/cool/, March 15, 2003); "Sassaby Deal Opens Mass Market to Estée Lauder," *NYT* (September 26, 1997): D4; Teenage Research Unlimited, (TRU, http://www.teenresearch.com/home.cfm, April 3, 2003); Marylin Johnson, "Hey Girls, Companies are Creating Cosmetics Just for you (and your Wallet)," *Atlanta Journal–Constitution* (May 2, 2002): 13GE; Betsy Schiffman, "Avon Likes Young Women," Forbes.com, (http://www.forbes.com/2002/01/24/0123avon.html, April 10, 2003).

6. David Carr, "Primedia Explores Sales of *Seventeen*," *NYT* (February 6, 2003): C1; James Sullivan, "Now Teens Have People, Too," *San Francisco Chronicle* (January 21, 1998): E1; Teresa Puente, "Culture Clash Complicated Latinas' Teen Years," *Chicago Tribune* (February 28, 1999): 1; Lynn O'Dell, "The Magazine Scene Proves It's, Like, A Teenage World," *Los Angeles Times* (April 23, 2000); Jim Rutenberg, "A Network that Serves Youth, and Sells it as Well," *NYT* (January 6, 2003): C1; The *Washington Post* announced in August 2000 that teenage girls are "flocking to the Internet. . . . [and] have made one of the biggest contributions to the growth spurt in female users." Alec Klein and Carrie Johnson, "Women Surf Past Men on Net," *Washington Post* (August 10, 2000): A1.

7. Bob Thompson, "The Selling of the Clickerati," *Washington Post Magazine* (October 24, 1999): 32.

Illustration Acknowledgments

Images from the following high school yearbooks courtesy of the Maryland Department, Enoch Pratt Free Library, Baltimore, Maryland. Reprinted with permission.
Agnesian, Mt. Saint Agnus High School
Bryn Mawrtyr, Bryn Mawr School
Eastern Echo, Eastern High School
Forester, Forest Park High School
Quid Nunc, Roland Park Country School
Rarebit, Oldfields School
Sidelights, Towson High School
Westward Ho, Western High School
Yearling, Cambridge High School

Images from the following materials courtesy of Walters Family Papers, Baltimore, Maryland. Reprinted with permission.
Arvilla Scholfield, Diary
Irene Scholfield, Movie Star Drawings
Arvilla Scholfield, Photograph
Shasta Daisy, Shasta Union High School

Images from *Ladies' Home Journal* courtesy of Meredith Corporation. Reprinted with permission.
Copyright September 1932, Meredith Corporation, *Ladies' Home Journal,* page 24
Copyright July 1935, Meredith Corporation, *Ladies' Home Journal,* page 63
Copyright February 1936, Meredith Corporation, *Ladies' Home Journal,* page 60
Copyright February 1938, Meredith Corporation, *Ladies' Home Journal,* page 6
Copyright March 1946, Meredith Corporation, *Ladies' Home Journal,* page 8

Images from the following high school yearbooks courtesy of the Charles Sumner School Museum and Archives, Washington, DC Public Schools
Libber Anni, Dunbar High School
Purple Wave, Cardoza High School

Images from the Frederick Douglass High School high school yearbook, *Survey,* courtesy of Frederick Douglass High School. Reprinted with permission.

Photograph from *Life* (February 21, 1938), page 5, by *The Birmingham News* All rights reserved. Reprinted with permission.

Index